New Ideas in

Strategic Thinking & Management

A Knowledge Tree of New Age Mantras

AF512051

New Ideas in Strategic Thinking & Management

A Knowledge Tree of New Age Mantras

Subhash Sharma
Director
Indus Business Academy (IBA)
Bangalore

NEW AGE MANAGEMENT

An Imprint of

NEW AGE INTERNATIONAL (P) LIMITED, PUBLISHERS
New Delhi • Bangalore • Chennai • Cochin • Guwahati
Hyderabad • Kolkata • Lucknow • Mumbai
Visit us at **www.newagepublishers.com**

Copyright © 2016, New Age International (P) Ltd., Publishers
Published by New Age International (P) Ltd., Publishers
First Edition: 2016
Reprint: 2016

All rights reserved.
No part of this book may be reproduced in any form, by photostat, microfilm, xerography, or any other means, or incorporated into any information retrieval system, electronic or mechanical, without the written permission of the publisher.

BRANCHES

- **Bangalore** 37/10, 8th Cross (Near Hanuman Temple), Azad Nagar, Chamarajpet Bangalore-560 018, Tel.: (080) 26756823, Telefax: 26756820 **E-mail: bangalore@newagepublishers.com**
- **Chennai** 26, Damodaran Street, T. Nagar, Chennai-600 017, Tel.: (044) 24353401 Telefax: 24351463, **E-mail: chennai@newagepublishers.com**
- **Cochin** CC-39/1016, Carrier Station Road, Ernakulam South, Cochin-682 016 Tel.: (0484) 2377303, Telefax: 4051303 **E-mail: cochin@newagepublishers.com**
- **Guwahati** Hemsen Complex, Mohd. Shah Road, Paltan Bazar, Near Starline Hotel Guwahati-781 008 Tel.: (0361) 2513881, Telefax: 2543669 **E-mail: guwahati@newagepublishers.com**
- **Hyderabad** 105, 1st Floor, Madhiray Kaveri Tower, 3-2-19, Azam Jahi Road, Near Kumar Theater Nimboliadda, Kachiguda, Hyderabad-500 027, Tel.: (040) 24652456 Telefax: 24652457 **E-mail: hyderabad@newagepublishers.com**
- **Kolkata** RDB Chambers (Formerly Lotus Cinema) 106A, 1st Floor, S N Banerjee Road Kolkata-700 014 Tel.: (033) 22273773, Telefax: 22275247 **E-mail: kolkata@newagepublishers.com**
- **Lucknow** 16-A, Jopling Road, Lucknow-226 001, Tel.: (0522) 2209578, 4045297 Telefax: 2204098, **E-mail:lucknow@newagepublishers.com**
- **Mumbai** 142C, Victor House, Ground Floor, N.M. Joshi Marg, Lower Parel Mumbai-400 013, Tel.: (022) 24927869, Telefax: 24915415 **E-mail: mumbai@newagepublishers.com**
- **New Delhi** 22, Golden House, Daryaganj, New Delhi-110 002 Tel.: (011) 23262368, 23262370, Telefax: 43551305 **E-mail: sales@newagepublishers.com**

ISBN: 978-81-224-3933-5

C-15-08-8683
Price: ₹ 250.00
Printed in India at Glorious Printers, New Delhi.
Typeset at In-house, New Delhi.

PUBLISHING GLOBALLY
NEW AGE INTERNATIONAL (P) LIMITED, PUBLISHERS
7/30 A, Daryaganj, New Delhi - 110002
Visit us at **www.newagepublishers.com**

Foreword

Prof. Subhash Sharma's thought provoking book, "Strategic Thinking and Management: A Knowledge Tree of New Age Mantras" is a timely and distinctive contribution to the field of strategic thinking, management and leadership. In the new age of global village, where local and global forces are influencing the entire world, a new approach to strategic thinking is needed. This calls for continuous creativity and innovation. Prof. Sharma's work challenges us to reexamine some of our current thinking by offering new models and new frameworks.

Prof. Sharma who is known for his "beyond the frame" thinking, has presented many of his ideas given in this book, in various Strategic Management Forum (SMF) conventions. He has been actively associated with the Forum from its formative years and has presented papers in most of the seventeen conventions held so far. His presentations always led to some animating discussions, which he has used to his advantage in refining his ideas and presenting it to wider community.

This book adds to literature on strategic thinking and strategic management emerging from India with roots in Indian experiences, Indian metaphors and Indian thought with a universal appeal. Ideas presented here have global implications as they provide a new macro-vision of 'Harmonic Globalization' wherein forces of Market, State, People and Self find a proper balance.

Prof. Sharma takes 'grounded praxis' route to research and knowledge creation and provides us some new insights that will be useful to policy makers, CEOs, as well as leaders from the NGO sector. Academic community and research scholars will find some new leads that can be taken up for further research.

This book is a welcome addition to Strategic Management thought and I recommend it to readers and researchers interested in inter-linkages between strategic thinking, management, leadership and grounded praxis.

Lucknow

Jan. 01, 2015

Prof. Krishna Kumar

Founder Secretary,
Strategic Management Forum (SMF)
Former Director,
Indian Institute of Management, Kozhikode

Preface

Transition from Industrial revolution to knowledge revolution and movement towards a new revolution of consciousness has necessitated need for new thinking in terms of new metaphors, new models, new mantras, and new yantras in strategic thinking, policy making and management. Challenges of globalization have also opened new windows, doors and corridors in new knowledge creation. My book, Management in New Age: Western Windows Eastern Doors (1996) envisioned a future direction for strategic thinking and management based on opening new windows and doors. This visioning and envisioning also found expression in my subsequent books *viz.*, New Mantras in Corporate Corridors (2007), New Earth Sastra (2012) and Wisdom & Consciousness from the East (2013).

Current book, New Ideas in Strategic Thinking & Management: A Knowledge Tree of New Age Mantras, builds upon the ideas presented in these books. In particular this book is largely based on my papers presented at the Strategic Management Forum (SMF) of India and also at AIMS (Association of Indian Management Scholars) International and other presentations in National & International forums within India and outside India, in US, Australia, Germany, France, Switzerland, Thailand, Bhutan and Nepal. These papers were published in various peer reviewed journals, conference proceedings and book chapters. It may be indicated that strategic thinking has implications for Corporates, Government and Ground realities expressed through capillary action initiatives. Hence, it is connected with strategic management, policy making and grounded praxis.

My involvement with Strategic Management Forum (SMF) started from its initial stage when Prof. Krishna Kumar, then Professor of Strategy at Indian Institute of Management (IIM), Lucknow, started it in 1998 and invited me to join this Forum. Since then I have been involved with this Forum and attended most of its Conventions and presented papers. These Conventions were held at IIMs *viz.*, IIM, Ahmedabad; IIM, Calcutta; IIM, Bangalore; IIM, Lucknow; IIM, Khozikode; IIM, Indore; and other leading institutes such as MDI, Gurgaon; XLRI, Jamshedpur; IIT, Kanpur; IIT, Mumbai; and IIFM, Bhopal. These SMF Conventions provided me an opportunity to present and test some new ideas which were further enriched because of feedback, discussions and dialogues with participants of the Conventions.

The ideas presented in this book were also field tested through 'grounded praxis research approach' during my interactions with Industry leaders and policy makers and also during several Management Development Programs. As founding Director of Indian Institute of Plantation Management, Bangalore, I had the opportunity to interact at the strategic and field level in the plantation industry in general and Indian Tea industry in particular through 'reach out training programs' and consulting. As an Executive Committee member of Bangalore Management Association and Indian Institute of Public Administration, Karnataka Regional Branch, I had an opportunity to get an understanding of strategic thinking and management issues in Indian Industry and Government. My association with Bangalore Management Association (BMA) and other professional bodies brought me in touch with senior managers in various industries and provided me an opportunity to field test some of these ideas.

My personal involvement in institution building from creation stage in 'creations from shunya' such as Indian Institute of Plantation Management, Bangalore, Women's Institute for Studies in Development Oriented Management (WISDOM), at Banasthali University, Banasthali, Rajasthan; Indus Business Academy (IBA), Bangalore and Greater Noida; also provided me opportunities to field test some of the ideas. These experiences led to some new insights leading to creation of some new tools and new ideas. Using creative meditative research approach such insights and new ideas were conceptualized through windows, doors and corridors view of knowledge creation and leading to some new management metaphors, mantras, and yantras, while retaining the flavour of model building approach. These ideas were then presented in National and International Conferences organized by SMF and other leading institutions.

Further, these ideas were also extensively class room tested at WISDOM (Women's Institute for Studies in Development Oriented Management), Banasthali University, Banasthali, Rajasthan; Indian Institute of Plantation Management, Bangalore; Indus Business Academy, Bangalore and Greater Noida; Calcutta Business School (CBS), Kolkata; and R K University, Rajkot, Gujarat; in Management Perspectives and related modules and in Management Development Programs (MDPs) and Faculty Development Programs (FDPs) that I taught at these institutions. These ideas were also tested in FDPs and MDPs of various other academic institutions and professional associations with which I got associated.

Thus, a triadic approach coupled with 3D model of Discussion, Dialogue and Discourse, has been used in creation, development and testing of these ideas. The triadic approach included, field testing through grounded praxis approach, action based research & consulting, and academic testing through presentations in conferences as well as through teaching & discussions with students, practitioners and faculty colleagues, during MBA classes, Management Development Programs and Faculty Development Programs. Further, some of these ideas have been used by research scholars in their Ph.D. research at WISDOM, Banasthali University, Banasthali, Rajasthan and R K University, Rajkot, Gujarat, and other institutions and universities in India. This triadic approach helped in planting this 'knowledge tree' with its origin in Indian experiences of new knowledge creation.

This book as a 'bouquet of ideas' is rooted in a variety of experiences that include research, consulting, teaching, MDPs & FDPs and institution building and is based on author's articles presented in SMF Annual Conventions and other conferences including Conferences organized by AIMS (Association of Indian Management Scholars) International, Houston, Curtin University, Perth, Zurich University, Zurich and India Trade Conferences, in Los Angeles and Indian School of Business, Hyderabad. Basic idea of this book is to link and align Management, Leadership and Policy Making Processes with Strategic Thinking. This idea is useful not only to the corporations but also to the national context. In the context of a nation, such alignments lead to good governance. New Age Mantras presented in this book arise from a synthesis of Western and Eastern models and experiences through the integration of 'Western Windows and Eastern Doors' (WWED) approach to new knowledge creation.

Since the book is primarily based on previously published papers, there are repetitions which have been retained to reinforce the ideas. As an acknowledgement to the journals and books in which author's articles have been published, a list of publications is provided in the researcher's corner. Articles and other previously published materials have been revised, extended and updated for the purpose of this book.

The book is divided into following five parts:

Part I: Knowledge Creation–In the knowledge era, strategic thinking requires creation of new ideas and new perspectives. New knowledge can be created through a variety of approaches *viz*., quantitative-empirical approach, qualitative-conceptual approach and creative-meditative approach. These approaches complement and supplement each other. While quantitative empirical approach dominates our thinking, new age thinkers bring new insights through creative meditative approach to knowledge creation. They use geometry of consciousness to gain insights into strategic thinking and management. Through knowledge generation windows and doors, they take us beyond Division (Divided vision) approach to creative approaches to new knowledge creation. Thus, we move beyond the rationality paradigm in strategic thinking to wisdom paradigm wherein both rationality and creativity are combined to get new insights.

Part II: Macro Perspectives in Strategic Thinking – In the era of Globalization, it is necessary to take a macro perspective of new changes, challenges and new thinking. New thinking is taking a holistic view of the development processes and identifying new connectivity between various roads to development. It also requires moving beyond the pyramid thinking that has dominated human thought since centuries. New thinking requires new metaphors. Responding to the needs of his times, Gandhi used *charkha* as a powerful metaphor for India's freedom struggle. Now the new thinking requires a new metaphor for holistic approach to integration of strategic thinking and policy making. 'Economic chapati making' serves as a new metaphor of 'harmonic globalization' which takes a holistic and integrative view of four forces of globalization *viz*., Market, State, People and Self. Strategic thinking in the context of Market has led to the development of 'strategic management', strategic thinking in the context of State has led to 'policy making' and strategic thinking in the context of people's movements and other capillary action initiatives has led to 'grassroots development thinking'. Holistic view of strategic thinking implies interconnectivity between these three streams of thinking.

Part III: New Models & New Mantras–New thinking at macro level requires new thinking at national and organizational levels. Hence, new models and new mantras are needed for Forward Engineering, Enterprise Performance Improvement Systems (EPIS) and Organization Development & Management (ODM). These models and mantras include, BEST Analysis, CINE Matrix, METRIC Analysis, SWAN & SPOT Analysis, STEPS Analysis, VSP Yantra, etc. These tools and techniques are helpful to managers and leaders in providing strategic direction to their organizations and also in growth and development of their organizations.

Part IV: Ethical Foundations–During recent years significance of the business ethics and corporate governance has been emphasized by the corporate leaders and management and social thinkers. It is now recognized that Character Competence of the Corporation should be given due importance in leadership and management of corporations. This is leading us towards the idea of Holistic Corporate Management (HCM), wherein Profit, CSR, Good Governance and Ecological concerns constitute the new foundation for a holistic view of corporations. It also implies a shift from Balanced Scorecard to Holistic Performance Scorecard. It may be indicated that Focus on Self (Spiritual Self in particular) has been a missing dimension in literature on Strategic Management, the idea of ethical foundations, aims to bridge this gap through the concept of Holistic Corporate Management (HCM) as presented in this book.

Part V: New Visioning & Envisioning–In Strategic thinking, we have moved from the age of rationality to the age of creativity and to the age of imagination. Recent focus on Innovation and Imagination in strategic thinking and management is an indicator of the same. Moon has always been connected with creativity and imagination, hence, the idea of Moon Ocean Strategy offers us a new approach taking us beyond the red ocean and blue ocean strategy.

In this book, three important management yantras that were earlier presented in my book, New Mantras in Corporate Corridors (2007) have been further refined and extended in the context of strategic thinking and management. These include, TCP yantra as foundation for the New Corporate Model, KTG yantra as a basis for ethical management & leadership, and VSP yantra with focus on Organization Development & Management (ODM). Their integration leads us to an ODM and institution building yantra. These yantras are based on an integration of 'Western models and Eastern mantras' and thereby represent the new age management thinking for corporates to evolve as social institutions in their journey from business entities to social institutions and as institutions of national and international significance. They also provide us new age philosophical and conceptual foundations for the idea of Holistic Corporate Management (HCM).

Bangalore **Subhash Sharma**

Acknowledgements

This book has received support from a number of persons with whom I have been interacting in my academic ventures. I particularly thank Prof. Krishna Kumar, Former Director, Indian Institute of Management (IIM), Kozhikode and Founder of Strategic Management Forum (SMF) of India, for his constant support. Interactions, discussions and dialogues with him enriched the ideas I presented in various SMF Conventions since 1999. I also thank my colleagues at SMF for their valuable inputs during my interactions with them.

I take this opportunity to thank Mr. B.M.L. Jain, Chairman, Indus Business Academy (IBA); Mr. Manish Jain, CEO, IBA Bangalore and Mr. Ritesh Jain, CEO, IBA Greater Noida for their sustained support and encouragement.

I thank Prof. Aditya Shastri, Vice Chancellor, Banasthali University; Prof. Siddharth Shastri, Vice President, Banasthali University and Prof. Harsh Purohit, Dean, WISDOM (Women's Institute for Studies in Development Oriented Management), Banasthali University, Banasthali, Rajasthan, for their encouragement and support and providing me an opportunity to extensively experiment and test these ideas at WISDOM since 1996.

I thank Prof. Omprakash Gupta, President AIMS (Association of Indian Management Scholars) International, Houston; Prof. Samir Chatterejee, Curtin Business School, Perth and Prof. Michael Zirkler, Zurich University, Zurich, for their encouragement and support. I thank Prof. S. P. Agarwal, Management Consultant, Mumbai, and Dr. Upinder Dhar, Amity University, Noida for their continuous encouragement and support. I also thank my colleagues at the Southern Economist Study Circle, Bangalore, also known as Bangalore Intellectuals Group (BIG) for their support and participation in discussions at various workshops and discussion sessions that we organized.

I thank my MBA-PGDM students, my doctoral students, MDP and FDP participants for their enthusiastic response to the new ideas presented in my writings. I thank faculty colleagues at WISDOM, Banasthali University, Banasthali, Rajasthan; Indian Institute of Plantation Management, Bangalore; Indus Business Academy (IBA), Bangalore; Indus Business Academy (IBA), Greater Noida; Calcutta Business School (CBS), Kolkata; and R K University, Rajkot for the interactions and discussions I had with them that led to enrichment of the ideas. I also thank my colleagues at Association of Indian Management Schools (AIMS) and AIMS International, for their support and encouragement. Last but not the least, I thank SMF Conventions participants for animating discussions and their comments and suggestions during my presentations, that further enriched the ideas.

I particularly thank Mr. Saumya Gupta, Managing Director, New Age International Publishers, New Delhi for his support in publishing this book.

Bangalore **Subhash Sharma**

Contents

Part II: Macro Perspectives in Strategic Thinking

Part III: New Models and New Mantras

Part I

Knowledge Creation

CHAPTER 1

Towards Creative Meditative Research*

Traditionally focus of social science research in general and management research in particular has been largely on quantitative approaches. Qualitative approaches to research found some acceptance and legitimacy during last three to four decades. During recent years, the idea of Creative research is finding its echo in social sciences (Ananta Giri, 2004, 2006, 2010). Sharma (2001) suggests scientific and Rishi approaches as routes to reality and thereby as approaches to research. In fact, with acceptance of creative research as a legitimate pathway to research, new doors to management research will open.

Broadly there are following three approaches to social science and management research:

1. Quantitative
2. Qualitative
3. Creative

Further, social science and management research can also be classified in terms of following three methodologies:

---

*Creative Meditative Research: Towards 'VITAL' Mode of Learning, Subhash Sharma, in Global Recession, Survival and Growth, Selected Papers of AIMS (Association of Indian Management Scholars) International Conference on Management, Om Prakash Gupta, V Nagdevra, Subhash Sharma and Shivprakash Agrawal (Eds), AIMS Houston, 2010, pp. 179–183. Also presented in a Workshop an Creative Meditative Research, at International Dialog amongst Research and Practice, School of Applied Psychology, Zurich University, Zurich, Sept 1–3, 2014.

1. Empirical
2. Conceptual
3. Meditative

When we juxtapose the approaches to research in terms of Quantitative, Qualitative and Creative, with methodologies employed in terms of Empirical, Conceptual and Meditative, we arrive at the following 3 × 3 research presented in Fig. 1.1, representing the typologies of research.

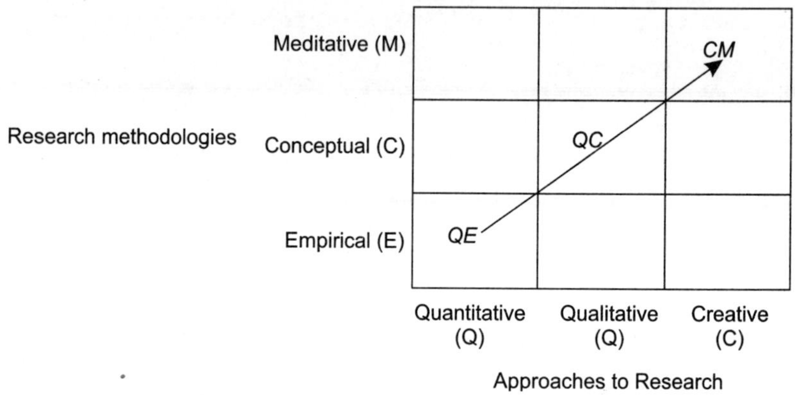

Figure 1.1. 3 × 3 Research Typologies Matrix

It may be indicated that most of the Quantitative research falls in the empirical category though research potentialities for conceptual and meditative research also exist in this domain. Similarly most of the Qualitative research falls in the empirical and conceptual categories though potentiality of meditative research also exists in this domain. In contrast to these, creative research draws upon all the three methodologies *viz.*, empirical, conceptual and meditative. In particular Creative-Meditative research offers us new frontiers in social sciences and management research. It may be indicated that the choice of a particular typology also depends upon the quantum state of the researcher's mind.

1.1 Research Pathways and Quantum States of Mind

Sharma (2005) identified following three quantum states of mind and explored its implications for research:

1. Division state of mind
2. D-vision state of mind
3. Direct vision state of mind

In Division state of mind, mind takes a divided-vision view of reality. It divides reality into segments and takes a 'silo' view. For example, in the context of an organization, problems are viewed from the perspective of marketing division, production division, finance division, HR division etc. Such an approach leads to a Division approach.

In D-Vision state of mind, mind takes a 'rainbow' perspective to look at the problems / issues from a holistic perspective.

In Direct Vision state of mind, mind operates at the Direct-perception (Darshan) level.

The above presented three thinking approaches / mind sets / quantum states of researcher's mind provide the conceptual foundations for the following three pathways to research and knowledge creation:

1. Rational-Analytic path (Critical thinking)
2. Intuitive-Creative path (Creative thinking)
3. Imaginative-Visionary path (Imaginative thinking)

These three pathways can also be considered as three models of research and they correspond to Quantitative-Empirical (QE), Qualitative-Conceptual (QC) and Creative-Meditative (CM) perspectives of research. These approaches also lead us to three models of thinking *viz*., critical thinking, creative thinking and imaginative thinking and a corresponding typology of thinkers in terms of rational-analytic thinkers, intuitive-creative thinkers and radial thinkers. Such thinkers can also be classified as scientists, artists and rishis. There is a fourth category of SAR (Scientist, Artist, Rishi) thinkers who combine all the three approaches to arrive at new insights and foresights in their field of enquiry. In Indian tradition to knowledge creation, they are like Rishi, thinkers as they engage actively in seeing and re-seeing reality in new ways and are engaged in reflection and contemplation. They combine 3 Is *viz.*, Intuition, Insight and Imagination to give new vision(s).

Analytic metaphors provide us interesting insights and they also represent a creative approach to research. Table 1.1 provides some illustrations of the same from social sciences and management.

Table 1.1. Illustrations of Metaphors and Models

Thinker / Researcher	Metaphor	Model
Freud	Iceberg	Conscious, Subconscious, Unconscious
Adam Smith	Invisible hand	Functioning of Markets
Maslow	Hierarchy	Hierarchy of needs
C. K. Prahlad	Pyramid	Bottom of pyramid
Thomas Friedman	World is Flat	World is flat
Michael Porter	Diamond	Nation's Competitive diamond
W. Chan Kim & Renée Mauborgne	Blue ocean	Blue ocean strategy

In this book, I have presented several new metaphors arising from my personal experiences of using metaphors to create new knowledge in the form of analytical models, mantras and yantras (geometrical representations). For example, flying swan led me to formulate SWAN (Strengths, Weaknesses, Achievements, Next step) analysis and moving clouds invoked in me the idea of SPOT (Space Pace Opportunities Threats) analysis. Rainbow led me to formulate SHARMAN model of mind and seven intelligences. Ashokan lions led me to formulate the idea of 'Holistic Globalization' based on four global forces and chapati making led me to formulate 'economic chapati making' model of holistic development. Coconut structure led me to formulate 'coconut model of society' to highlight role of the middle class in contrast to pyramid model of society used by C.K. Prahlad and others, etc. Discussions on these metaphors leading to new concepts in strategic thinking, policy making, management and leadership are presented in this book in different chapters.

1.2 Towards 'VITAL' Model of Learning

Above discussion has implications for learning. The discussion leads us to, 'VITAL' model and thereby 'VITAL' model of learning wherein by 'VITAL' we imply the following:

Vi: Vision

T: Thought

A: Action

L: Learning

Thus, in the VITAL model of learning there is an integration of Vision, Thought, Action and Learning. This model is useful to the practicing managers as they are continuously involved in learning process through implementation of vision and new ideas originating from new thoughts. We can also refer to this model as CH^3 (Consciousness, Head, Heart and Hand) as vision is the function of consciousness, thoughts (that include new insights) are the function of head & heart, and action is represented by hand. For effective learning there should be harmony between them. It may be indicated that Creative-Meditative research has a linkage with consciousness as in this research mode mind operates from Direct Vision / Direct Perception (Darshan) level and Direct Vision & Darshan (DVD) leads to intuitive insights.

'VITAL' model of learning is particularly useful in organizational learning wherein managers continuously engage in action. Further, it is also useful in fields like 'Business Ethics' where managers face dilemmas in decision making and action. This model can also be referred to as 'grounded praxis' model of learning as managers learn from their actions and impact of actions on the ground reality.

1.3 'Diya' (Lamp) Metaphor of Research

The three pathways to research suggested above can also be explained metaphorically through the 'Diya' (Earthen lamp) metaphor. Three researchers *viz.*,

Quantitative-Empirical researcher, Qualitative-Conceptual researcher and the Creative-Meditative researcher would look at the 'diya' presented in Fig. 1.2, in three different ways.

Figure 1.2. Three Research Interpretations of 'Diya' (Knowledge Lamp) Metaphor

A Quantitative-Empirical (QE) researcher would be interested in understanding relationships between variables such as height of the flame and its relationship with the quantity of oils in the lamp and the chemical composition of the oil etc. A rational-analytic thinker would follow this approach.

In contrast to the above, Qualitative-Conceptual (QC) researcher would be interested in knowing what meaning 'Diya' has for people. His research question would include various subjective meanings that people attribute to 'Diya'. An intuitive-creative thinker would follow this approach.

A Creative-Meditative (CM) researcher will see a higher meaning and higher order reality in 'Diya'. In my interpretation, base of 'Diya' represents Consciousness (we can see the base as C and letter C is the first letter in the word Consciousness). One can also see the mathematical symbol of infinity and therefore light of the lamp can be interpreted as 'Light of Infinity' spreading in all directions. Thus, a creative-meditative interpretation can provide us a deep insight that can expand the frontier of knowledge by providing new creative meaning to a phenomenon. A meditative-visionary thinker / wisdom thinker would follow this approach.

Thus, a scientist, an artist and a rishi would 'look' at the 'Diya' (lamp) in above discussed three ways. Above presented 'Diya' metaphor clarifies our thinking to three routes to reality *viz.*, Scientist's, Artist's and Rishi's route to reality. These three pathways to research and knowledge creation can also be captured by the metaphors of 'Western Windows', 'Eastern Doors' and 'Wisdom Corridors'. In the field of management, the expression, Management Guru, has become quite popular. It may be noted that Management Guru and Management Rishi essentially explore the third pathway to provide new insights. Further, there is a subtle difference between Management Guru and Management Rishi, as Management Rishis like the ancient Rishis, also get involved in action. They not only provide insights and foresights for new directions and vision but also consciously or unconsciously use the 'VITAL' model of learning and demonstrate feasibility of their ideas by converting ideas into reality.

Candle light experiment of creativity (Sharma 1999, 2007, 2013) in addition to providing insights into creativity provides us an insight into various research approaches to observe a phenomenon.

1.4 Some Tools of Creative-Meditative Research

In my creative-meditative research I have experimented with following tools of creative-meditative research and Imaginative Thinking (IT):

1. Action-Reflection-Wisdom
2. 3 D: Discussion, Dialogue, Discourse
3. Shabd-yoga / Word talk / Shabd-darshan
4. Rishi as Re-see
5. Darshan / Direct Perception / Radial Visioning
6. Mind walk
7. 'META' synthesis
8. Evolution of Mind towards WIESDOM

A discussion on these tools is available in author's various writings. A brief discussion is as follows:

1. **Action-Reflection-Wisdom:** Paulo Frerie (1970) suggested the action-reflection approach to learning in the social context. Schon (1983) suggested the idea of 'reflective practitioner'. We can extend these ideas to Action-Reflection-Wisdom framework of learning and research. When this 'reflective learning' approach is combined with creative-meditative interpretations of a phenomenon, we get some new insights in the form of new knowledge that may be expressed in the form of 'new mantras' and 'wisdom statements'. Further, insights gained through wisdom also lead us towards new foresights. Many social thinkers and visionaries have intuitively used this approach to create new vision (s) for the society and their organizations. Quite often, vision and mission of an organization are a result of action-reflection-wisdom process. Action-reflection-wisdom model can also be referred to as 'Wisdom model of research'. Because of the action dimension inherent in this model, this model of research can also be referred to as 'Grounded Praxis' model of research.
2. **3D: Discussion, Dialogue, Discourse:** With roots in *Upanishadic* tradition as well as in the dialectical methodology of Position-Opposition-Proposition, 3D model of Discussion, Dialogue and Discourse leads to new insights. At Indus Business Academy (IBA), Bangalore and Greater Noida, this model is a foundational model of learning. Author's experience indicates that it leads to new perspectives about managerial and social issues as it facilitates conversation through participative and democratic approach. It also leads to pooling of

creative insights of different individuals through the process of 'mind pooling'. It may be indicated that the idea of 'round table discussions' has been in existence, 3D model facilitates this process through creation of 'Omega circles' within the organization.

3. **Shabd-yoga / Word talk / Shabd-darshan:** Importance of 'word power' has been recognized since ancient times. Words have inspirational meaning. Shabd-yoga suggests that a word can reveal its deeper meaning by 'talking' to the researcher. Yoga implies connectivity. Shabd-yoga implies connectivity with nature or a phenomenon through words. When a person establishes a deep connectivity with a word, he/she finds new meanings and interpretations and thereby leading to creation of new concepts and new knowledge. To some extent this is also reflected in the popularity of acronyms. Many researchers create new acronyms to communicate their ideas. However, acronyms should be differentiated from 'mantras'. Mantras are deeper revelations of the word. They indicate deeper connectivity with the words. It may be indicated that a 'word view' can reveal a 'world view'. Hence, 'shabd-darshan' is important for the researcher. In my book, Western Windows Eastern Doors (1996), I made an extensive use of the shabd-yoga to develop many new conceptual models and some of them have now become part of 'received knowledge' in 'Indian Management'.

4. **Rishi as Re-see:** Rishi approach of creative-meditative research is rooted in a new definition of Rishi, as an individual who can 're-see' a phenomenon in new perspectives (Sharma, 2001). Many paradigm shifting ideas even in natural sciences have originated because an 'anomaly' was seen and re-seen by the researcher/scientist in new ways leading to development of new thoughts.

   Corporate application of Rishi approach implies that a CEO should have ability to re-see the events, opportunities and threats around him/her in new ways. Thus, his / her Rishi (Re-see) competence should be high. In academic context, an 'Academic Rishi' provides a new pathway.

5. **Darshan / Direct Perception / Radial Visioning:** The word Darshan implies Direct-Perception leading to a new insight. It also implies 'radial visioning' wherein full picture of a phenomenon is seen by the person in a holistic manner. It is like standing on the beach and looking at the horizon and seeing the ocean and the sky merge. Such a darshan can take one's mind to the creative-meditative level sometimes leading to new insights through poetic creations and poetic vision.

   Radial visioning has many managerial applications. It is said that Dhirubhai Ambani had the 'radial visioning' experience when he visualized the football stadium full of his shareholders. Mahatma Gandhi had the radial visioning experience when he was thrown out of the train. Martin Luther King communicated his radial visioning experience through his catch phrase, 'I have a dream'. In general, 'Radial thinkers' take a full circle / 360 degree / 'Omega circle' view to integrate and synthesize different perspectives and thereby provide new insights.

6. **Mind walk:** Technique of mind walk or mind travel is rooted in yoga, meditation and mind-stilling. Yoga, meditation and mind-stilling exercises help in stilling/calming the mind. In a still or peaceful situation mind can 'walk' easily and can travel at high speeds and thereby it can explore new perspectives and create new knowledge. During dream state of consciousness, mind can even fly. It is beyond the laws of gravity. Many times, dreams lead to insights and insights provide new solutions and new vision. There are many illustrations of creative meditative influences via 'knowledge creating dreams' from the field of natural sciences. Examples of 'knowledge creation through dreams' include scientific discoveries such as Benzene structure, Periodic Table, Double helix, etc.

   One can also train one's mind through yoga, meditation and mind-stilling exercises to undertake mind walk, mind travel and mind flying during waking state of consciousness. This becomes possible because three interrelated ideas *viz.*, yoga, meditation and mind stilling lead to liberation of mind from existing constraints. It may be indicated that mind flying state of consciousness can also be referred to as '789' state of consciousness wherein mind is at the 'seventh heaven, eighth chakra and ninth cloud'. At this state of consciousness, mind displays 'charismatic creativity'.

7. **'META' synthesis:** Nature has endowed every individual to experience 'Moments of Enlightenment, Transcendence and Awakening'. Learning from such 'META' experiences leads to a higher level synthesis of ideas. Such a synthesis takes us beyond Hegelian approach of Thesis-Anti-thesis and Synthesis. While Hegelian dialectical approach is useful in developing new insights and creating new knowledge as was demonstrated by Karl Marx and many others, creative-meditative approach with its origin in Eastern mysticism can lead to new creative insights. Mahatma Gandhi's insightful ideas during the freedom struggle of India are a pointer towards the same. Now in changed social scenario a similar 'META' approach is needed to create new perspectives.

8. **Evolution of Mind towards WIESDOM:** WIESDOM implies World of IQ, EQ, SQ, DQ & Oceanic Mind, wherein IQ represents Intelligence Quotient, EQ represents Emotional Quotient, SQ represents Spiritual Quotient, DQ represents Divinity Quotient and OM represents Oceanic Mind. This WIESDOM model is a five steps model of evolution of mind from IQ (Head) to EQ (Heart) to SQ (Consciousness) to DQ (Divinity) to OM (Oceanic Mind). At the Oceanic level, mind is creative, meditative and expansive leading to charismatic creativity. Ancient Rishis have described this state of mind through many evocative metaphors. It may be indicated this WIESDOM model is also a model of leadership.

Creative-Meditative research can open new frontiers of knowledge complementing the Quantitative-Empirical and Qualitative-Conceptual research approaches. 3 × 3 Research Typology Matrix presented earlier provides us a new framework of research that is useful to the social sciences as well as to the management discipline. Three pathways to research and knowledge creation suggested here, can also be described as paths that are usually travelled by a scientist, an artist and a rishi. We have referred to these research pathways as 'Western windows', 'Eastern doors' and 'Consciousness corridors'. In the field of management, the travelers of the second and third paths usually emerge as 'Management Guru' and 'Management Rishi'. While Management Gurus, largely give advice to the practicing managers and leaders, Management Rishis experiment with new insights and demonstrate the feasibility through their direct or indirect involvement in the process of implementation. We also suggest some techniques of creative-meditative research and Imaginative Thinking (IT) to make the travel on the third path easy for Creative-Meditative researchers.

❑

CHAPTER 2

Towards A New Geometry of Consciousness*

Broadly there are two approaches to consciousness *viz.*, **the Scientific and the Rishi**. In the scientific approach consciousness is an emergent phenomenon of matter. This can be referred to as the matter route to consciousness. In the Rishi route consciousness is an infused phenomenon wherein matter is infused with spirit. īśā vāsyam idaṃ sarvaṃ, yat kiñca jagatyāṃ jaga, Ishopanishad declares. It implies all matter is infused with consciousness. This can be referred to as the spirit route to consciousness.

Now there is a need to combine the two approaches to consciousness. It implies recognizing the impact of consciousness on Space and Time and on Energy and Matter. This also implies viewing the world through the lens of STC (Space Time Consciousness) and EMC (Energy Matter Consciousness).

David Bohm proposed the idea of Implicate and Explicate order. He further suggests the triad of EMI (Energy Matter Information) to understand the linkage between implicate and explicate order. Bohm's EMI triad can be viewed as EMC triad wherein Consciousness represents the implicate order that finds its expression in the explicate order in terms of matter and energy. We can also represent this idea in terms of AUM (All Unmanifest & Manifest). AUM finds its expression in the form of EMC triad and a general relationship in terms of $E = MC^n$ (Sharma, 1999).

*Towards a New Geometry of Consciousness, Subhash Sharma, The International Journal of Transformation of Consciousness, Vol. 1, No. 1, 2013. Dialogical Workshop on Spiritual Pragmatics and New Geometry of Consciousness, IBA center for C-School, Asian Forum for Social Theory, R K University, Rajkot, Indus Business Academy, Bangalore, 28th Aug. 2013.

This AUM expression can also be represented in terms of 'Geometry of Divinity' (GOD) that we observe in nature through 'Great Order & Disorder' (GOD).

In ancient times, 'Geometry of Divinity' was represented through yantras. In fact, yantras can be considered as an ancient geometry of consciousness because consciousness was represented through various yantras *i.e.*, geometrical figures. With the advent of science, a new geometry of consciousness is needed to integrate two routes *viz.*, scientific route / scientific formulations and rishi route / spiritual formulations. This requires a new approach *viz.*, Re-see approach wherein we re-see both Science and Spirituality in new ways and provide new interpretations to symbols used in science and spirituality.

Above discussion can also be viewed in terms of a historical perspective. Ancient India explored consciousness and gave *Upanishads* to the world. Modern science focused on the exploration of matter. Now both these traditions *viz.*, *Upanishads* and Science, are finding a new convergence in Consciousness studies leading to a new geometry of consciousness. This historical perspective can be represented as USCS (*Upanishads* – Science – Consciousness Studies) flow:

Upanishads (U) → Science (S) → Consciousness Studies (CS)

(Rishis) (Scientists) (Scientists-Rishis / Modern Rishis)

2.1 Some Symbols of New Geometry

New geometry of consciousness can be represented through symbols that are widely in use both in science and spirituality. A brief discussion on such symbols is as follows:

1. **Plus, Multiplication and Spiral (+, × and ◎):** Three symbols *viz.*, +, × and ◎ (plus, multiplication and spiral) can be considered as fundamental symbols of the new geometry of consciousness. These three symbols are interrelated and a number of phenomenon of nature can be explained with the help of these symbols. When + is rotated, we arrive at × and when × is rotated at a very high speed it generates an upward moving force of spiral like a tornado.

   In nature we observe following three types of changes:

   (*i*) Changes that are incremental in nature represented by + symbol.

   (*ii*) Changes that are multiplier in nature and therefore lead to multiplier effect represented by ×.

   (*iii*) Changes that are spiral in nature and lead to fundamental change in the configuration *e.g.*, revolutions in societies. An event in a society can influence the entire nation and can even change the course of history.

   Like the changes in nature, changes in organizations and societies can also be viewed in terms of these three symbols of the new geometry of consciousness. Organizations and societies experience incremental changes, radical changes and disruptive / revolutionary changes arising from spiral like effects.

2. **Languages as Geometry of Consciousness:** It may be indicated that geometry of consciousness also finds its expression through various languages. An illustration of geometry of consciousness is the very first letter (क) of *Devnagri* script which is a combination of symbol of infinity (∞) and the symbol T. It is a symbol of infinity combined with **a vertical and a horizontal line**. As a symbol of the new geometry of consciousness, it represents the idea of consciousness as infinite and unbounded in its vertical and horizontal expanse. This *Devnagri* letter can also serve as an analytical model of dialectical synthesis wherein symbol of infinity represents thesis and anti-synthesis intertwined. This illustration from the Devnagri script leads us to a general view that alphabets of various languages represent a geometry of consciousness.

   Popular usage of the phrase, From Alpha to Omega can also be interpreted in terms of evolution of consciousness from Alpha state to Omega state. In fact, all languages can be considered as expressions of nature's geometry of consciousness. In view of the same, there is an underlying unity of all languages. A unity in diversity can be experienced when languages are considered as different expressions of geometry of consciousness.

   T as a symbol is indicative of vertical and horizontal dimensions of knowledge and consciousness. T letter symbolizes vertical and horizontal dimensions of knowledge. It also symbolizes Truth. 'In Truth we trust' finds its echo in *Upanishadic* wisdom, '*satyamev jayate*' (Truth always prevails). When T symbol is included within a circle, it acquires a new meaning and represents three views of knowledge and consciousness *viz.*, vertical, horizontal and integrative. For example, 'scientific precision'/ domain specialization, can be represented by vertical dimension and 'creative art'/ creativity approach by horizontal dimension. These two are balanced by including them in a circle. Thus, T within a circle is a metaphor of vertical, horizontal and integrative approaches to knowledge creation, decision making and problem solving. Many universities are now recognizing the need for these three dimensions of knowledge in development of curriculum. Figure 2.1 presents this symbol as a symbol of a new geometry of consciousness.

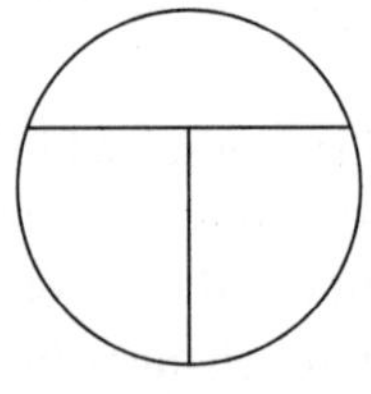

Figure 2.1. A Symbol for Vertical, Horizontal and Integrative Perspectives

Above illustrations indicate that the shapes of letters from different languages across the world can provide us some new insights to the geometry of consciousness.

3. **Seven Tempers of Mind as SHARMAN Circles of Consciousness:** Full circle rainbow is another illustration of new geometry of consciousness.

Full circle rainbow in the outer sky has a mirror image as an inner rainbow with ROYGBIV circles representing seven expanding circles of consciousness. Table 2.1 provides interpretations to various colours of consciousness and this model can also be referred to as rainbow model of mind.

Table 2.1. Colours of Consciousness

Red (R)	Orange (O)	Yellow (Y)	Green (G)	Blue (B)	Indigo (I)	Violet (V)
Reason	Intuition	Wisdom	Insight	Revelation	Imagination	Vision
Scientist (S)	Humanist (H)	Artist (A)	Rishi (R)	Muni (M)	Awakened (A)	Nirvana (N)
Scientific Temper	----------------	----------------	----------------	----------------	Spiritual temperament	

(**Source:** Wisdom & Consciousness from the East, Subhash Sharma, IBA Publications, Bangalore, 2013, p. 119.)

In the above presented interpretation, scientific temper is the starting point of awareness and as awareness increases we finally reach the stage of awakening leading to transcendental vision. Visionaries operate from higher levels of consciousness and thereby they provide transcendental vision to the society. While Philosophers operate from rationality end of the 'spectrum of knowledge', poets, saints, sages and wise gurus operate from higher levels of consciousness and therefore provide new insights based on their transcendental vision of reality. In essence this rainbow model of mind represents seven tempers of mind and seven approaches to knowledge creation. It also suggests seven intelligences of mind in terms of reason, intuition, wisdom, insight, revelation, imagination and vision. These seven expanding circles of consciousness also represent the idea of Theory O and are represented by SHARMAN circles wherein SHARMAN stands for Scientist, Humanist, Artist, Rishi, Muni, Awakened/Avatara like and Nirvana states of consciousness. Thus, rainbow model can also be considered as SHARMAN model of consciousness as well as SHARMAN model of knowledge creation and seven approaches to problem solving. A proper understanding of these seven circles of consciousness and corresponding seven approaches to knowledge creation and problem solving, is very useful to managers and leaders because many problems require solutions from higher states of consciousness. This model also provides us a framework for typology of minds and it may be interesting to find linkages of this typology with different areas of brain. This model also has implications for education wherein focus is on development of all seven tempers of mind and not just the scientific temper. Further, this model can also be referred to as Thinker to Thirthankar model of mind. While scientific temper represents the Thinker and knowledge creation through thinking based on reason, spiritual temperament represents the Thirthankar and knowledge creation through imagination and vision is the essence of the same.

Inner rainbow model presented above also has equivalence with Indian model of mind in terms of waking state, dream state, deep sleep and transcendent states of mind. Many 'revelations' have emerged from dream state *e.g.*, Kekule's insight on Benzene structure, Mendeleev's insight of periodic table, Watson's insight of double helix etc. It is speculated that Martin Luther King had a dream in his dream leading to the famous statement, 'I Have a dream'. Human history has been deeply influenced by the 'dream actualization' of the insights originating from the dreams. Thus dreams have the potential of changing the reality in the waking state, in addition to being a source for new knowledge creation.

4. **Expressions of Consciousness in Human Society: From Fight to Fullness:** In the context of human society, we find expression of consciousness in terms of 5F *viz.*, Fight, Flow, Fly, Float and Fullness. Geometry of this evolutionary model of human consciousness can be represented by various symbols as presented in Table 2.2.

Table 2.2. From Fight to Fullness

Fullness	•
Float	∞
Fly	○
Flow	△
Fight	□

In this geometry of human consciousness, rectangle represents Fight consciousness as it represents territory for which human beings fight in their survival. Triangle represents flow like the flow of river from the top of the mountain. Circle represents the fly like the flight of the bird and ∞ represents the floating like floating of the cloud and *shunya* (dot) represents the fullness state of consciousness. It may be indicated that fullness state of consciousness is also represented by many phrases such as *Fanna, Nirvana, Moksha etc*. These phrases represent the 'fullness experiences' in different languages. As more and more human beings evolve on this ladder of consciousness (from fight to fullness), we can visualize a shift in consciousness from 'Darwinian existence' to 'Enlightened existence' with dignity and divinity oriented worldview. It may be indicated that 'full moon' (*poornima*) is indicative of fullness and a simple exercise of looking at the full moon on the full moon day can create a shift in consciousness from Fight to Fullness and this simple exercise can be used for stress management. Prominent and influential Western thinkers such as Freud, Marx and Darwin have emphasized Fight aspect of human existence. World is now discovering the higher truths of human nature in terms of Fullness dimension and thus a shift in consciousness is taking place at the global level.

It may be indicated that above presented model can be reduced to three levels model *viz.*, Fight, Delight and Light levels. At Fight level, mind thinks in Darwinian terms and views reality around him / her in terms of Darwinian jungle and highlights 'areas of darkness' and accordingly seeks solutions to various problems within this framework. At Delight level, mind views nature as a source of positive energy and celebration and at Light level, it sees 'areas of light' and thereby its focus is on experiencing fullness in every human endeavor. It may be indicated that these three worldviews are in consonance with Indian Guna theory which classifies nature's energies in terms of *tamas* (violent), *rajas* (vibrant) and *sattava* (silent / non-violent) energy.

5. **Π, ϕ, ψ and Sky: Four Circles Model of Consciousness:** Π, ϕ and ψ are three well known symbols that can also be considered as symbols of the geometry of consciousness. It may be indicated that in terms of their meaning in social sciences, these symbols are considered as symbols of Politics (Π), Philosophy (ϕ) and Psychology (ψ) and Spirituality (Sky).

   These symbols have their equivalence in Body, Mind and Spirit model of human beings as well as in energy *chakras*. As symbols of consciousness they represent evolution of consciousness from Body to Mind to Spirit to Cosmic consciousness. As an individual's consciousness evolves, it reaches the sky level *i.e.*, yoking with cosmic consciousness. This four levels consciousness model has implications for individual, collective and organizational consciousness. It can also be represented as a model of four concentric circles of consciousness representing expansion in consciousness.

6. **Dialectical Chakra, Swastika Analytics and Whirlpool/Spiral Geometry:** Three concepts that capture the essence of the geometry of consciousness and its application to society's analysis include dialectical *chakra, swastika* analytics (analyzing horizontal & vertical axis of an issue) and whirlpool geometry. A dialectical *chakra* arises from the multiplicity of dialectics that we observe in society. This multiplicity could arise from caste, class, gender, culture, religion, etc. Dialectical *chakra* can also take the shape

of *swastika* and as a result of the rotation of *swastika*, whirlpool / spiral is generated. Thus, small events in society turn into huge spirals and influence the whole society through the process of the dialectical *chakra* turning into *swastika* and then becoming a whirlpool / spiral. This process can be seen in communal and other types of riots in the society. Social media has also speeded up this process as information is communicated instantaneously. Thus, we can find a large number of examples of 'local event' having 'global impact'. These have created new challenges for the modern State. Social sciences have not yet grasped a proper understanding of this geometry of consciousness as many tools of social sciences are rooted in models drawn from natural sciences. An understanding of three tools *viz.*, dialectical *chakra*, *swastika* analytics and spiral analytics can lead to new insights and thereby new solutions for the social and managerial problems and issues.

7. ***Shunya,* Matrix and the *Swastika:* Matrix as *Swastika* and *Swastika* as Matrix:** Popularized by Harvard Business School, 2 × 2 matrix is widely used as an analytic tool in Management. The dynamic aspect of 2 × 2 matrix is revealed when the matrix is viewed in terms of its origin from *Shunya* and transformation into a *Swastika*. Figure 2.2 presents this view of the 2 × 2 matrix.

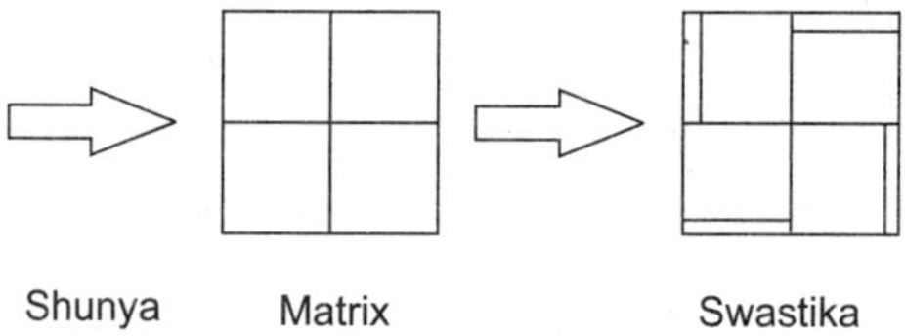

Figure 2.2. *Shunya*, Matrix and *Swastika* Inter-relationships

Thus, 2 × 2 matrix does not represent a static phenomenon as inherent within the matrix is a *swastika*. As the matrix rotates, it can become a spiral because of hidden *swastika* within it. Further, 2 × 2 matrix is hidden in *shunya*. When *shunya* expands in terms of horizontal and vertical axis, a 2 × 2 matrix is generated with a hidden *swastika* in it. Rotation at a high speed then leads to a spiral. Thus, there is *shunya* and spiral connectivity via a matrix and *swastika*. In essence, the Geometry of *shunya* (*shunya* matrix) finds it expression in many forms such as matrix, *swastika* and spirals. In 'creations from *shunya*' we can feel the presence of this geometry in varying forms.

8. **Western Windows, Eastern Doors and Consciousness Corridors: Three Models of Thinking:** New geometry of consciousness also leads us to a new architecture of consciousness in terms of 'Western windows, Eastern doors and Consciousness corridors'. Western Windows (WW) represent the Western enlightenment tradition reflected in scientific approach to

knowledge creation wherein we look at the outer reality through the windows. Eastern Doors (ED) represent the Eastern awakening tradition wherein we experience inner reality through the doors. Consciousness Corridors (CC) provide us opportunity to study reality from higher levels of consciousness. Every knowledge domain particularly in the field of social sciences can be studied from the perspective of Western windows representing the scientific-analytic approach, Eastern doors representing the intuitive-creative approach and Consciousness corridors perspective representing imaginative-visionary or the higher consciousness approach. These three models of thinking also correspond to left brain, right brain and central line connecting the two sides of the brain.

9. Omega Circle as a Symbol of Integration, Synthesis and Strategic Thinking:

Rooted in the Jainism concept of *syadvad* and *anekantavad*, Omega circle is a symbol for new geometry of consciousness emphasizing the concept of integration and synthesis. This circle also represents 360 degree approach, wherein we look at reality from various angles and thereby move in the direction of holistic view of reality. This integration and synthesis is of particular significance in case of strategic thinking, decision making and problem solving.

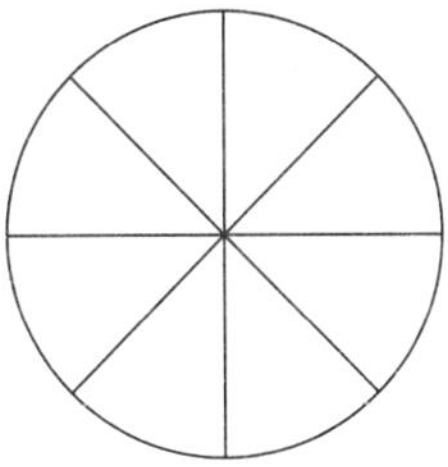

If we put alpha to omega in an ascending order, omega also represents a top of the mountain view. Thus omega circle has two interesting implications for strategic thinking *viz*., taking a top of the mountain view and achieving an integration and synthesis of various analytical results. Hence it can be considered as a symbol for strategic thinking. Further, it represents a geometry of consciousness that takes us from analysis to synthesis. We can also find the echoes of the SHARMAN circles of consciousness in moving towards meta synthesis of ideas originating from analytics. It may be indicated that *chakra* in the Indian flag also represents the omega circle view of strategic thinking. Further, it also represents the idea of One and Many (OM), wherein center of *chakra* represents One and its spokes represent Many. Hence it is symbol of unity in diversity. In strategic thinking, we need to integrate diverse perspectives to create a vision.

2.2 Science and Spirituality Connections

Geometry of consciousness helps us in seeing connectivity between science and spirituality. While science is 'matter' (outer search) route to reality, spirituality is 'spirit' (inner search) route to reality. It is indeed interesting that while the two routes are different in its approach, there are interesting parallels. Capra (1976) provides many interesting parallels. Chandrankunnel (2008) takes us in the direction of 'quantum holism' and 'cosmic holism'. Wilber (2000) suggests the need for 'Integral Psychology'. In the discussion below we point out parallels between some well known symbols from science and spirituality. These include symbol of atomic power and *atmik* power, double helix symbol of DNA and *Kundalini* symbol, medical symbol of intertwined snakes and *Kundalini* structure, symbol of psychology and symbol of trident etc. These are presented in Table 2.3.

Table 2.3. Symbols from Science and Spirituality

Symbols from Science	Symbols from Spirituality
 (Atomic power)	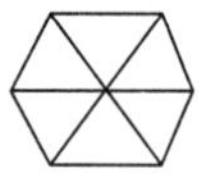 (Heart *Chakra* hexagon / diamond (A symbol of *Atmik* power)
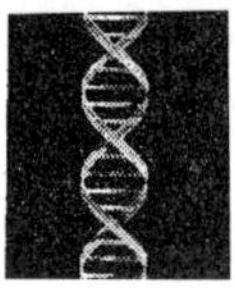 (Double helix)	 (Kundalini double helix)
 (Medical symbol)	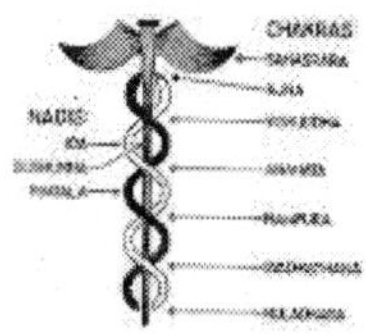 (Kundalini structure)
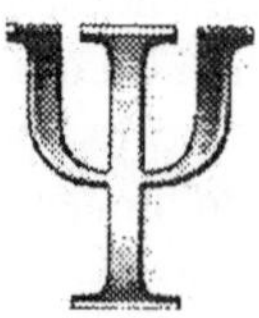 (Psychology)	 (Trident: Spirituality)

Thus, we observe interesting connectivity with some primordial symbols that are common across cultures. This indicates that ancient geometry of consciousness is being rediscovered through the route of science. This is bridging the gap between science and spirituality. Science has recently discovered the 'God particle', in spirituality, '*shunya* particle' represents the 'inner spirit' of the matter. In future, we may discover the bridge between the 'God particle' and the '*shunya* particle' *i.e.*, between the 'atom' and the '*atma*'. Such a discovery could come from the scientific route or the Rishi route or a combination of both approaches. It will lead to deeper understanding of expressions of One and Many (OM), both in matter and spirit leading to the ultimate search of unity of unities between matter and spirit. This search has been a core idea in Vedanta and now it is finding its expression in consciousness studies. In fact, science and spirituality integration in the form of integration of 'scientific temper' with 'spiritual temperament' is leading us towards 'new age modernity' (namo).

Linkage between science and spirituality can also be understood through the metaphor of river and a 'quantum bridge' connecting two sides of the river. This metaphor helps us in understanding linkages between Matter, Mind and Consciousness. We can imagine a hut on the West side or the left of the river, housing three eminent scientists *viz.*, Einstein, Newton and Darwin (END) representing 'END' of science. On the East side or the right side of the river, there is another hut housing three great thinkers and seers of humanity *viz.*, Mahavira, Buddha and Aurobindo ('MBA') representing 'Spiritual MBA' view of consciousness. Flowing river represents Mind and whirlpools in river represent whirlpools in mind. Two sides of the river represent the matter and consciousness view of universe and human beings and the flowing river represents the mind of human beings. These two sides are connected through a 'quantum bridge'. A person standing on the quantum bridge across the river, sees these two huts on both sides and also his own reflection in flowing water and thereby thinks of integrating Matter-Mind-Consciousness (MMC). As she/he looks at the rainbow in the sky and starts meditating on the seven colours of the rainbow, she/he gets a feel of the seven SHARMAN circles of consciousness leading to holistic view of knowledge creation. Figure 2.3 provides a diagrammatic representation of this visualization.

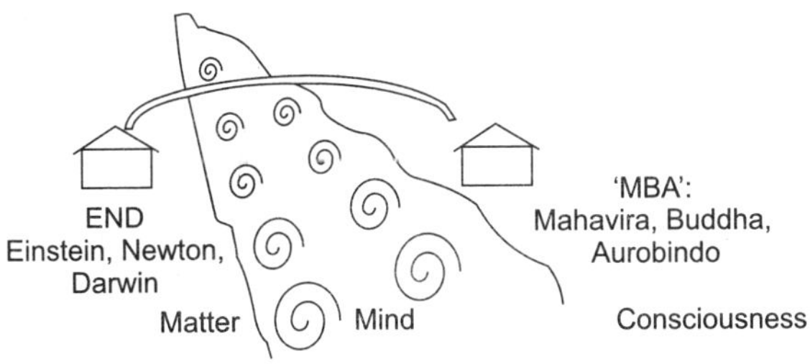

Figure 2.3. Quantum Bridge as a Metaphor for Science Spirituality Integration

This metaphor of river also has implications for knowledge creation. Left side of the river also represents 'Western Windows' (WW) approach to creation of knowledge, wherein outer world is explored through scientific approach and right side of the river represents the 'Eastern Doors' (ED) and 'Consciousness Corridors' (CC) approach with focus on exploration of the inner world. For a proper understanding of the whirlpools in the river representing the whirlpools in the world in the form of events, WW, ED, CC approaches are needed. This will lead to an integrative and holistic understanding of knowledge creation for the benefit of both West and East through a new synthesis of 'scientific temper' with 'spiritual temperament'. This idea can also be represented through the metaphors of Harvard-Haridwar-Himalaya. In Fig. 2.3, Harvard is visualized on left bank of the river, river is flowing through Haridwar and Himalayas provide the backdrop. Visualization of Fig. 2.3 is from my visit to Rishikesh, well known for its iron suspension bridge known as 'Laxman jhula'.

2.3 Application to Social and Management Thought

To understand application of the geometry of consciousness to social sciences and social studies and Management thought, we consider the following four stages model of evolution of knowledge creation approaches in the field of social and management thought:

Natural sciences → Social sciences → Neuro sciences → Consciousness sciences
(I) (II) (III) (IV)

Methodology of the natural sciences deeply influenced the development of social sciences. However, with the development of neuro-sciences, social sciences are undergoing a transformation. Further, with the impact of 'consciousness sciences'/ 'consciousness studies', many fields of human knowledge are finding some new directions. In particular geometry of consciousness can lead to new directions of research in social studies, Management studies and Management thought.

In social contexts, geometry of consciousness finds its expression through individual and collective consciousness. An individual's consciousness can transform a society *e.g.*, Gandhi's impact on society through the combined affect of +, x and spirals of awakening created by him. Similarly, collective consciousness of a society can also transform a society *e.g.*, French revolution and Russian revolution. Revolutions can be considered as 'tornadoes of collective consciousness' leading to fundamental change in the society and its structure. A better understanding of geometry of consciousness can provide us some lessons in understanding disruptions and transformations in society and nations. Giri (2013) suggests the need for 'Planetary realizations' for social transformation that can be facilitated through the new geometry of consciousness. Sharma (1996 & 2006) and Meera Chakraborty (2010) outline contours of the 'colors of mind' for individuals, society and organizations. Further, Sharma and Albuquerque (2012) explore implications of consciousness approach in the context of corporations.

2.4 Towards Theory O of Consciousness*

O is symbol for *shunya* / zero as well as alphabet O, and can be considered as a fundamental symbol in the geometry of consciousness. As *shunya* symbol it represents consciousness and as the radius of the circle increases, **the circle** of consciousness increases. When radius becomes infinite, one reaches the realm of infinity. Thus, consciousness expands to infinity. SHARMAN model of consciousness represents expansion of consciousness. In fact, Full circle rainbow is an interesting metaphor for the expanding circles of consciousness and therefore it captures the essence of Theory O.

Theory O implies realization of deep rooted Oneness of everything in cosmos from quantum level to cosmic level through 'Quantum ropes' and 'Quantum threads' (Sharma, 1999). This was the Vedantic view and in Physics, string theory envisages the same. Once such a realization of deeper connectivity dawns an individual, her / his circle of consciousness expands and her / his world view becomes inclusive and holistic. A person moves away from Division (Divided vision) approach to Cosmic vision approach to life, living, relationships and even management and leadership.

Theory O of consciousness aims at evolution of consciousness towards Oneness with cosmos. Since cosmos is infinite, Theory 0 implies expansion of one's consciousness to infinity. This leads to fullness experience that has been variously described as experience of bliss, *nirvana etc*. When such experiences are brought into play in day to day activities, it leads to harmony and peace through wisdom. Such a workplace becomes '*pragyasthan*' *i.e.*, a place where people experience oneness and bliss and decision making is based on 'wisdom (*pragya*) approach' also represented by 'wisdom circle' represented by an integration of science and art (represented on x–axis), philosophy and spirituality (represented on y–axis). This is the basic idea of Theory O that has wide application in social sciences, management, leadership and good governance. In all 'creations from *shunya*', entrepreneurs, leaders and institution builders experience an expansion in their consciousness starting from the initial state of zero / a start from the scratch. Such experiences help in broadening of mental horizons. Figure 2.4 presents the concept of wisdom circle.

*First presented by Prof. Subhash Sharma at a discussion session with faculty at the School of Applied Psychology, Zurich University, Zurich, June 27, 2013. This idea of Theory O was also presented in a Workshop on Wisdom & Consciousness, Alsace-Rhindia, ARC Evolution, Strausbourg, France, June 28, 2013.

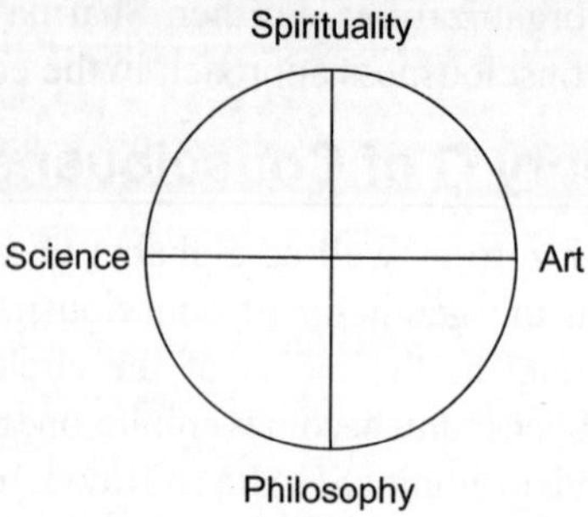

Figure 2.4. Concept of Wisdom Circle

In essence, Theory O implies expansion of consciousness and as consciousness expands, it creates conditions for inclusive approach. Divisions disappear and entire world becomes one family. When Swami Vivekananda addressed the Parliament of Religions through his famous words, Brothers & Sisters, he expanded the circle of consciousness to include everyone. Thus, Theory O of consciousness was unconsciously at work. Now the time has come to consciously use this approach for individual, organizational and social transformation.

❑

CHAPTER 3 Knowledge Generation Windows and Grounded Praxis*

With the advent of 'new economy', a new paradigm of management has been emerging. While, the concept of Total Quality Management (TQM) belonged to the brick and mortar economy, the idea of Total Knowledge Management (TKM) belongs to the 'new economy' and the high tech era. A transition from TQM to TKM has already occurred with the recognition of 'knowledge' as an important asset of organization. The focus of new age management thinking is on knowledge, knowledge leadership and knowledge workers.

3.1 Total Knowledge Management

Nonaka and Takeuchi (1995) provide us the concepts of 'explicit knowledge' and 'tacit knowledge'. In organizational context, Total Knowledge can be defined as a summation of the explicit and tacit knowledge. Thus, the idea of Total Knowledge can be captured through the following equation:

$$\text{Total Knowledge} = \text{Explicit Knowledge} + \text{Tacit Knowledge}$$

$$TK = EK + TK$$

Given this as a definition of Total Knowledge, the concept of Total Knowledge Management could be defined in terms of managing the 'Total Knowledge' of the organization with a view to enhance competitive advantage of the organization.

*Sharpening & Strengthening Knowledge Competence of Corporates: Knowledge Management in Enterprise Context, Subhash Sharma, Decision, IIM Calcutta, Jan–Dec. 1999, Total Knowledge Management (TKM): Enhancing Competitiveness Through Knowledge Management Systems, Subhash Sharma, *Journal of Scientific & Industrial Research*, CSIR (Council of Scientific & Industrial Research), Aug–Sept, 2000, 59, 673–682.

It may be indicated that the field of knowledge management is essentially an inter-disciplinary area. Research in several other disciplines has contributed to the development of the idea of knowledge management and the idea of Total Knowledge Management is a natural extension of the concept of knowledge management. It may also be mentioned, recognition of knowledge as an asset has gained importance due to developments in Information Technology as well as other high tech industries.

The idea of learning organization (Peter Senge, 1990) as well as developments in cognitive sciences, artificial intelligence and study of consciousness provide the foundation for emergence of the concept of knowledge management. In addition, Everett Roger's (1983) work on 'adoption of innovations' has also influenced the developments in the field of knowledge management. Indeed, knowledge, when considered in a broader context, can be viewed in terms of learning at the level of individual, organization and society, facilitated through the idea of innovation. Thus, TKM can also be conceptualized as an interactive process for knowledge generation and development at the individual, organization and society level influenced by the circle of innovations or circles of innovations.

As a backdrop to the idea of knowledge management, it may be indicated that the most well known knowledge management window is the model given by Nonaka and Takeuchi (1995) who consider 'knowledge management' in terms of an interaction between 'explicit' and 'tacit' knowledge leading to four modes of knowledge creation, *viz.*, tacit to tacit mode or the 'socialization' mode, tacit to explicit mode or 'externalization' mode, explicit to tacit or 'internalization' mode and explicit to explicit or 'combination' mode.

As a supplement and complement to Nonaka & Takeuchi (1995), knowledge generation window in the form of interaction between explicit and tacit knowledge, Sharma (1999) suggests three knowledge generation windows. These include (*i*) A taxonomy of approaches to knowledge building; (*ii*) Old wine–New wine metaphor; and (*iii*) Knowledge generation matrix.

3.2 Knowledge Generation Window I: ETOS (Explicit–Tacit Objective–Subjective)

The taxonomy to knowledge building adds the dimension of objective and subjective methodology to the explicit and tacit typology of knowledge. This gives us four combinations:

1. Objective–Explicit (Knowledge is explicit in nature and has been gained through Objective methodology).
2. Subjective–Explicit (Knowledge is explicit in nature but has been gained through Objective methodology).
3. Objective–Tacit (Knowledge is tacit in nature but has been gained through Objective methodology).

4. Subjective–Tacit (Knowledge is tacit in nature but has been gained through Subjective methodology).

3.3 Knowledge Generation Window II: Old Wine–New Wine

The Old wine–New wine concept of knowledge building uses the well known wine–bottle metaphor to classify knowledge in terms of old wine–old bottle, old wine–new bottle, new wine–old bottle, new wine–new bottle. In addition to this classification, knowledge could also be developed on the basis of 'refined wine and refined bottle'.

3.4 Knowledge Generation Window III: Theory–Practice Window

In the field of management, knowledge is continuously generated at two levels *viz.*, by the practitioners in their day-to-day context and by the scholars and researchers. Given this understanding of knowledge creation, there could be a four-fold classification of knowledge in the form of concepts and ideas:

1. Known to practitioners and known to scholars
2. Known to practitioners and unknown to scholars
3. Unknown to practitioners and known to scholars
4. Unknown to practitioners and unknown to scholars

Once we put this classification system in a matrix somewhat similar to Johari window, we get an analytical model that can be referred to as 'knowledge generation matrix' or the 'knowledge window'. This matrix is presented in Fig. 3.1.

		Scholars	
		Known	Unknown
Practitioners	Known	I Text-books / Work-books	II What they don't teach in management schools
	Unknown	III Available in the journals	IV What is unknown to companies and management schools

Figure 3.1. Knowledge Generation Matrix

A brief on the four cells of the knowledge generation matrix is given below:

Cell–I: It refers to ideas that are known to both practitioners and scholars. These ideas find their way in standards textbooks on the subject.

Cell–II: It refers to ideas known to practitioners but not known to scholars. This knowledge may be in practitioner's head and is usually not taught at the Harvard Business School or any other management school.

Cell–III: It refers to ideas unknown to practitioners but known to scholars through their insights and subsequent conceptualization. Such ideas may be lying in scholarly journals inaccessible to practitioners.

Cell–IV: It refers to the ideas terrain that is neither known to practitioners nor scholars. This represents the 'black box' and it offers new horizons for innovative thinking and creativity and has the greatest potential for paradigm breaking knowledge. Clues to the contents of this black box could come from the intuitive insights of workers, customers and others interacting with the organization. For new ideas, this black-box needs to be explored.

Ideas which are known to practitioners and have been empirically tested and re-tested by the researchers and scholars, become part of the 'received knowledge' of the subject. Thus, they become the 'standard elements' of the subject matter and are reproduced in textbooks and workbooks for learning by the new entrants in the field. In this case, theory and practice both tend to converge because theory is based on practice and practice is influenced by theory.

Ideas that are known to practitioners but have not been studied by scholars or have not yet been tested, belong to category II. These ideas are based on the 'empirical intelligence' of the practitioners. They are the intuitive flashes, and brainwaves that practitioners generate in the course of their day-to-day confrontations with reality. Since, such ideas have not yet become part of the 'received knowledge', they belong to the category of "what they don't teach you at the Harvard Business School" or "what they don't teach at the management schools". This represents the case of a practice that is yet to be theorized. Scholars can gain considerably from such 'practitioners' knowledge', as practitioners' insights could be converted into models and concepts.

Ideas that are known to scholars from their insights and interactions with field situations and have been conceptualized and theorized but are not yet available to practitioners, belong to category–III. If published, such ideas may be available in journals. It could represent the case of a theory that is yet to be practiced. Practitioners can enhance their 'knowledge circle' by accessing such knowledge.

Ideas that are neither known to practitioners nor to scholars in the field represent the 'dark spaces' with 'dotted spots'. There are many examples of new and innovative ideas coming from people outside the field leading to opening up of new knowledge doors. For example, many physicists have contributed to development of stock market theory. Since, they didn't belong to the field, they offered some fresh insights in an unrelated knowledge area.

This knowledge generation window also provides us a framework to understand the academic–industry interaction. It recognizes the fact that contributions to knowledge building could came from both the academicians as well as practitioners. While practitioners provide the experience-based insights, academia provides the intellectual expertise of conceptualizing the ideas. The interaction between the two creates synergy for new knowledge building. If the two pursue their different routes, such synergy may be lost. At times new ideas originate from industry and at times they originate from academician's head. Through an interaction, both industry and academia gain. Because of this usefulness of the knowledge generation window, it could also be referred to as 'knowledge development matrix'.

The knowledge generation window also has implications for curriculum design in management institutes. In most cases, the focus of the curriculum is on ideas belonging to Cell–I of the window, because it represents the standard body of knowledge in the subject. However, there is a need to go beyond the Cell–I and find out ways to develop innovative methods to explore the knowledge from other cells of the knowledge generation window. While such efforts are left to the imagination of the individual teachers, a conscious approach on the part of the management schools would not only ensure a closer industry-academia interaction but also lead to generation of new knowledge and enhancement in intellectual capital.

3.5 Implications for Learning and Knowledge Building: Learning Context, Learning Models and Grounded Praxis

The above discussion on knowledge generation window leads us to the next question. What is the learning process by which knowledge in the quadrants I, II, III and IV is acquired by the knowledge seekers who could be students or practitioners?

In respect of quadrant–I knowledge, the standard learning model of mathematics *viz.*, the question-answer model is quite useful. We attempt a question and look at the end of the textbook for the correct answer. Since, elements of the subject are nothing but the 'received knowledge' there is only 'one' correct answer. Through repeated practice, we learn to arrive at the correct answers.

In respect of quadrant–II knowledge, we can use the action–reflection–conceptualization model of learning. Schon's (1983) idea of 'Reflective Practitioners', provide us the learning model for "How Professionals Think in Action". Similarly Paulo Freire's (1970) well known model of learning, action–reflection leading to praxis could also form the basis of learning in quadrant–II. These models of learning fall in the category of 'Praxis mode of learning'. We suggest the term, 'grounded praxis' as practice is grounded in reflective action. Further, the conceptualization of experience is also rooted in ground reality. This 'wisdom' model of 'grounded praxis' incorporates the 'reflective action' idea and indicates the relationship between knowledge and wisdom. This relationship also provides us the learning cycle through a feedback between wisdom and knowledge leading to refined knowledge and refined wisdom, is presented in Figure 3.2.

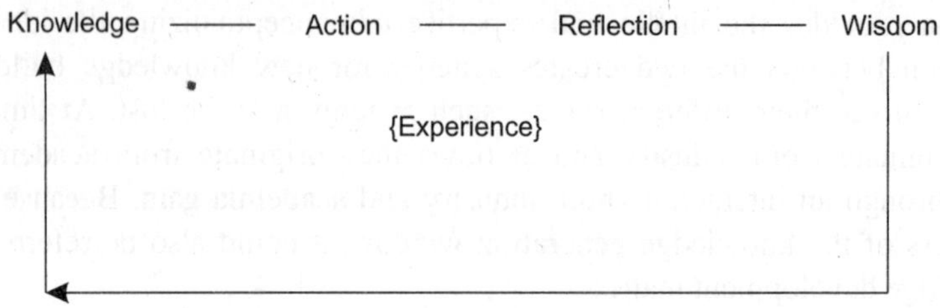

Figure 3.2. Knowledge–Wisdom Learning Cycle

A practitioner develops his/her insights in the form of 'managerial wisdom' on the basis of his/her knowledge about theories and the reflective action. This ensures that his/her praxis is rooted in action and ground reality. Wisdom equation, W (Wisdom) = Reason (R) + Intuition (I), also captures the essence of the knowledge–wisdom cycle presented above (Sharma, 1999).

In grounded praxis, the conceptualization of one's experience is rooted in ground reality. It may be indicated that the idea of 'grounded praxis' is distinct from the concept of 'grounded theory' which has emerged as a research tool for qualitative research in social sciences. In fact, insights from grounded theory could be useful for grounded praxis. During recent years, grounded theory has been applied in study of management and organizations (Locke, 2001). 'Action based research' could also throw up insights for grounded praxis. The grounded praxis could also be considered distinct from Marxist praxis thought though some insights from Marxist praxis may also be useful. In essence, grounded praxis is a learning model and a tool for new knowledge generation. Hence, it is useful for knowledge management. It may also be indicated that for all practical purposes, 'grounded praxis' could be considered a new approach and a new learning model, though it draws from reflective–action model of learning. Grounded praxis not only reduces the theory–practice gap but can also provide links between macro and micro realities.

The concept of grounded praxis can also be applied to management research. Knowledge–wisdom cycle constitutes the foundational basis for grounded praxis approach to research. In this approach, experiential insights available from practitioners provide clues for formulating new concepts and ideas leading to development of new knowledge.

In respect of quadrant–III, testing mode of learning could be used. In the testing model of learning, theory or idea is field tested and thereby a theory is converted into practice.

In respect of quadrant–IV, the interactive mode of learning could be used. Interactions with people from other fields could yield new knowledge. Brainstorming sessions, creativity networks, creativity circles, mind pooling through 'Discussion sessions' or simply the 'bull sessions' could provide new insights. The 3D model of learning *i.e.*, Discussion, Dialogue and Discourse, is also a useful model for this quadrant. 3D model is a three step model. In step 1 learner is at the Discussion stage. Once the ideas are understood and internalized, learner moves to the second step *viz.*, Dialogue stage, wherein the learner is able to engage in a dialogue with the teacher/mentor/guru. Once the learner has internalized ideas to such an extent that he/she is able to extend ideas through commentary, the learner enters the third stage *viz.*, Discourse. Thus, the 3D model of learning is evolutionary in nature, wherein learning takes place in three distinct but overlapping stages of discussion, dialogue and discourse.

From the above discussion, it can be inferred that corresponding to each quadrant we have a specific learning model; For quadrant–I: The question–answer mode of learning; For quadrant–II: Grounded Praxis mode of learning; For quadrant–III: Testing mode of learning; For quadrant–IV: Interactive mode of learning. Table 3.1 provides a summary of various learning models in consonance with the knowledge generation window.

Table 3.1. Learning Models for Knowledge Management

	Learning Context	Learning Model
1.	'Received knowledge' (Textbooks/ Workbooks)	Repeated Practice, one correct answer approach to learning
2.	What they don't teach at Management Schools	Grounded Praxis
3.	Theory that is yet to become a Practice	Field Testing
4.	Opening New Windows and New Doors to Knowledge	Interactive Learning through 3D (Discussion, Dialogue and Discourse), Brainstorming sessions, Mind pooling, Group discussions, Creativity circles, Bull-sessions and similar other interactive techniques.

3.6 Five Steps to Knowledge Building

While the above discussion has focussed on the knowledge generation window and the learning models, in the discussion below we provide another perspective on knowledge building. In this perspective, we divide the knowledge in the following five categories:

1. Routine Type Knowledge
2. Analytical Approach to Knowledge Building
3. Creative & Path Finding Approach

4. Paradigm Breaking Approach
5. Re-see Approach (High competence to see and re-see reality in new ways)

In the routine type approach to knowledge building, there is reproduction of the 'received knowledge' through para-phrasing methodology and empirical repetitions. It is a typical cook-book or the recipe approach of knowledge compilation and reproduction. In the analytical approach to knowledge building, aim is primarily at puzzle solving within a known paradigm. The well-known 'scientific approach' of hypothesis formulation and hypothesis testing belongs to this category. Creative and path-finding knowledge building aims at creation of new and novel ideas. Development of novel concepts and creation of a new tributary of knowledge belongs to this category. The paradigm breaking knowledge building aims at radically new perspectives, which are developed by seeing through the anomalies (Kuhn, 1962) as well as through subjective insights by "looking at the spaces that no one has looked before". The fifth category of knowledge generation is the Re-see approach, which implies generation of new knowledge by re-seeing the ideas in new perspectives. We can also refer to this as Rishi approach. Rishis are those who can re-see the ideas, events and things in new perspectives. We are familiar with the ancient Rishis. During modern times, Vivekananda, Aurobindo, Gandhi, are examples of 'Modern Rishis' who opened new consciousness corridors. Now in the corporate era, 'Corporate Rishi' is one who can see **and re**-see events, threats and opportunities in new ways.

Figure **3.3 presents** the five steps framework of knowledge building. In this figure, rishi **or re-see** step has been metaphorically represented as Buddha *i.e.*, an enlightened **one.**

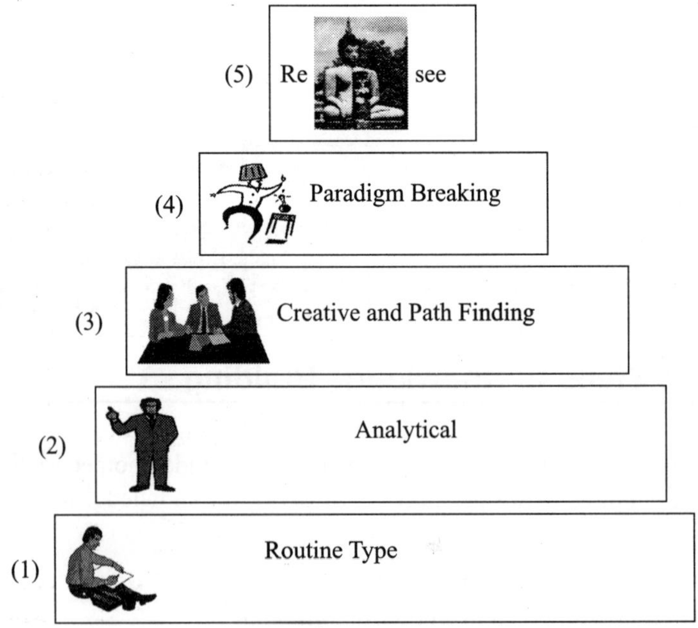

Figure 3.3. Five Steps Model of Knowledge Building

This five steps model also integrates the following three approaches to knowledge creation:

1. Rational–analytic (critical thinking)
2. Intuitive–creative (creative thinking)
3. Imaginative–visionary (imaginative thinking)

As the mind's windows, doors and corridors open, critical thinking, creative thinking and imaginative thinking get enhanced and we move towards gaining holistic understanding of reality. This holistic understanding comes through Rationality, Intuition, Wisdom, Insights, Revelation, Imagination and Vision, represented by the rainbow model in terms of SHARMAN model of seven circles of consciousness, seven intelligences, seven types of minds and seven approaches to knowledge creation. These seven approaches also represent seven rivers (*sapt sindhu*) of knowledge. Each river represents a 'stream of knowledge' based on its source in reason, intuition, wisdom, insights, revelation, imagination and vision. Hence, in each discipline of study (*e.g.*, Economics, Political science, Sociology, Management, Leadership, Spirituality) knowledge creation can take place through these seven approaches and knowledge created in the discipline can be categorized in terms of above presented categories. As a researcher or knowledge creator evolves in his/her consciousness, his/her ability to create new knowledge beyond the quantitative-empirical approach increases and he/she provides new insights and vision to the discipline and thus creates paradigm shifts. For a manager and a leader an understanding of the seven circles of consciousness and seven approaches to knowledge creation and problem solving, is very useful because of inter-linkages between consciousness, intelligences, knowledge creation and problem solving. Hence, this model can be used as a model for imparting management education in particular and holistic education in general.

Table 3.2 provides an indicative list of Western and Eastern knowledge creators, who have used in varying ways, various approaches presented above.

Table 3.2. Western and Eastern Knowledge Creators — An Illustrative List

Western windows	Eastern doors
Newton	Aryabhatta, Ramanujan
Einstein	S.N. Bose
Darwin (Evolution of matter)	Aurobindo (Evolution of mind), J.C. Bose (Plants have feelings)
Freud	Osho (Spirituality)
Maslow	Raman Maharishi, Mahesh Yogi (Spirituality)
Marx	Vivekananda, Gandhi

Many other names can be added to both sides. When this exercise is done in the class with students, many new insights emerge *e.g.*, names of C.V. Raman, S. Chandrashekhar and others get cited with respect to Eastern doors. When this exercise is done to identify seven modern rishis (modern *saptrishis*) of India, names such as Vivekananda, Gandhi, Aurobindo, Osho, Mahesh Yogi, Radhakrishnan …, emerge as part of general consensus.

3.7 From Knowledge to Truth

'Satyamev jayate' (Truth ultimately prevails) is the key mantra of Indian Constitution and thereby Indian State. In fact, 'In Truth We Trust' has been the voice of ancient Rishis and sages. It finds its echo in *Upanishads* and during recent times in Gandhi's 'My Experiments with Truth'. Science is also always in search of Truth. Each scientific discovery takes us closer to the Truth. Idea of Truth represents the 'Religion of Religions' because searching for the 'Light of Truth' is the essence of all religions. According to ancient Rishis, 'Truth Actualization' represents the essence of human existence. It may be indicated that the idea of 'Truth Actualization' takes us beyond Maslow's concept of Self-actualization.

Earlier we presented the link between Knowledge and Wisdom. Wisdom paves the way for higher Consciousness, which in turn paves the way for Enlightenment. Enlightenment leads us to 'see' the Light which in turn leads us to realization of the Truth. This process can be represented in terms of a flow with broad equivalences with six chakras, as presented in Table 3.3.

Table 3.3. From Knowledge to Truth

Knowledge →	Wisdom →	Consciousness →	Enlightenment →	Light →	Truth*
(K)	(W)	(C)	(E)	(L)	(T)
(I)	(II)	(III)	(IV)	(V)	(VI)

*Satyamev jayate

As the circle of consciousness of an individual expands, a person evolves from being an expert to become a wise person and then evolves to higher consciousness leading to enlightenment. In case of managers and leaders as their circle of consciousness expands, they become Enlightened Leaders and their decision making becomes more intuitive, imaginative, inclusive, integrative and holistic. In Corporate context, such a leader is a 'Corporate Rishi'. In academic context, a Teacher and a Researcher evolves as a Guru and as an 'Academic Rishi', as she/he understands above indicated linkages.

To conclude, in this chapter we have presented the concept of knowledge generation windows. For practicing managers, a number of windows are available. However, most important one is the knowledge generation matrix, which recognizes the contribution of the practitioners to knowledge generation. We have also presented five steps model of knowledge building. Individuals and organizations can identify the step/level at which they are currently operating. They can plan and evolve their strategies and action plans to move up the 'ladder of knowledge' from level 1 to level 5. If individuals and organizations are able to reach level 4 and 5, they become the 'knowledge leaders'. For a society to develop, the proportion of individuals and organizations at levels 4 and 5 should increase. In essence, leadership in knowledge era is provided by 'knowledge gurus' who operate from level 4 and 5 of the knowledge ladder. At level five, 'knowledge gurus' see the light of Truth and use this experience to create a 'spiritual awakening' among masses. For example, Gandhi through his experiments with truth created an awakening that transformed the world.

❑

CHAPTER 4

Three Paradigms of Management*

100 years of the journey of Management Thought can be viewed in terms of a start from Science in Management (SIM) to movement towards Spirituality in Management (SIM). This journey can also be referred to as transition from Taylor to Transcendence. We can classify this journey in terms of four stages *viz*., Scientific Management, Human Side of Management, Ethics and Values in Management and Spirituality in Management. These evolutionary stages developed as a result of imperatives of the times. From 1900 to 1950s, Scientific Management played dominant role. 1960s to 1990s, Human Side acquired importance. 1990s onward, Ethics and Values became important imperatives for Good Governance of Corporations and after 2000, Spirituality in Management started emerging as a new paradigm as a result of imperatives of environmental concerns and well being *etc*. It may also be indicated that management thought initially evolved in the context of stable environment and the factory context of industrial revolution. Over the years stable environment has given way to complexity and change and new concerns have emerged and 'campus' has emerged as a dominant metaphor in the knowledge driven economy.

4.1 Evolutionary Journey of Management Thought

During each stage of development of management thought, different disciplines impacted the field of management. During Scientific era, Engineering and Economics played dominant role as the major concerns were productivity and

*Three Paradigms in Management: American, Japanese and Indian, Subhash Sharma, *International Journal of Organization Theory & Behavior*, Spring 2013, 16 (1), pp. 30–41. A version of this paper was presented at the Fifth International Conference on Contemporary Business, Curtin Business School, Curtin University, Perth, Sept. 15-16, 2011.

cost. Hence, associated tools and techniques were largely rooted in task focus and production focus.

During Human Side period, discipline of Psychology acquired dominance and concern for people became an important concern. This was also reflected in human dimensions related concepts and tools and techniques such as MBO, Blake and Mouton Grid, Transformational Leadership *etc*. However, ethics and values had not yet fully entered the field of management. Once the concern for Good Governance became important, the discipline of Philosophy as a foundation for Ethics and Values impacted the field of management. This led to emergence of new concepts such as Principle Centered Leadership.

After new concerns such as environmental issues, sustainability and well being became important, the idea of Spirituality in Management gained acceptance and ideas from the field of Spirituality / Consciousness Studies started impacting the management thought. New concepts such as Triple Bottom line, Spiritual leadership, Wisdom leadership, Leadership by Consciousness and Transcendent Organizations (Gustavsson, 1992) became part of the discussion and dialogue in management thought and books such as Tao of Physics (Capra, 1976), The Turning Point (Capra, 1992), Seven Spiritual Laws of Success (Chopra, 2002), Integral Psychology: Consciousness, Spirit, Psychology, Therapy (Wilber, 2002) *etc*., started influencing the field of management and leadership. In future all four stages will have varying influences for future development of management thought and practice. Table 4.1 sums up this discussion.

Table 4.1. Evolutionary Journey of Management Thought

	Scientific Management	**Human Side Management**	**Ethics & values**	**Spirituality**
Concern	Productivity, Cost	People Dimension	Good Governance	Environment, Sustainability, well being
Influencing Discipline	Engineering & Economics	Psychology	Philosophy	Spirituality / Consciousness
Major focus	Technical side	Human side	Ethics side	Spiritual side
Illustrative Tools	Time and Motion studies	MBO, Blake & Mouton grid, Transformational Leadership	MBHO: Management by Higher Objectives	HOPE: Higher Order Purpose of Existence
			Principle Centered Leadership	Triple bottom line, Wisdom Leadership

Future

It may be indicated that tools and techniques developed during different stages of development of management thought arose from the meta-vision and meta-perspectives of management thinking during that period. As new thoughts emerged, new tools and techniques were developed. Four stages led to four sides of management *viz.*, Technical side, Human side, Ethics side and Spiritual side. Now the new house of management with all the four walls is leading us towards a holistic vision of the concept of management. This holistic vision represents the future of management thought.

4.2 Three Paradigms: American, Japanese & Indian

There is another way of understanding the evolution of management thought *viz.*, in terms of the nations and their management thinking. Up to 1970s, American Management dominated the field of management thought. Subsequently, with success of Japanese Corporations, the idea of Japanese Management emerged. During recent years, the idea of Indian Management has been emerging as a result of success of Indian companies particularly Indian IT companies as well as from the soft power exhibited by many successful Indian spiritual movements. A recent book, The India Way (Peter Cappilli *et al.*, 2010) published by Harvard University Press, outlines some distinctive features of Indian Management styles. Another recent book, American Veda: From Emerson and the Beatles to Yoga and Meditation How Indian Spirituality Changed the West (Goldberg, 2010) captures the influence of India's soft power through its spiritual movements. As a result of such developments, over the past century, 'one best way' approach popularized by American Management has given way to 'Pluralist Management' recognizing the diversity of approaches to management and leadership. Further, Globalization with its interdependence across nations has brought spotlight on culture. Japanese Management emerged from its cultural roots and the Indian Management seeks its rootedness in the knowledge seeking ethos and spiritual heritage. It may also be indicated that American Management had roots in Taylorian techniques that were suitable to production methods of assembly line and hard power view of the world. Now the world has become more complex and has become knowledge driven and soft power view is capturing the imagination of the world. There is also a pressure on corporations to move towards ecological sensitivity and society-centric approach in their functioning. Indian Management with its philosophical foundations is now relevant for such a context. In fact, in the 'new world' that managers are encountering, moral and social goals are becoming important in addition to economic goals. This is also leading to search for new paradigms to overcome some of the weaknesses of existing dominant paradigms.

Sharma (2007) in his book, New Mantras in Corporate Corridors (p. 56), captures these ideas in terms of Kola, Kaizen and Knowledge metaphors reflecting the essence of American, Japanese and Indian management approaches. Kola derived from 'Cola' (Coca Cola) is indicative of a competitive approach based on aggressive approach to every managerial activity to ensure the presence of the brand across the world. It reflects primacy of economic goals over moral and social goals. Kaizen approach to management is based on continuous improvement and focus on quality. Knowledge metaphor indicates achieving competitive advantage based on Knowledge and Talent. In Indian Management, focus is on Knowledge as 'Knowledge seeking ethos' represent the essence of Indian ethos and have defined India since ages.

Three paradigms represent three types of CEOs *viz.*, Kola oriented CEOs, Kaizen oriented CEOs and Knowledge oriented CEOs who are Creative Enlightened and Organic (CEO) leaders. In future Corporations may need a new breed of CEOs who will combine the Kola, Kaizen and Knowledge approaches to managing corporations.

Kola, Kaizen and Knowledge define the DNA of American, Japanese and Indian Management. However, as indicated above, for new competitive advantage we need a 'recombinant DNA' in the form of K^3 model of management and leadership. This model can be represented as K^3 formula given below:

$$K^3 = \text{Kola} * \text{Kaizen} * \text{Knowledge}$$

It may be indicated that K^3 formula suggested above is an integrative model and has universal relevance and is a new age mantra.

Significance of K (knowledge factor) has been widely recognized in the knowledge economy. Earlier the focus used to be on Cost (C) and Quality (Q) factors. Japanese demonstrated importance of Q factor in achieving competitive advantage. In 21st century, 'KQC Triad' represents the new mantra of competitive advantage, wherein all the three factors *viz.*, Knowledge, Quality and Cost are considered as important determinant of the competitive advantage.

4.3 Key Aspects of Three Paradigms: Towards AJIN (American, Japanese, Indian, New Age) Integration

Key aspects of three paradigms *viz.*, American, Japanese and Indian can be understood in terms of the following three levels:

1. Philosophical Foundations
2. Leadership Dynamics
3. Sustainability

Foundational Philosophy of three paradigms represents the meta-vision of the paradigm. It could be viewed in terms of following dimensions:

1. Vision of Life
2. Influencing Thinkers
3. Dominant Ethos
4. Foundational Theories

American paradigm's Vision of Life, is rooted in Struggle for Existence and Survival of the Fittest. Japanese paradigm's Vision of Life, is rooted in Struggle for Betterment and Indian paradigm's Vision of Life is rooted in Struggle for values and recognizing co-existence and the fact that everything in nature is interconnected and we owe our existence because other things exist. Accordingly, influencing thinkers include Darwin in case of American paradigm, Zen philosophers in case of Japanese paradigm and Vedantik and other social thinkers, such as Vivekananda, Gandhi and Aurobindo in case of Indian paradigm (Chakraborty, 2003). This is also reflected in terms of dominant ethos of these paradigms *viz.*, spirit to dominate in case of American paradigm, spirit to improve in case of Japanese paradigm and knowledge seeking and social concerns & social purpose in case of Indian paradigm.

It may also be indicated that Japanese Management introduced the notion of super-ordinate goals thereby taking us beyond Peter Drucker and his Management by Objective (MBO) idea as an overarching idea. Super-ordinate goals also reflect the idea of Higher Objectives. Indian Management thinkers suggested the need to link Management with the 'Purpose of Existence' and introduced the notion of HOPE (Higher Order Purpose of Existence, Sharma, 2007, p.177) as an overarching idea for developing institutions and organizations with society-centric approach. Thus, three thought currents have roots in Objectives, Super-ordinate Goals and Purpose of Existence as foundational basis for development of management concepts and associated tools and techniques.

Above indicated thought processes are also reflected in terms of foundational theories defining the respective paradigms. American paradigm is based on Theory X and Theory Y and Maslow's Hierarchy of Needs as a basic concept. Japanese Management is based on Theory Z and the idea of continuous improvement-Kaizen. Indian paradigm is based on Theory K (Theory of collective energy of community and thereby collective advantage, Sharma, 1998) and the idea of 'Basket of Needs' (Sharma, 1996 & 2006, p. 96) and Nurturant Task Leadership (Sinha, 1980).

Leadership dynamics of the three paradigms is reflected in terms of decision making approaches. As a result of Western Enlightenment tradition, American paradigm is largely dominated by Head *i.e.*, rationality perspective of decision making. Accordingly, its tools and techniques have been developed on the basis of rational approach to decision making. Because of Zen influences, Japanese paradigm emphasizes Head coupled with Heart approach. Its tools and techniques such as quality circles etc. reflect a combination of rationality and intuition. Indian paradigm because of spiritual heritage, consciously or unconsciously reflects a combination of Head, Heart and Consciousness (Spirituality) with greater reliance on Heart and Consciousness. Incorporation of the consciousness dimension (spiritual dimension) in decision making, relationships, communication processes *etc*., represents the essence of the Indian paradigm or the 'India Way' (2010). In fact, need for 'Joining of Heart and Spirit' (JHS) is being felt in all walks of life.

Three paradigms can also be viewed from the viewpoint of sustainability. As the awareness of sustainability is spreading, American paradigm is slowly responding to it. The idea of Triple Bottom line is making some inroads, however, American paradigm has not yet moved beyond the 'Balanced Scorecard' to 'Holistic Performance Scorecard' (Sharma, 2007, p. 503). Japanese paradigm is evolving towards sustainability because of Zen influences and in case of Indian paradigm, idea of sustainability is inherent in its spiritual traditions and has some new ideas to offer. For sustainability idea to catch imagination, we need to write a new book that may as well be titled as Karma-Kapital. It would provide to the world a philosophy of holistic and sustainable development and management, wherein development is based on positive actions (*Karmas*) for the benefit of all stakeholders ('*sarvodaya*') and is in tune with the requirements of environment. It would take us beyond Karl Marx's Das Kapital as well as beyond 'Kola Capitalism'. It also implies need for a new approach to competitive advantage within the paradigm of spirituality, sustainability and social responsibility through positive actions. It may be indicated that echoes of this philosophy can also be heard in recently popularized phrase, Karma Capitalism that has a touch of Indian paradigm. Further, it also suggests a movement towards 'Holistic Advantage' concept based on an integrative view of competitive advantage, collective advantage and *Karma* advantage. While the idea of competitive advantage has its origin in market competition, collective advantage has its origin in social action / community and *karma* advantage has its origin in spirituality. In organization context, collective advantage also manifests itself in team building and karma advantage manifests itself in ethics, values and environmental concerns. In holistic approach to management and leadership, these three are combined for the benefit of the organizations, society and individuals. This is the foundation for *Karma-Kapital* (Sharma, 2011). Table 4.2 sums up the above discussion and provides a foundation for development of New Age Mantras originating from an integration of three paradigms. This can be referred to as AJIN (American, Japanese, Indian & New Age) model for creation of new age mantras in the field of management, leadership and strategic thinking.

Table 4.2. Key Aspects of Three Paradigms in Management

	Key aspects	American	Japanese	Indian
1.	Vision of Life	Struggle for existence	Struggle for betterment	Struggle for Values
2.	Influencing Thinkers	Darwin...	Zen Thinkers	Vedantik & other social Thinkers, Vivekananda, Gandhi, Aurobindo
3.	Overarching idea	MBO	MBHO: Management By Higher Objective	HOPE: Higher Order Purpose of Existence
4.	Dominant ethos	Spirit to dominate	Spirit to improve	Knowledge seeking ethos
5.	Foundational Theories	Theory X Theory Y	Theory Z	Theory K, Nurturant Task approach
6.	Leadership	Head, Rationality First	Head + Heart, Rationality + Creativity	Head + Heart + Consciousness, Rationality + Creativity + Spirituality
7.	HR perspective	HR as Human Resource with focus on managing others	HR as Human Relationships with focus on managing teams	HR as Human Responsibility with focus on managing self
8.	Sustainability perspective	Evolving	Evolving	Inherent in spiritual traditions

New Age Mantras based on AJIN (American, Japanese, Indian & New Age) foundations

4.4 Darwinian Jungle, Neurons and Nirvana: Towards New Mantras

Following three metaphors have emerged in discussion, dialogue and discourse on human existence, human society and views of life:

1. Darwinian Jungle
2. Neurons
3. Nirvana

Darwinian view of life views life in terms of natural selection, natural violence and natural competition. This thinking in the context of organizations and society over emphasizes jungle metaphor of competition, struggle for existence, survival of the fittest and natural fight. It views corporate jungle as full of violence where only fittest survive. It rejects other view of jungle as celebration of life through cooperation and connectivity. 'Big fish eats the small fish' was also noted in the ancient literature. However, it was also observed that big fish eats the small fish only to satisfy its hunger and thereby it coexists with small fish. There is a need to look at nature from this perspective also.

With emergence of neuro sciences, metaphor of neurons has been emerging as a new metaphor to view life. Neurons are interconnected and cooperate with each other. They display 'natural connections' and 'natural delight'. Thus, neuron metaphor highlights cooperation and connectivity in the society. Organizations and human society are discovering this metaphor as a new metaphor and use it to emphasize the importance of cooperation (*e.g.*, '*jugalbandi*' in music) and connectivity in management and leadership.

In nirvana metaphor, life is Light and celebration ('*Jai ho*') and nature in itself is a celebration. There is 'natural light' and 'natural celebration' all around. In this view, life is not a struggle for existence and essentially represents 'joy of existence'. As Gandhi noted, 'There is enough for every body's need and not for everybody's greed'. The metaphor of nirvana provides us a consciousness view of life and it suggests that human beings are striving for expansion of human consciousness from its narrow perspectives to cosmic perspectives. In this perspective, whole world is one interconnected web of life. Hence, an organization should view itself as part of that interconnected world.

It may be observed that these three metaphors also correspond to Body, Mind, Spirit (BMS) perspectives of human and social existence. They also correspond to Fight, Delight and Light perspectives on Life, Living and Leadership with roots in struggle for existence and joy of existence.

Above metaphors lead us to a new understanding of the way we view Self and Others through SO-SO (Self-Other, Self-Other) window. In this window, Other could be viewed as Enemy or Competitor. This is Darwinian view of human existence, wherein Other is your enemy and should be eliminated or defeated. In human history such a view has led to violent wars and colonialism wherein others were dominated, oppressed and suppressed. Other (s) can also be viewed as Friend, Partner, Brothers & Sisters. This is Humanistic view of 'Co-existence'. In Spiritual view Others are members of the cosmic family representing cosmic unity. Further, evolution of Self leads to a state of consciousness wherein 'Other is Self and Self is Other'. This is Vedantic view. This framework of SO-SO window view of Other (s) can be viewed in terms of social transformation from Darwinism to Humanism to Spiritualism and Vedantic view reflected through Fight, Delight and Light perspectives on Life, Living and Leadership. This discussion of SO-SO window is presented as a five steps model in Fig. 4.1 and can also be considered as a five steps model of Self evolution, wherein there is a transformation of an individual's mindset of viewing others as enemies and competitors to others as friends, brothers and sisters and ultimately Other (s) as extension of Self.

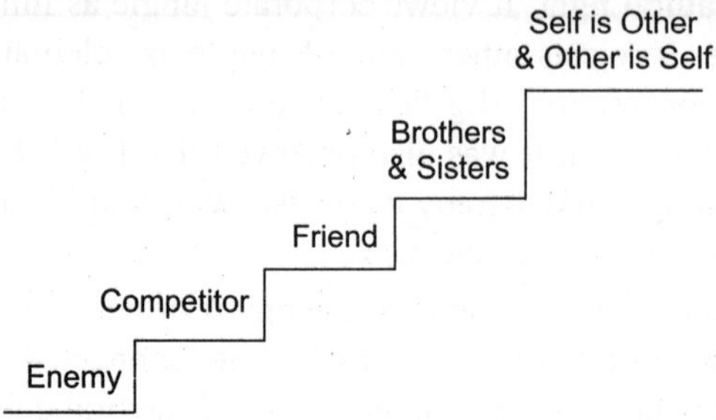

Figure 4.1. SO-SO Window Views of Other (s)

Above indicated SO-SO window views of Others, combined with neuron and nirvana metaphors, lead us to following three principles of life that have implications for management and leadership:

Principle I: Life is celebration (Joy / Joy of living / Jai HO – Hope & Optimism / Joy HO) – Idea of life as celebration is reflected in nature *e.g.*, rainbow reflects the idea of celebration.

Principle II: Other is your friend (*Mitwa*). Everyone is a friend (a *mitwa*).

Principle III: Others are brothers & sisters and co-travelers (*Musafir*) in the journey of life as celebration. We are all community of co-travelers.

These three principles have implications not only for individual evolution but also for organization development as in the 'New Age of the Global Village', it is being recognized that everything is interconnected and therefore neurons and nirvana provide us a better metaphors for future development of human society. This is also influencing the management, leadership and social thought. In an intuitive manner, Indian Managers have been using '*Jugaad*, *Jugalbandi* and *Jai ho*' as metaphors to find new creative solutions for responding to ground realities. These new mantras have global application in view of shift in strategic thinking from Darwinian view to neurons and nirvana view of human existence.

Our discussion of three paradigms of management and three metaphors *viz.*, jungle, neurons, and nirvana, has implications for future of management thought. This implies a movement towards an integrative model of management and leadership based on convergence and confluence of the three paths or paradigms through a process of mutual influencing, blending, melding, co-mingling and harmony. Ralston (1993) suggested the phrase 'cross-vergence' for such processes. Chatterjee (2007, 2009) studied them in the context of Asian Management Perspectives.

For this new architecture of management and leadership, Sharma (2007) suggests the metaphors of Western Windows, Eastern Doors and Consciousness Corridors reflecting Head, Heart and Spirit (Consciousness) approaches to management and leadership. They can also be referred to as American Windows, Japanese Doors and Indian Corridors leading us towards New Age Mantras. An architecture based on these approaches can become a 'House of HOPE: Higher Order Purpose of Existence'. Challenge before managers and leaders of twenty first century is to create such a 'House of HOPE' to ensure environmental sustainability, social responsibility and well being of all the stakeholders ('*sarvodaya*'). This implies a shift towards Holistic Corporate Management (HCM) wherein lessons from American, Japanese and Indian Management approaches as well as Rationality, Creativity and Consciousness / Spirituality approaches are harmonized for the benefit of the entire humankind. Holistic Corporate Management (HCM) also implies an integrative view of competitive advantage, collective advantage and *karma* advantage driven by Higher Order Purpose of Existence (HOPE) and Harmonic Globalization (HG).

❑

Part II

Macro Perspectives in Strategic Thinking

CHAPTER 5 Holistic Globalization and Holistic Development*

For the holistic development of the world, we need a holistic view of globalization. In fact, the concept of society's growth, development and progress should be viewed within the framework of a holistic vision of development. While the three terms *viz.*, growth, development and progress are interrelated, there is a subtle difference between the three. Growth largely refers to the economic dimension, development refers to social dimension and progress refers to holistic approach that includes the spiritual dimension.

5.1 Four Forces Model of Holistic Globalization (HG)

In contemporary context, following four fundamental forces are influencing individuals, organizations, nations and the world at large:

1. Force of Market
2. Force of State
3. Force of People / Community
4. Force of Self (Spirituality)

Dynamic interactions between these four forces shape the social configurations across the globe. Force of Market finds its expression in the form of business

*Development Matrix and Development Discourse: Towards A Framework of Strategic Gearing of the NBUs, Subhash Sharma, 4th SMF Convention, Indian Institute of Management (IIM), Ahmedabad, May 24–26, 2001, Towards A New Development Vision, Subhash Sharma, 5th SMF Convention, Management Development Institute (MDI), Gurgoan, April 25–27, 2002, Beyond Pyramid and Pyramid Thinking, Subhash Sharma, 13th SMF Convention, Indian Institute of Management (IIM, Lucknow, Noida campus, May 27–29, 2010.

organizations. Force of State finds its expression in the form of Governmental institutions. Force of people / community finds its expression in the form of social movements and through capillary action in the form of grassroots organizations. Force of Self (spirituality) finds its expression in the form of spiritual movements and corresponding institutions.

Discourse between force of Market and force of State has been reflected in terms of role of State. This can be expressed in terms of empire and umpire roles. In empire role, State acts as an empire and appropriates to itself many economic activities. This was the case in the ideology of Socialism, where State acquired 'commanding heights'. In its umpire role, State acts as a regulator just as the umpire in sports. During recent years, there has been a shift from empire to umpire role of the State as far as Market is concerned. Its role with respect to people is to ensure Good Governance, through a reach-out approach, wherein state reaches out to the people. Discourse on the significance of self and its expression in Market, State and Society has not received adequate attention. In general, this has been a missing link in Management and Social Sciences, though some attention has been drawn to during recent years in the ethics literature.

Figure 5.1 presents this Four Forces Model in *Swastika* diagram. In this *Swastika* theory, Market-State axis is represented as horizontal axis and Self-Community as vertical axis. It captures the essence of the dynamic interaction between four forces that we observe at the global level as well as at the national level. In the global village, '*swastika* dynamics' in one nation leads to '*swastika* spirals' across various nations.

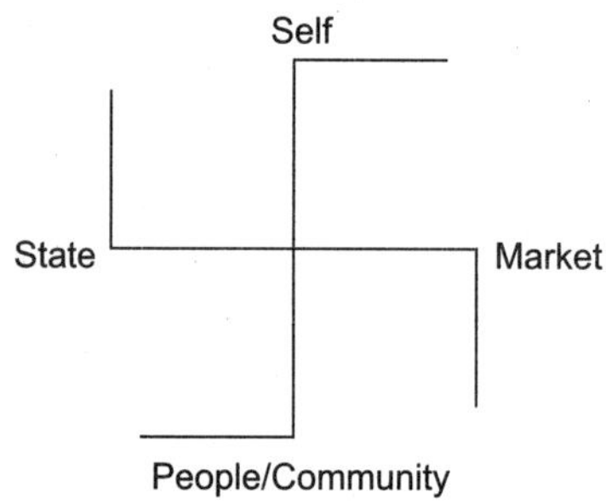

Figure 5.1. Swastika Model representing Four Forces of Holistic Globalization (HG)

When these forces act in harmony, synergy is generated and when they act in conflict and opposition to each other, there is negative energy (negergy). We refer to this model as a model of Holistic Globalization to differentiate it from the current ideology of globalization that is rooted in the global spread of the force of Market through the Corporate approach.

Social configurations of different nations differ depending upon the intensity of these forces. At one point of time, during the communist regime, Russia represented the dominance of State through 'commanding heights' ideology and forces representing market, society and self were not allowed to develop and manifest leading to chaos and disorder that in turn led to fall of communism. Social configuration of America has always been in favor of market. Gandhi suggested the need for community organizations. Traditionally India represented the force of spiritual self in the form of force of spirituality. This is reflected in the popularity of *yoga* and many Indian spiritual movements that have worldwide popularity. However, now the time has come to take a balanced view of the four forces.

In contemporary time, four nations *viz.*, India – China – America – Russia (I-C-A-R) have emerged as global players and they represent varying configurations of Holistic Globalization model. This I – C – A – R model has global level economic, political and social significance as it indicates mutual interdependence and interconnectivity of these four forces in the 'new age of global village'. This model can be represented as I- C- A- R global *swastika*, wherein I–C (IC) represent the vertical axis and A – R (AR) represent the horizontal axis. We can observe the interplay of this global *swastika* in varying forms in economic, political, social and psychological dimensions of contemporary societies. In this model both East (represented by IC) and West (represented by AR) find a new connectivity through the concept of Holistic Globalization.

Four forces model presented above can also be represented by four lions Ashokan symbol that is also a symbol of India as a Nation-State. It can also be found on every Indian currency note. This symbol can be reinterpreted to represent the four forces of Holistic Globalization as discussed above. Figure 5.2 presents the four lions model of four forces shaping the global village.

Self (S)

State (S) ——  ——Market (M)

People (P)

Figure 5.2. Four Lions Symbol Representing Four Forces MSPS Model

It may be indicated that three lions are visible *viz.*, lions representing Market, State (Government) and People. Fourth lion representing the Self is a hidden lion. In fact, intellectual discourse during last 150 years or so has been largely between the two lions *viz.*, lions representing the Market and lion representing the State. Ideologies of capitalism and socialism originated from such a view. From time to time, third lion represented by People roars in the form of social movements and social upheavals. During recent years environmental movements represent the third lion. Fourth lion *viz.*, hidden lions, representing the Self represents the spiritual energy. In general, lions representing the people and self, have not been incorporated in the social discourse dominated by Market and State. In this respect Indian Guna theory and its integration with Market, State and Society provides us a new insight to the dynamics between the four forces.

It may be indicated that in Indian context, Gandhi wanted the force of Self / Spirituality and force of People to emerge strongly, however, under Nehruvian vision, India borrowed the Russian model and opted for the dominance of the force of the State. It may be observed that during recent years, force of People has also emerged in the form of NGOs and Self Help Groups etc. The philosophy of Liberalization, Privatization and Globalization (LPG) represents the emergence of the force of Market and the expression 'economic reform' implies reducing the influence of the State and allowing the greater role for Market. A new vision requires a balanced approach rooted in the strengths of the nation represented by four lions symbolism representing Holistic Globalization (HG) and thereby it provides conceptual foundations for the vision of Holistic Development & Management (HDM). This new vision implies a paradigm shift from LPG to HDM. Thus, India's development journey can be viewed in terms of Socialistic vision to LPG to HDM.

In today's Nation-States, we can witness the dynamic interplay between the above identified four forces that influence nation's or region's growth, development and progress. This interplay is also influenced by four forces Swastikas of other nations.

5.2 Foundations of Four Forces: Market Equilibrium, Social Equilibrium and Personal Equilibrium*

Deeper roots of above four forces are in the following ideas and values:

1. Profit, competition and self-interest (PCS);
2. Justice, rights and duties (JRD); and
3. Love, compassion and devotion (LCD).

Market force expresses itself through PCS (Profit, competition and self -interest) mode of thinking and these three (PCS) represent the market values. People force expresses itself through JRD (Justice, rights and duties) mode of thinking and these three (JRD) represent the social values. Force of Self / Spirituality expresses itself through LCD (Love, compassion and devotion) mode of thinking and these three (LCD) represent.

With roots in Profit, competition and self-interest, Market promotes a Transactional (T1) worldview. In contrast, Society wants a Transformational (T2) approach to society's growth, development and progress through Justice, rights

*Expressions of Self in Market, Society and Spirituality, Subhash Sharma, International Seminar on Practical Spirituality and Human Development, Institute of Sociology, University of Freiburg, Freiburg, March 25, 2007.

and duties. Spirituality suggests a Transcendental (T3) approach through Love, compassion and devotion, in order to create harmony within society. Transactional (T1), Transformational (T2) and Transcendental (T3) values define a nation through an interplay of market, social and spiritual values. There is a need to find an appropriate balance between the three. This is also the essence of Theory T (T = T1 + T2 + T3) of creating a harmonic society. It can also be considered as a foundational theory for 'harmonic globalization'.

Thus, for creating a new social order that takes us beyond the current concept of globalization, there is a need to balance market values represented by PCS, social values represented by JRD and spiritual values represented by LCD. It may be indicated that the concept of 'globalization' takes a narrow view of life as it is largely based on PCS or Transactional view of life. Figure 5.3 presents a harmony model of achieving a balance between market values, social values and spiritual values representing market, society and self. In this 'harmony yantra,' demand supply diagram represents the market equilibrium, balance represents the social equilibrium achieved through social values and '*chakra*' represents personal equilibrium achieved through spiritual values and Y represents balancing these three equilibriums. Circle represents the grand equilibrium as a vision for the world.

It may be indicated that in the language of isms (idea spirit-manifestations), PCS represents the 'spirit of capitalism', JRD represents the 'spirit of social responsibility' and LCD represents the 'spirit of spiritualism / spiritual concerns' that finds its expression in good governance. In the 'harmony yantra,' all the three spirits find unification. This is the essence of the harmonization paradigm for a new social order.

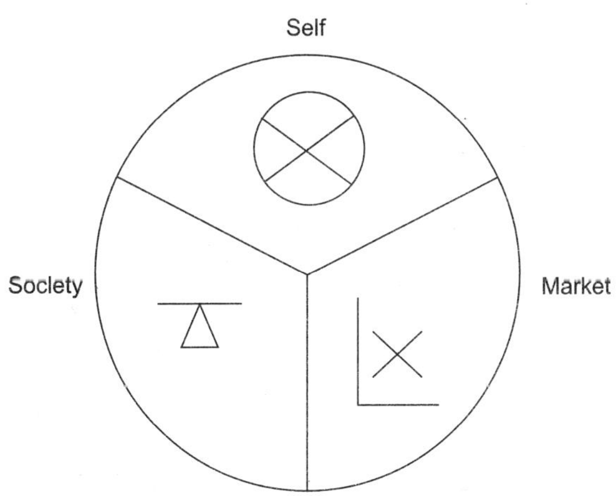

Figure 5.3. Harmony Yantra Model of Balancing Market, Society and Self

In the above discussion of harmony model, role of the State is minimal. Role of the State is more in the form of umpire and to facilitate creation of harmonic society. It may also be indicated that over a period of time, State's role of social justice has largely been taken over by NGOs and other social institutions and movements. This has further diluted the role of State. In fact, through the 'reforms', State has been reducing and redefining its own role. In its new role it should focus on achieving a balance between Market, Society and Self (Spiritual force).

5.3 Three Wise-men Metaphor for Holistic Corporate Management (HCM)

In consonance with the above discussion, there are three paradigms of development *viz.*, economic development, sustainable development and holistic development. Economic development is primarily based on profit, competition and self-interest (PCS) approach. However, such an approach leads to over exploitation of resources and ignores the environmental dimension. The concept of sustainable development incorporates the environmental dimension as well as inter-generational equity. In a limited way, it accommodates the justice, rights and duties concept. In corporate context, the concepts of Environmental Management Systems (EMS) as well as Corporate Social Responsibility (CSR) reflect the application of sustainable development in business organizations.

The concept of holistic development takes us one step beyond the sustainable development. In holistic development, ethical dimension is part of the development thinking. Further, it incorporates the spiritual dimension reflected through love, compassion and devotion, as an integral aspect of development process; it also draws our attention to 'My Social Responsibility' (MSR) to create an awakening among human beings towards their social responsibility at individual levels. Further, in corporate context, it implies concern for good governance.

The concept of holistic development can be viewed in terms of an integrative approach wherein various aspects of development that include, efficiency, equity, ethics, social concerns such as environment, gender equality, etc., and transcendental / spiritual concerns are integrated.

This model can also be explained through the imaginative metaphor of "Three Wise-men walking on Development Road". First wise-man, Adam Smith is walking on the right side of the road and all the corporate leaders and managers are following him chanting the mantra of efficiency and profit, competition and self interest. Second wise-man Karl Marx, is walking on the left side of the road and the factory workers are following him chanting the mantra of social equity and justice, rights and duties. Both these wise-men are following the third wise-man, *viz.*, Gandhi and all others including social activists, unorganized workers, etc., are following him chanting the mantra of ethics and truth. As Marx follows Gandhi, he realizes the futility of the violent approach to create change and he abandons the violent path and adopts the democratic approach.

It may be indicated that the three wise-men also represent three worldviews *viz.*, 'economics', 'politics' and 'good governance' and their integration implies a holistic view of the world.

In an extended imagination of this metaphor, we can imagine the spiritual masters or the realized beings such as Swami Vivekananda and others guiding the three wise-men through 'spiritual awakening'. This metaphor of three wise-men in the company of the spiritual masters, provides us an integrative view of development, wherein various isms such as capitalism, socialism, ethicism, environmentalism, feminism, spiritualism, etc., find space as well as integration in the form of holistic development. In corporate context, three wise-men metaphor presented here leads us to the idea of Holistic Corporate Management (HCM) rooted in the philosophy of Holistic Development, wherein profit, CSR and Good Governance are integrated in corporate management practices.

It may be indicated that in India, spiritual awakening has been a powerful method for creating social change and silent revolutions in contrast to violent changes and violent revolutions. Indian history is witness to the same. During medieval times Bhakti movement was a movement centered around spiritual awakening and during modern times, India's freedom movement was based on spiritual awakening. In the age of globalization, we may expect a similar awakening in future. This will lead us to a new vision for a new social order and a new corporate awakening.

5.4 Towards A New Social Order

The world needs a new vision,
To see the world through a new prism,
The world needs a new mission,
To go beyond all isms…

It was earlier observed that 'globalization' is based on the narrow worldview of life, in terms of an economic vision rooted in 'Market' or transactional approach to life. Further, it is largely corporate or MNC oriented. There is a need to move beyond this vision of globalization. The holistic model can provide us a new foundational premise for a new vision, wherein there is a proper balancing between Market, State, Society and Spiritual Self to create a new social order.

The new social order can also be referred to as vision of sacro-civic society, wherein there is a touch of transcendence in all human activity. Such a vision, would aim at a balanced view of life earlier presented as harmony circle. This circle finds its manifestations in the society in terms of various organizations and movement such as corporates, Government institutions, people's institutions and spiritual movements. In sacro-civic society, these institutions play complementary part and are not in antagonism to each other.

The vision of sacro-civic society has following three essential components:

1. Its view of life is rooted in eco-sattavik perspective. In ecological-sattavik perspective of life, transcendental concerns are the guiding values for day to day activities and actions. Life is driven by HOPE *i.e.*, Higher Order Purpose of Existence and not by 'survival of the fittest to eliminate the rest'.

2. Its view of society is rooted in the concept of harmony. Hence, 'harmonic society' is its aim, wherein all factors of creation *viz.*, Knowledge, Power, Capital and Labour (KPCL) operate in harmony. Further, there is harmony among various isms and religions. Thus, in contrast to conflict model of society, harmonization paradigm is its essence.
3. Its view of leadership and management is reflected in Divine-Democratic approach and style. It implies that democracy should evolve further and should lead to divine like synergy in the society and its institutions. Thus, it suggests a shift from authoritarian approach to democratic approach to divine-democratic approach. In divine democratic approach, love; compassion and devotion (LCD) is part of the leadership style.

It may be indicated that in a sacro-civic society; a business organization is not merely an economic entity, it is a sacro-economic entity and business activity is sacro-economic in nature. The roads to development presented in above discussion with proper connectivity with the holistic development framework, can lead us towards the new vision of establishing sacro-civic society, wherein there is holistic growth, development and progress for everyone.

5.5 Towards RICH Model*

Concept of RICH model provides us a basis for nation's development. Components of RICH model include the following:

1. Per Capita Resources
2. Per Capita Income
3. Per Capita Consumption
4. Per Capita Happiness

RICH model focuses on four factors of development *viz.*, Resources, Income, Consumption and Happiness. It may be indicated that the concept of per capita happiness is derived from the concept of 'Gross National Happiness' (GNH) suggested by Government of Bhutan.

Figure 5.4 presents the concept of RICH model as development wheel or the '*Vikas chakra*'. Because of its focus on happiness, this model includes spiritual dimension as an important parameter of development. Hence, this model integrates the economic and spiritual aspects of development and represents a model of Holistic Development. It may be indicated that RICH development wheel moves with the support of Institutions and Technology. Societies that develop institutions and take the help of technology are able to give better momentum to the development wheel. As over exploitation and non-sustainable use of resources can

*Per Capita Income, Per Capita Happiness and Per Capita Bliss: Integrating Economics, Psychology and Spirituality in Modern Societies, Subhash Sharma, in Workshop on Happiness, Well being and Ananda, Gaeddu College of Business Studies, Royal University of Bhutan, Oct. 10, 2013

have adverse impact on per capita happiness, this model suggests sustainable use of resources leading to sustainable income and sustainable human development.

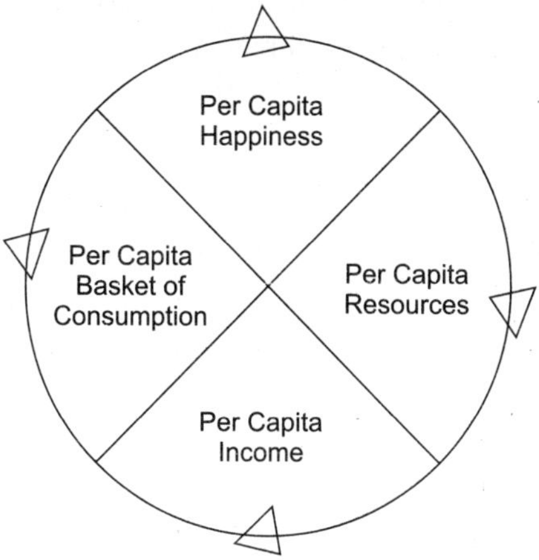

Figure 5.4. RICH Model of Holistic Development

5.6 Nation's Business Units (NBUs)

The development wheel of a nation moves through Nation's Business Units (NBUs). The idea of SBUs (Strategic Business Units) is widely discussed in strategic management literature. When it is extended to a nation's context, we arrive at the idea of NBUs *i.e.*, Nation's Business Units. Indeed, in consonance with the development matrix discussed earlier, the spectrum of economic activities of nation could be viewed in terms of six distinct forms / sectors / models *viz.*, the MNC sector, India Incorporated: Indian private sector, public sector, co-operative sector, self managing micro enterprises sector or the 'people's sector', or the 'small growers' sector. Entrepreneurship and start up businesses could also belong to the people sector. Figure 5.5 presents this spectrum which could also be referred to as Coca cola – Coconut spectrum. It may be indicated that all the six models of NBUs have their own strengths and weaknesses, plus points and negative points and in any development strategy, due consideration should be given to the Full Spectrum rather than only one end of the spectrum.

An analysis of the contribution to employment generation by each sector is critical to understanding the focus of government's policy, as it indicates the degree of economic relevance of each sector in a country like India. Instead of focusing merely on the market shares and market growths, the GNP shares and employment generations also need to be focused. In the hype created by advertising, the issues related to employment generation are quite often forgotten, as the focus is on 'Fortunate 500' rather than the masses.

Focus of Government policies should be to achieve a balance. It can be argued that what is needed is a correction or reform in favour of the people's sector side of the spectrum to improve its market competence to effectively complete at the market place. In essence, a balanced approach is needed wherein corporate sector, public sector, co-operative sector and people's sector play partnership and complementary roles in the development process, and thereby contribute to generating the required momentum for the development wheel to move forward.

MNC	**India Inc.**	**Family owned Business**	**Public Sector**	**Co-operative Sector**	**People's Sector**
Large, Organized Mega Structures	Large, Organized Structures	Large size and Mid size	Large, Organized, Government Supported	Large and Mid size	Mid size, Micro-Enterprises, Self Managing Nano enterprises

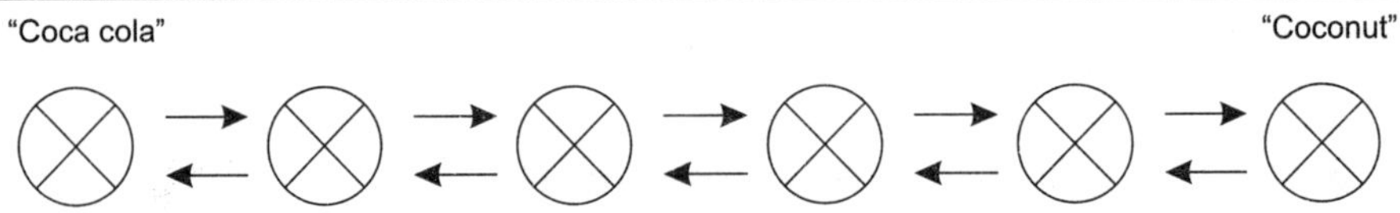

Figure 5.5. Spectrum of Economic Enterprise – NBUs of a Nation

5.7 Towards Development STEPS for Holistic Development and Management (HDM)

To operationalize the above suggested ideas in contemporary global context, there is a need for a new vision statement for holistic development at the national and global levels, *viz.*, 'modernization of villages and spiritualization of cities'. Modernization of villages implies taking science and technology to the villages and putting it in the service of rural masses. Appropriate institutions and latest technology are needed for the development of villages as economic and socio-cultural units. In addition to the *Panchayatiraj* institutions, new technological innovations should be brought to the door step of the villages. While Information Technology is very useful to provide market information on prices of commodities and opening doors for market access, it is also important to provide new "packages of technologies" to the villages. In essence, modernization of villages implies a "reach-out model" approach to development process wherein new institutional structures are created to take the technology to the people. Modernization of villages also implies employment generation and work creation at the grassroots level. This would also reduce the need for migration to cities.

Cities have taken the benefit of technology and have relied upon the positive dimensions of market mechanisms to induce the development processes. However, cities need spiritualization to overcome the 'existential stress' created due to intense competitive pressures. Thus, spiritualization of cities is an important aspect for the holistic development of the Nation.

Vision of the sacro-civic society can be realized through the STEPS development model of Holistic Development & Management (HDM). By STEPS we mean the following dimensions of development (Sharma, 2001).

S : Social

T : Technological

E : Economic

P : Political

S : Spiritual

First dimension of Development STEPS is Social (S) aspects of a society. Social development implies promotion of art, culture, literature and related soft aspects of human development. A vision that ignores this dimension of human existence and human development, could only be a partial vision. Hence, for holistic development, this aspect cannot be ignored. It may be indicated that values such as equity, human rights, etc. are important aspect of social development. Further, societies differ on individualism – collectivism spectrum and some societies strive to achieve a balance between the two through a search for 'middle space solutions' – mid range solutions. Pendulum metaphor as pendulum model is useful in understanding search for middle space solutions. Individualism and collectivism represent two extreme positions of social pendulum. However, most societies are looking for the balance represented by mid-range solutions as suggested by pendulum metaphor. We observe that when things go to extreme, a dialectical process emerges to achieve a balance.

Second dimension of development STEPS, is the technological (T) dimension. Use of technology is critical to human and social development. It may not be necessary to reinvent the technology wheel as it may require huge investments in Research and Development. While technology or new ideas may be invented in any part of the world, what is important is the development of required skills in use of technology and new ideas for the benefit of people. Societies should use technology for peaceful purposes and not for dominating others. History of technological developments indicates that quite often technology has been used to dominate others.

Third dimension of development STEPS, is the Economic (E) dimension. Harnessing the markets and promotion of entrepreneurial spirit of people are critical inputs for economic development. This can be achieved through the LPG (Liberalization, Privatization, Globalization) and LPGM (Local Products in Global Markets). Development of the different sectors of the economy is important for the economic development of the Nation. Hence, a sectoral development approach is very much required as a part of economic development. This could be based on the mantra of 'self sufficiency through cost efficiency'. Unless we take care of the QC factors *i.e.*, Quality and Cost, we cannot achieve competitive advantage. For

LPGM to become a reality, we need a "full spectrum approach", wherein proper competence is developed within each economic sector to take advantage of both ends of the market spectrum. For example, the IT industry should not only focus on the lower end of the market spectrum, but should also work in the direction of the higher end of the market.

Fourth dimension of development STEPS is the Political (P) dimension. There has been transition from authoritarian political systems to democratic institutions. Political dimension implies development of political institutions to ensure good governance. Democratic institutions with a decentralized approach to their development, need further strengthening to ensure a synergy between the Markets, State and People. State should play the facilitation and 'umpire role' in unleashing the entrepreneurial spirit of its people and providing good governance to people. It should follow pro-people policies coupled with accountability.

Fifth dimension of development STEPS is the Spiritual (S) dimension. It implies making human beings as better human beings and exploring the inner dimensions of self-development. A touch of spiritual aspect would ensure, material prosperity is used for social purposes. It also implies that human beings also set higher order purposes as their life's goals and make contributions to the society. In fact, making "contribution to society" can be considered as an essence of spiritual dimension of development. Inclusion of spiritual dimension in the development model takes us a step towards creation of a "sacro-civic society" facilitating HDM (Holistic Development & Management). Values such as "concern for environment" and "concern for the weakest", can as well considered as part of the spiritual dimension of development.

If all the five dimensions are taken care and a harmony is ensured between them, there will be Prosperity (P), Justice (J) and Peace (P) in the nations and the global village. Figure 5.6 presents the Development STEPS model for Holistic Development & Management (HDM).

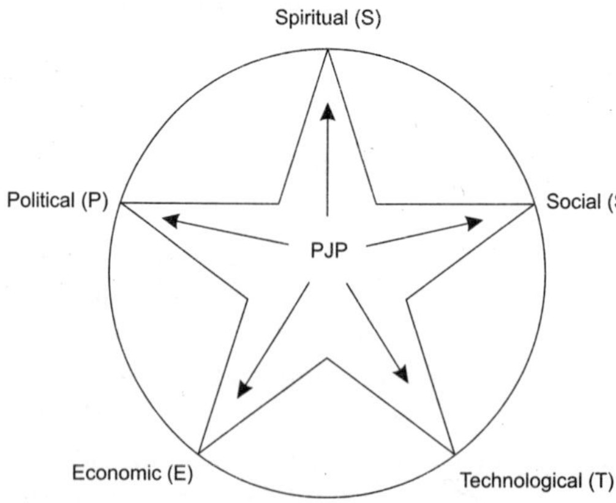

Figure 5.6. Development STEPS Model of HDM

The STEPS development model presented above is the model "*Panchmukhi Vikas*", five-fold development of the Nation by emphasizing five dimensions of the development STEPS. It goes beyond the existing models rooted exclusively in technology or markets, which end up producing "mal-developed societies". For a holistic development of the nation and the world, there is a need to expand the horizons of the development process by going beyond the existing models of development. The STEPS development model takes us towards an "ideal State", wherein there is a proper balance between five dimensions of development, leading to establishment of an ideal "sacro-civic" society.

Societies differ in their STEPS configurations because of differing beliefs in Social, Technological, Economic, Political and Spiritual aspects of existence. STEPS model can also be used to analyze various dialectical processes within nations such as individualism-collectivism dialectics (social dialectics), socialism and free market dialectics (economic dialectics), democracy – authoritarianism dialectics (political dialectics), violence and non-violence dialectics (spiritual dialectics) etc. Model suggests that we need to move beyond such dialectics and move towards Holistic approach to ensure Prosperity, Justice and Peace for all nations and all people of the global village. This is the essence of Holistic Globalization and HDM (Holistic Development & Management).

5.8 Holistic GDP: Towards Holistic Performance Scorecard of Nations

Discussion and conceptual frameworks provided in this chapter lead us to the concept of Holistic GDP, wherein GDP stands for Growth, Development and Progress. This GDP can be viewed in terms of Economic, Social and Psycho-Spiritual GDP of a nation. Economic GDP is reflected through 'Gross Domestic Product', Social GDP is reflected in terms of 'Human Development Index' and Psycho-Spiritual GDP is reflected in terms of 'National Happiness Index'. Idea of Holistic GDP integrates these three ideas about 'Human Development'. Traditionally concept of 'Development' was viewed only in terms of 'Gross Domestic Product' and policy making was driven by this philosophy. This was a narrow view of the idea of Development. In the broader view of Development, we need to include not only Economic perspective but also Social and Psycho-spiritual perspectives. Hence, for developing Holistic Performance Scorecard of Nations, we need the concept of Holistic GDP taking us beyond existing ideas of ranking of nations based on Per capita income and Human Development Index (HDI). Following 'Holistic GDP equation' can form the foundation for Holistic Performance Scorecards for Nations and their ranking.

Holistic GDP = Economic GDP + Social GDP + Psycho-Spiritual GDP

It may be indicated that ideas of HRD, HSD (Human & Social Development) and HQD (Human Quality Development) correspond to the Holistic GDP equation.

❑

CHAPTER 6

Beyond Pyramid Thinking*

The idea of 'Holistic Globalization' represented by the four forces model (Market, State, People, Self) has implications for Development Thinking as well as for the field of 'Strategic Management'. The intellectual roots of Strategic Management are rooted in the 'Force of Market' and thereby in Competition paradigm. In contrast, the intellectual roots of 'Public Policy' are rooted in the 'Force of State'/ Role of State. Intellectual roots of social movements and grassroots economic activity in the form of Capillary Action can be traced to many social thinkers such as Gandhi. In Strategic Thinking, there is a need to connect the triad of Strategic Management, Public Policy and Social movements.

The traditional terminologies of the 'Right' and 'Left' approaches at the political level also reflect the role of Market vs Role of State / Government in the development thinking. However, there is need to incorporate the Force of People / Community in the form of 'Capillary Action' and 'Collective Action', not only in the arena of social movements but also in the arena of economic development. The metaphor of Capillary Action from Physics provides us the conceptual foundations for the development of grass root institutions and social movements. It also implies

*Holistic Globalization & Rotating the Pyramid, Subhash Sharma, Key note presentation at ICOQM8, AIMS International, Assumption university, Bangkok, Oct. 17, 2007, Beyond Pyramid and Pyramid Thinking, Subhash Sharma, 13th SMF Convention, held at Indian Institute of Management (IIM), Lucknow, Noida campus, May 27–29, 2010, Holistic Thinking in Strategic Management, Subhash Sharma, SMF International Conference, Challenges to Inclusive Growth in Emerging Economies, Indian Institute of Management (IIM), Ahmedabad, Dec. 15–17, 2010, Coconut Model of Society and Rise of The Bottom for Holistic Development, Subhash Sharma, Southern Economist, Golden Jubilee Volume, Vol. 50, No. 1, 2011, pp.7–11.

the importance of the role of 'grassroots economic units'. Naxalism is dominant in those regions of India where there is very little grass root economic activity. It may be indicated that Capillary Action could also be in the form of NGOs and it could also manifest in the form of social movements such as environmental movements that we have been witnessing. In fact, Capillary Action model provides us a better understanding of the social movements and 'uprising of the bottom' in varying forms including some social revolutions. In exceptional cases Capillary Action gets transformed into Tornado model with immense amount of social energy (like the tornado in nature) leading to complete transformations of societies. History is witness to such social phenomenon.

We also need to recognize the role of 'Self' in the form of 'Spiritual self' as part of the development thinking. Popularity of Yoga, Meditation and Spirituality (YMS) is a pointer in this direction. Thus, in the model of holistic globalization suggested above, the role of Self is duly recognized. It may be indicated that the Globalization and the 'Inclusive Globalization' models do not recognize the role of 'Spiritual self'. They only recognize the role of 'Self' in the form of self-interest. The idea of 'Higher self'/ Spiritual self (beyond the self-actualizing self) has not been the part of discourse in these models. For example, Amartya Sen gives no role to 'Spiritual self' in his development thinking.

We need to expand the intellectual horizons of Strategic Management by linking it with the idea of Holistic Globalization and also linking it with intellectual thinkers representing the four forces of holistic globalization. This would imply moving beyond the narrow confines of intellectual roots of Strategic Management in the Market and MNC paradigm. This would lead to development of new concepts in the field of Strategic Thinking & Management (STM), as its intellectual roots will be broadened beyond the Competitive paradigm. Such an approach would lead to a greater synergy between Public Policy, Capillary Action Paradigm / Social movements and Strategic Management.

6.1 Coconut Model of Society

Today World is a global village. But what is the structure of this village. Different thinkers have used different metaphors to define the structure of the global village. Traditional conceptualization has been in the form of Pyramid metaphor.

Social Pyramids are in general oppressive in nature. In history, we find that Feudal pyramid was replaced by Communist Pyramid in USSR and it turned out to be equally oppressive. In contemporary times, Prof. C.K. Prahlad popularized the idea of Pyramid in Management Thinking and Strategic Management through his well known book, 'Fortune at the Bottom of Pyramid'.

During recent years another view about the structure of the global village has emerged. Roots of this view are in cyber revolution and knowledge economy. Its advocate, Thomas Friedman suggested that 'World is Flat'.

These two models have dominated the intellectual discourse in Management thinking in general and Strategic Management in particular.

However, world is neither a Pyramid nor Flat, hence, need for a third model to view the world. In fact, in contemporary society and economy we need another framework to understand the changes in the society. In my paper on 'Asian Mode of Thinking' at the Workshop on 'Social Theory and Asian Dialogues' held at Chulalongkorn University, Bangkok, Dec. 15–16, 2009, I suggested the Coconut metaphor for study of societies and social structures*. This generated considerable interest among the scholars and they considered it as a useful analytical tool for 'social-analytics' to study structural configurations of various societies. Emergence of middle classes in various societies makes it imperative to go beyond the Pyramid metaphor of societies as societies are undergoing transition from Pyramids to Coconut like structures. Coconut model recognizes the importance of middle class in social action and creating a change in society. In the past such a role has been denied to the middle class by the social thinkers. Focus of social thinkers has been either on the top of the pyramid or the bottom of the pyramid.

Coconut model has important implications not only for social sciences and development theorists but also for Management Thought and Strategic Management. In 13th SMF Convention, held at Indian Institute of Management (IIM), Lucknow, Noida campus on May 27–29, 2010, I presented the Coconut model of society to the participants of SMF Convention and thus this model was brought to the attention of Strategic Management scholars, researchers and thinkers. It created interesting discussion and dialogue leading to some new insights. 2014 elections in India brought its significance in political context as 'neo middle class' played a decisive role in this election.

Earlier we noted that with the expansion of middle class, societies are becoming more like Coconuts. Prosperity at the 'Bottom of the society' can come from developing Capillary Action in the form of grassroots economic activity and grassroots institutions. It is here that this idea differs from Prof. C.K. Prahlad's model of the 'Bottom of the Pyramid' that reflects the top down approach. In his model the implied inclusiveness is a top down inclusiveness. There is an indirect influence of 'colonial thinking' and 'colonialism' implied in his top down approach to development. Coconut model corrects this bias by giving due focus to Capillary Action model of Development and linking the paradigm of development with holistic globalization. Thus, Coconut model of society takes us beyond Prof. C.K. Prahlad and his top down Pyramid view of society. Figure 6.1 presents the three contrasting models of the global village.

---

*Asian Mode of Thinking, Subhash Sharma, Workshop on Social Theory and Asian Dialogues, Institute of Social Research, Chulalongkorn University, Bangkok, Dec. 15–16, 2009.

World is Pyramid: C.K. Prahlad | World is Coconut: Subhash Sharma | World is Flat: Thomas Friedman

Figure 6.1. Three Models of the World (Coconut diagram from google images)

It may be indicated that Coconut model also has implications for Organization Structure. In knowledge economy, Knowledge Organizations are becoming more like coconut structure rather than pyramid structures that was largely an outcome of Industrial revolution. Further, Coconut model also has implications for the field of Marketing. In what different ways the 'Bottom of the Coconut' reflecting the micro-enterprises, can market their ideas and products in a global context?

At the global level, different societies and nations differ in their social structures just as there are coconuts of various shapes and sizes. Coconut model is a new approach to analyze societies, particularly, in the field of International Business. In essence, this model has relevance not only for the Policy makers in the Government but also for the field of Strategic Management, Marketing as well as International Business. To the social scientists it provides a new way of analyzing societies going beyond the Pyramid view. It also recognizes the role of middle class in initiating social change. Thus, this model also has 'political significance', as political parties need to consider the middle class in their political calculus in addition to the bottom class of the societies. India's 2014 Election has brought out its political significance as the development discourse of various political parties gravitated towards the middle class in contrast to earlier elections.

Thus, while Prahlad suggested Pyramid model and Friedman suggested the idea of 'World is Flat' to indicate the impact of Information Technology on societies, Coconut model provides us a more realistic picture of contemporary societies because today's world is neither Pyramid nor completely Flat. In fact, social 'Pyramids' have been tumbling as the recent experience of Egyptian revolution and other uprisings in Middle East show. Further, middle class is playing a more active role in political and social context beyond being passive spectator and consumer of goods and services. Such a role has been denied to it in the Pyramid model of the societies.

6.2 Rise of The Bottom and Rise of the Weakest

Broadly in consonance with the categories of Fittest, Fit, Weak, Weaker and Weakest, Sharma (1996, 2006, 2007, in Management in New Age: Western

Windows Eastern Doors, p. 53 and New Mantras in Corporate Corridors, p. 415) suggests a five classes model in terms of identifies following classes in a society:

1. Ruling class
2. Professional class
3. Working class
4. Struggling class
5. Suffering class

Figure 6.2 presents this five classes model of society in a diagrammatic form.

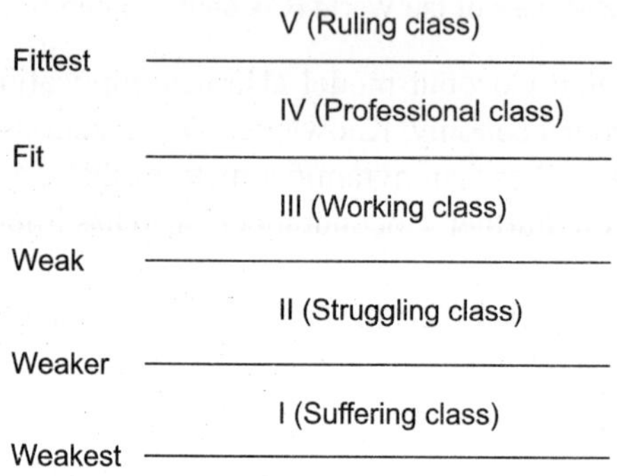

Figure 6.2. Five Classes Model of Society

Above discussed five classes model of society is universal as it can be observed in every nation and also at the global level. It takes us beyond Marxist classification of two classes model of society and provides us a better understanding of the dynamic interaction between the five Classes.

Societies can also be segmented on the basis of region, religion, castes, rural, urban, gender and other categorization. Further, societies can be viewed as a Matrix based on classes and other categorizations. Such a matrix of five classes and other segmenting variables such as region, religion, castes, rural-urban, gender etc. can be represented in terms of 'global matrix model'. This 'global matrix' of 'global village' rooted in coconut model of society, is presented in Fig. 6.3.

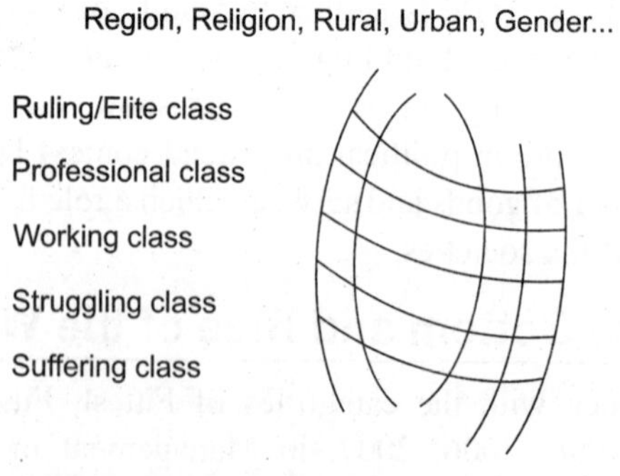

Figure 6.3. Social Matrix Represented as a Global Matrix Model

This 'Global Matrix, Model' also helps us in appreciating the idea of 'Rise of the Bottom' and 'Rise from the Bottom'. In fact, 'rise of the bottom' has been part of the social discourse in one form or other. If there is no rise of the bottom, there is 'Uprising of the Bottom' as the experience of history indicates. From time to time social thinkers have reflected on this theme and have provided solutions for the same. Some illustrative examples are as follows:

1. Swami Vivekananda suggested the idea of 'uplifting of the masses' through Education. According to him, rise of the bottom can be achieved through Education.
2. Mahatma Gandhi suggested the idea of 'grass root democracy' and development through micro-level activities in the villages.
3. Sardar Patel inspired creation of Amul by organizing farmers in the form of cooperative dairy. Risk of bottom can be achieved through such capillary action initiatives. Other illustrations of Capillary Action Organisations (CAOs) include Dabbawalas, SEWA, Lijjat Papad, *etc.*
4. Social Entrepreneurship model developed by Mohd. Yunus through his innovation of Grameen Bank for micro-credit revolution.
5. Through GRID (Grass Root Institutional Development) and empowerment of the masses. The empowerment can be achieved through decentralization of decision making at the grass roots level.

We can also cite the spiritual thinkers who designed ways and means for the rise of the bottom. For example, rise of the bottom was an underlying philosophy of Bhakti movement saints and sages. During modern times Vivekanand, Gandhi & Patel (VGP) provided moral and intellectual foundations for economic rise of the weakest.

It may be indicated that Corporate model is primarily based on the idea of creating organizations for the Fit and the Fittest of the society. Quite often, this model represents the 'Fittest paradigm' and 'fittest organizations' represented by organizations of the fittest, by the fittest and for the fittest. In contrast the challenge before societies is creation of organizations for the weak and the weakest through a participatory approach.

When rise of the bottom takes place, society loses its Pyramid structure and becomes a coconut like structure because many rise from the bottom and become part of the middle or close to the middle part of the social structure.

6.3 From Local to Global: Strength to Strategy*

Globalization has thrown up new challenges. Following three processes can be observed across many nations:

*New Mantras in Corporate Corridors: From Ancient Roots to Global Routes, Subhash Sharma, New Age International Publishers, New Delhi, 2007, pp. 61–63.

1. Globalization
2. Glocalization
3. Local to Global (LG): Local-Global Interactions and 'Viswanization'*

Ideology of globalization has led to standardization of many products and services across nations. This approach assumes that cultural barriers can be easily broken as the globalization process speeds up. However many Multinationals are discovering that local adaptations are needed if they wish to penetrate national and regional markets. This led to the idea of Glocalization – Go local wherever needed. For example, Glocalization has been adopted as a strategy in case of food industry.

Spread of Globalization has also led to LG (Local to Global) response by many companies. For example, many Indian products such as Yoga, Meditation and Spiritual Movements have used this approach to spread these ideas across the globe. Indian Tea is another illustration. LG Strategy leads to the idea of LPGM (Local Products in Global Markets). LG model implies that a nation in its policy making should focus on its internal strengths and thereby on LPGM, in its Liberalization, Privatization and Globalization policy. It implies that government's policy of Liberalization, Privatization and Globalization should focus on Local Products and their marketing in global markets. In strategic thinking, it implies that corporate should globalize the local products, local ideas and local innovations and this process can be referred to as 'Viswanization'.

In the Local-Global interactions, the idea of Local-Global alliances has also been taking roots. As a result, we can find many Local-Global alliances across the world. Sanskrit word for globe is Viswa. Interestingly it can be decoded as videshi + swadeshi. In Viswa, vi stands for 'videshi' and swa stands for 'swadeshi'. Thus, in this word two evocative expressions merge in one form. When we use them as two categories, Local-Global alliances imply Viswa (Videshi + Swadeshi) alliances. Local Global interactions can be referred to as Viswa vision in the form of VG (Viswanization + Globalization) vision. Figure 6.4 presents this vision in the form of a Viswa Matrix. This matrix is essentially a Product Market matrix based on Videshi – Swadeshi categories. It can also be considered equivalent to LG (Local-Global) matrix, wherein Local-Global competition is analysed in terms of local and global organizations.

---

*Idea of 'Local to Global' has been expressed metaphorically, in phrase, 'Jhansi se Jahan tak', by the author during his presentation at 11th SMF Convention IIT Kanpur, May 8–10, 2008. It is also included in author's poem 'Jhansi se Jahan tak', Shunya Poems, Subhash Sharma, IBA Publications, Banglore, p.18.

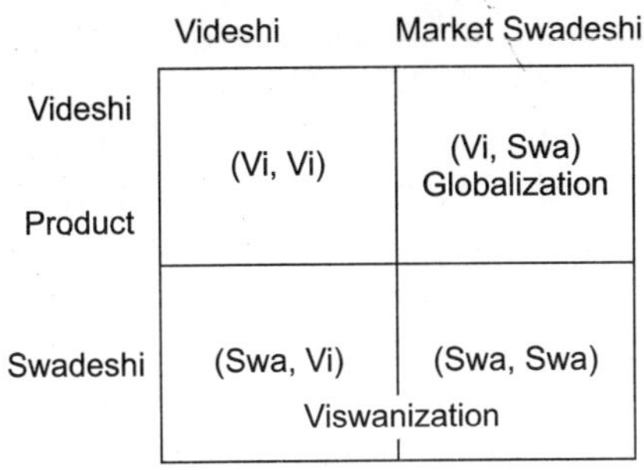

Figure 6.4. Viswa Matrix, Viswanization and Globalization

Viswa matrix is useful both for policy making and Strategic Management. It helps in understanding the tilt of the Government policies. Is Government providing level field playing to every one or is it excessively tilted towards one side or the other? Is it balancing Viswanization by focussing on internal strengths and Globalization that is biased in favour of global corporations.

Different nations have their 'natural strategic advantage' because of geographical and other advantages. Further, they can also develop their 'acquired strategic advantage' in their areas of strength. Their policy making and strategy formulation should take into consideration both *viz.*, natural strategic advantage and acquired strategic advantages that represent their internal strengths.

In today's global village four forces are influencing the world in one form or other and these are India (I) – China (C) – America (A) – Russia (R). They can be represented in the form of I-C-A-R global chakra presented in Fig. 6.5. Within each nation, there is Market (M) –State (S) –People (P) –Self (S), swastikas are operating to provide dynamism to the nations. Further, there are global level interactions among MSPS swastikas of various nations providing us a perspective of emergence of global MSPS forces as an aggregate of national level MSPS swastika forces.

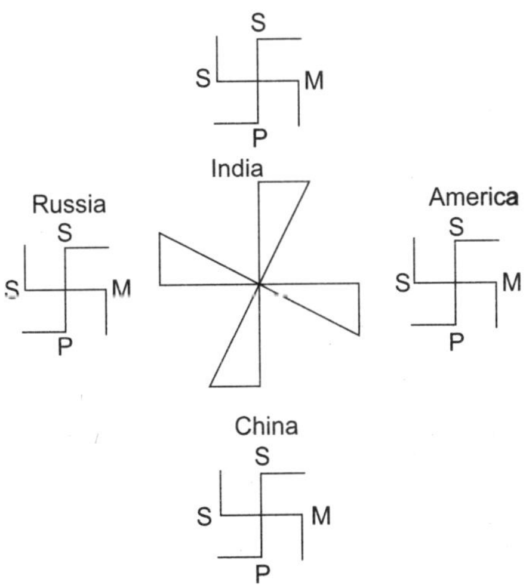

Figure 6.5. I-C-A-R Global Chakra

In I-C-A-R global chakra, horizontal axis represents America and Russia, and vertical axis represents India and China. This model has implications for strategic thinking not only for India but also for other nations. In terms of strategic thinking in India, this model implies looking for new market spaces across these nations through Viswanization and thereby creating new linkages with China, Russia and America. When represented as a matrix, I-C-A-R matrix can help us in mapping such linkages by mapping India's strengths with opportunities in these and other nations.

It may be indicated that for India's Viswanization thinking, there is an interesting lesson from Arthasastra with respect to the idea of natural strategic advantage and its usefulness for strategic thinking and strategy formulation:

'A dog on land drags a crocodile, a crocodile in water drags a dog.'

'By day a crow kills an owl, at night an owl kills a crow.'

(*Arthashastra, Book 9, Ch.1, Sutra 29 and 31*)

These observations when used in the business context provide us interesting insights for formulating strategies and in developing a nation's or an organization's 'natural strategic advantage'. These metaphors also provide us an interesting management lesson *viz.*, strategy should flow from strength.

A corporate organization needs to identify its natural strategic advantages and thereby it could either be an 'owl' type, 'crow' type, 'dog' type or 'crocodile' type. The dog-crocodile metaphor is indicative of the space (read market space) advantage while crow-owl metaphor indicates the timing advantage. These metaphors also indicate another important management lesson *viz.*, creating competition rather than merely facing the competition should be the key driving force for any competitive advantage.

In the context of liberalization and globalization, it is imperative on the part of business organizations to identify their natural strategic advantages in terms of being an 'owl', 'crow', 'dog' or 'crocodile' companies and also identify the competitors in terms of these metaphors with a view to devise effective strategies. It may be indicated that the well-known BCG matrix in strategic management also uses similar interesting metaphors. Thus, use of such metaphors is ancient yet modern.

We can also apply this lesson from Arthasastra in the context of a nation. India enjoys natural and acquired strategic advantage in several sectors of economy*. By making a sector by sector analysis we can identify the 'owl', 'crow', 'dog' and 'crocodile' sectors of the Indian economy vis-a-vis our competitors. This would help us in making sector specific strategies for enhancing Indian competitiveness in the domestic and the world market. For the purpose of illustration we can cite the many sectors of Indian economy where India either already enjoys or has a potential for a natural or the acquired strategic advantage. Table 6.1 provides an illustrative list.

Table 6.1. India's Natural and Acquired Strategic Advantage Representing its Internal Strengths

Illustrative Economic Sectors
• Information Technology
• Space program
• Nuclear research program
• Education, particularly higher education
• Indian cinema ('*Shor sharaba*')
• Herbal medicine sector
• Indian Tea
• Indian Food ('*Dhaba*')
• Co-operative dairying
• Yoga, Meditation
• Indian dance and music
• Indian spirituality ('*Baba*')
• Handloom and handicrafts

It may be observed from Table 6.1 that there are many areas of 'Soft power', in which India has a natural strategic advantage because of its mythology, history and culture. It is also reflected across the globe, by an evocative catch phrase, 'Baba, Dhaba, Shorsharaba' (Sharma, 2012).

*India: Land of New Opportunities, Subhash Sharma, Panel discussion presentation, 4th India Trade Conference 2011, Quanta Consulting, The Port of Los Angeles, Network of Indian Professionals and U.S. Commercial Services, Los Angeles, June 23, 2011.

Once we identify the sectors where we enjoy strategic advantage, the next question we need to ask is whether the Government policies are towards enhancing the strategic advantage or towards reducing the same. In essence, where is the focus of Government policies? Indeed 'strengthening the strengths' *i.e.*, Viswanization, should be the policy objective. In economic context it implies facilitating strengthening of domestic industry in those areas where it already has natural and acquired strategic advantage and thereby improved its internal strengths. When a nation or an organization is strong in its internal strengths, it can influence the external environment. It may be indicated that emergence of Indiapuras ("Mini-Indias") across the globe offers a new opportunity for the LPGM and Viswanization strategy at the policy making and strategic thinking levels. This is particularly relevant for the soft power domains of India. The lesson of the strength and strategy linkage is useful not only at the nation's level but also for the corporates.

In making an analysis of natural and acquired strategic advantage, an organization or a nation can undertake SWAN Analysis. SWAN Analysis (Sharma, New Mantra in Corporate Corridors, 2009 p.403), stands for following:

S : Strengths

W : Weaknesses

A : Achievements

N : Next step

For extending corporate frontiers from Local to Global ('Viswanization'), it is important to undertake SWAN analysis. In SWAN analysis, focus is on next step, keeping in view the current achievements, in addition to focusing on Strengths (Natural and Acquired Strategic Advantage) and Weaknesses (Areas needing improvement).

6.4 Three Roads to Development*

In the context of Globalization and associated ideas of Liberalization and Privatization, we can identify following three roads to development:

1. **Corporate Road:** It represents development through the corporate organizations. It is essentially a 'top down' approach to development. It is also referred to as Reform model and includes FDI (Foreign Direct Investment) approach to development and gives primacy to Corporate Management Systems (CMS). For example, corporates are advised to reach the 'Bottom of the Pyramid' (Prahlad, 2005).

*Sharma, Subhash, Three Roads to Development: Need for Grounded Praxis Approach to Strategic Management & Policy Making, 8th SMF Convention, Strategic Issues in Development Organizations and Corporate Social Responsibility, Indian Institute of Forest Management (IIFM), Bhopal, May 9–11, 2005.

2. **Capillary Action Road:** This is the 'bottom up' approach to development metaphorically represented by the concept of capillary action. It is also entrepreneurial model and is essentially Gandhian approach to development. It could also be referred to as 'Gram road', wherein 'gram' implies 'grassroot action and management'. It also represents self-management'. It also represents self-managing approach to development. Small business and micro enterprises are in general self managing in nature.
3. **Linkage Road:** This represents the connecting road between the corporate road and the capillary action road. Metaphorically. Corporate road is the highway, capillary action road is the village road and linkage road is the road connecting the two. Thus, 'GRAM' (Grass Root Action & Management) is linked with 'globe' *i.e.*, micro-entities are linked with macro-structures. Examples of this model include, Amul, e-chaupal of ITC, self-help groups and their connectivity with macro structures, contract farming, etc. Linkage model can also be referred to as 'Grounded Praxis' model because in grounded praxis, the attempt is to create linkages between the micro realities and macro initiatives as well as micro initiatives and macro realities, through Grounded Praxis Management (GPM) and reach-out approaches and corresponding Grounded Praxis Management Systems (GPMS). Hence, this road could also be referred to as 'link road'.

It may be indicated that the focus of globalization policies has been largely on the corporate road to development. This is also reflected in policy making at the Government level. Unless, we recognize the complementarity and inter-connectivity of the three roads, holistic development would not take place. For society's growth, development and progress, all the three roads to development should be properly developed. Since all the three roads lead to generation of employment, the focus of policy making should be to simultaneously develop all the three roads and also create 'development bridges' across the three roads. It may be indicated that while C. K. Prahlad advocated Corporate driven development, Amartya Sen advocates the need for Government to get involved in development process to 'reach the unreached'. Capillary action / Rise of the bottom approach suggests the collective action at the grass root level. Maitreyi (1992, 2013 in personal communication) explored creation of self help groups and grassroots institution building through collective action and strategic linkages to emphasize the need for linkage roads.

When these approaches are interconnected with 'development bridges', we arrive at the holistic perspective of the development of a nation/society. For this we need to connect strategic thinking with strategic management, policy making and ground realities and capillary action. Figure 6.6 presents this integrative approach to strategic thinking through a Holistic Perspective on Development.

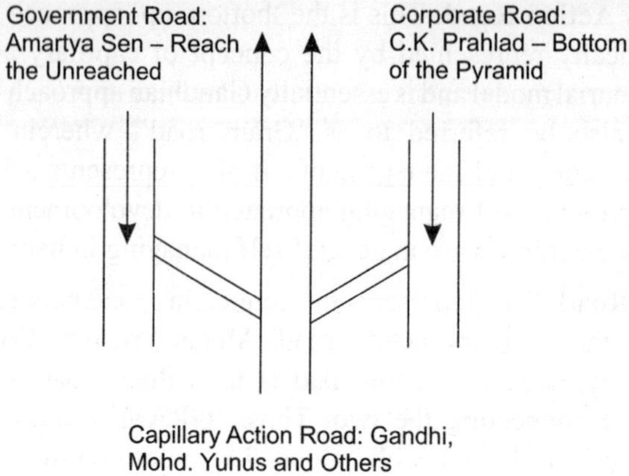

Figure 6.6. Integrative Approach to Strategic Thinking: A Holistic Perspective on Development

Thus, holistic approach to development provides us a linkage between Strategic Management by the Corporates, Policy making by Government and Collective action and Capillary action within societies. There is a mutual interaction and influence among these three processes. If they act at cross purposes, resources of the society get wasted. Strategic Thinking and Management (STM) should pay due attention to achieve a synergy between the Corporates, Government and Community. It also implies a new Public-Private-Community Partnership (PPCP) for the Holistic Development of the nation.

In this chapter, we emphasized the need for going beyond the pyramid thinking and think of new metaphors of social analytics. Coconut model brings out the emerging role of middle class that is ignored in pyramid model. Five classes analysis and associated global matrix model brings out the dynamic nature of society taking us beyond the simplistic view of two classes at 'war' with each other. The ideas of natural strategic advantage and acquired strategic advantage supported by SWAN analysis provide us a basis both for policy making as well as strategic thinking. Further, the idea of three roads of development with development brides across the three roads provides us a holistic perspective on the development of a nation.

❑

CHAPTER 7

Economic Chapati Making*

History of India's development experience since 1947 can be divided in terms of following eras:

Era I: 1947–1991: Socialistic era – During this period development vision was based on Nehruvian vision of socialism wherein State played a dominant role in development.

Era II: 1991–2013: LPG era – During this period, development vision was based on the idea of Liberalization, Privatization and Globalization.

Era III: 2014: HDM era – Limitations of both Socialistic and LPG (Capitalistic) vision have now been realized and a new holistic vision in the form of HDM (Holistic Development & Management) has merged. 2014 marks a beginning of this new thought beyond Socialistic and LPG visions. The new vision is represented by Holistic approach of 'Harmonic Globalization' (HG) and thereby 'Holistic Development'. This vision implies a policy shift from LPG to HDM. This vision envisages path of Holistic Globalization leading to Harmonic Development and Holistic Corporate Management (HCM) to create Prosperous, Harmonic and Happy Society.

7.1 Four Streets View of India: Swastika Theory

To appreciate the idea of emerging Holistic era and the idea of a new India, we take four streets view of India *viz.*, Dalal street (representing various Corporate streets / India Inc.), Parliament street (representing State / Government), Jantar-Mantar and

*Economic Chapati making: A New Metaphor for Harmonic Capitalism, Subhash Sharma, 17th Annual Convention of Strategic Management Forum (SMF), IIM Calcutta, June 12–14, 2014.

similar other streets (representing People street/Protest street from where voice of common people can be heard) and Haridwar street representing spiritual heritage.

In Fig. 7.1, Dalal street on the right side represents the Corporate India that believes in top down approach to business and society and prosperity. It also represents the traditional capitalistic vision with excessive focus on economic GDP. Its performance is measured by Dalal Street or Sensex. Fluctuations in sensex are in general indicative of the health of the economy. Dalal street represents the power of Corporate Indians.

Parliament street shown on the left side in Fig. 7.1 represents the power of the State expressed through bureaucrats and politicians. As per Constitution, it is expected to create social equity and create a just society. Traditional economic and political discourse has been on the role of these two streets in the affairs of a nation. This discourse has been labeled as 'Rightist' and 'Leftist' or neo-liberal and socialist.

However this discourse ignores two other critical aspects of human existence. In Indian context they are represented by Jantar-Mantar and Haridwar street. Jantar-Mantar has emerged as a metaphor of protest and social movements. Haridwar street represents spiritual movements as many spiritual movements have originated from Haridwar.

Cross roads of Dalal street, Parliament street, Jantar-Mantar and Haridwar street constitute a Swastika and offer a new vision not only for India but for the entire world. When this Swastika is out of balance, there is chaos in the society and the world. The new holistic vision is based on a balancing of four forces swastika represented by Market (Dalal street), State (Parliament street), Capillary action (Jantar-Mantar and similar other streets) and force of Self (Haridwar street).

This vision can be represented through Ashokan four lions symbol wherein four lions represent four fundamental forces of Holistic Globalization *viz*., Market, State, Community and Self. Figure 7.1 presents four forces globalization model through a swastika metaphor. This model provides us a conceptual foundation for Swastika Theory of Harmonic Capitalism and Holistic Development wherein all four forces are in balance at the national and global level.

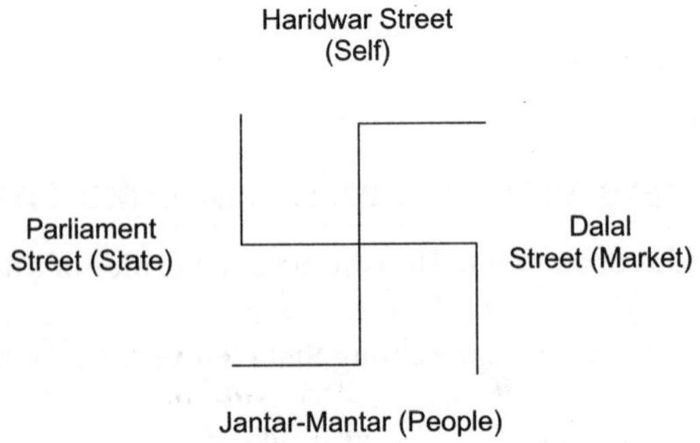

Figure 7.1. Four Forces Swastika Model as Foundation for a New Holistic Vision

7.2 Economic Chapati Making as a New Vision

New holistic vision presented above requires new metaphors. Indian metaphors of economic chapati making and dialectical chakra – dialectical wheel (Western Windows Eastern Doors – WWED, p. 56 and other related writings of the author) provide us a new ways to understand the idea of Harmonic Capitalism leading to Holistic growth, development and progress of a society.

Economic chapati making uses the metaphor of chapati making to economic policies and management. It takes us beyond the rightist and leftist approaches to policy making as it suggests the proper allocation of resources for the benefit of the victims of market forces. Science and art of chapati making suggests that in order to make a proper chapati, proper movement in all four directions is needed. It implies both horizontal and vertical movements. Traditional thinking in Political and Economic thought is only in terms of Rightist and Leftist approaches. These approaches ignore the vertical axis of capillary action economics and Sustainability economics. Chapati making metaphor suggests to the policy makers a need for a holistic approach taking us beyond the rightist and leftist social discourse in Economics and Society. Figure 7.2 presents the idea of economic chapati making in a diagram form. This metaphor also takes us beyond the growth vs equity debate (*e.g.*, debate between Jagdish Bhagwati and Amartya Sen) by incorporating the vertical axis ideas represented by grassroots economics and sustainability and provides us a framework of 'Holistic Economics'.

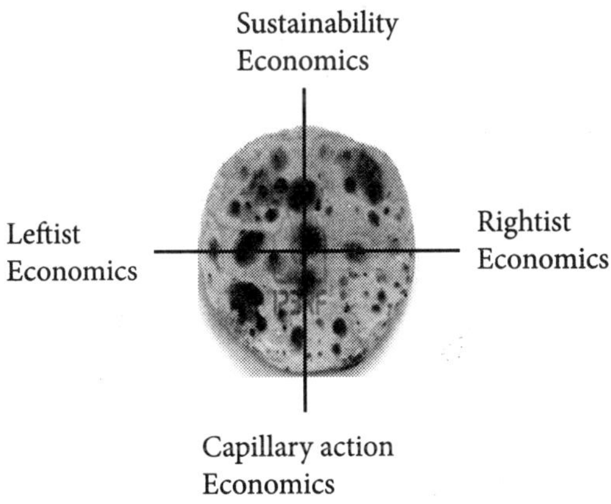

Figure 7.2. Economic Chapati Making Metaphor for Holistic Economics

Idea of economic chapati making also has a broader philosophical implication beyond Economics and Politics. It suggests that we need to go beyond the horizontal dialectics of Market (Right) and State (Left) that has dominated the social discourse. This can be done by incorporating in the social discourse, the vertical axis of Soil and Soul, advocated by Gandhi and during recent years highlighted by Satish Kumar (2012) and others involved in ecological movements. An important question we need to ask is whether Market and State are having adverse impact on

Soil and Soul or are creating conditions for positive impact on this vertical axis. Figure 7.3 presents this interpretation of the chapati making metaphor.

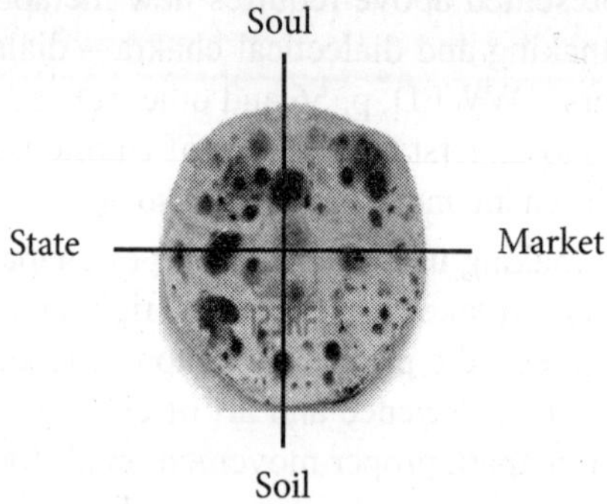

Figure 7.3. Economic Chapati making Model of Social Discourse incorporating Soil-Soul axis

It may be indicated that the horizontal axis of Market-State has been dominant in social discourse represented by ideas of Adam Smith (Rightist) and Marx (Leftist) and it has inspired many Indian thinkers. However this discourse is incomplete as it does not include the vertical axis represented by Vivekananda (Soul) and Gandhi (Soil). Figure 7.3 provides us a holistic model taking us beyond rightist-leftist discourse to a holistic view of social discourse.

7.3 Dialectical Chakras in Society

To further understand the science, art and wisdom involved in economic chapati making, we need to analyze the Dialectical chakras within a society. Dialectical chakras imply a look at the society from the view point of multiple dialectics manifested through caste, class, culture, gender and other factors. Through various intensities of dialectics the 'social chakras' move and lead to 'dialectical spirals' in the society that at times take violent forms in the form of negergy (negative energy) spirals.

'Action-Reaction cycles' arise from 'dialectical tensions' and 'dialectical intensities' in a society. Human history can be seen in terms of an unfolding of 'action – reaction dynamics' leading to unpredictability in the direction of change. This dynamics creates dialectical chakras and thereby negergy - synergy spirals with unpredictable consequences. Thereby it also facilitates ARIMA (Action – Reaction – Interaction – Mutual Adjustment) process in society. Deterministic models of history are inadequate in explaining these aspects of events in human history. Essence of theory of 'dialectical tensions' can be captured through the see-saw model of dialectical tensions and dialectical intensities. When dialectical tensions and dialectical intensities between two individuals, communities, nations, go out of control, it has disastrous consequences. For example, racial riots, communal riots, wars etc. are indicative of dialectical tensions and dialectical intensities going out of control. In such situations, 'actions and reactions make vectors change directions' (Sharma, 1999, in Quantum Rope). We can also see dialectical tensions and dialectical intensities in many forms in organization context. Role of an enlightened leader is to effectively manage dialectical tensions and dialectical intensities in organizations and society. This is a lesson from the science and art of chapati making.

In the context of Economics, Demand Supply curve is essentially a demand-supply swastika arising from high and low (hilo) dynamics in demand and supply, leading to demand-supply chakra. This in turn leads to bloom or gloom spiral depending upon the nature of swastika rotation. Figure 7.4 presents this dynamics arising from demand-supply swastika. This dynamics in turn can also set in motion other dialectical chakras in society leading to non-controllable disorders and thereby new changes in the society. It may be indicated that behavior of stock markets can also be analyzed through 'dialectical chakra' based on dialectical swastika wherein x-axis represents demand-supply and y-axis represents bulls-bears psychology. This is a psycho-economic model of stock market swastika. It may be indicated that dialectical chakras in stock markets can set dialectical chakras in society and vice versa.

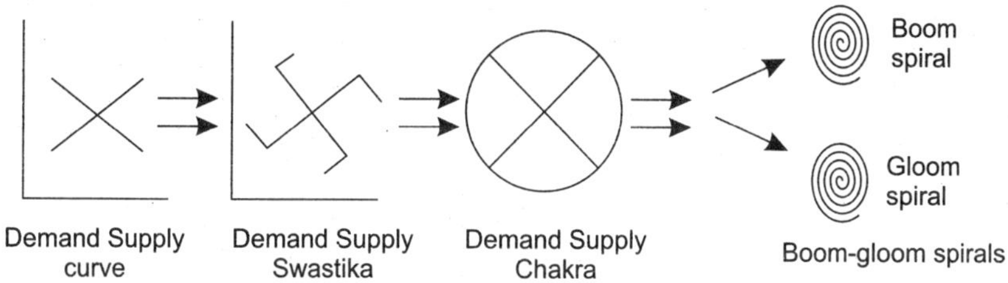

(Wisdom and Consciousness from the East, Subhash Sharma, 2013, p. 166)

Figure 7.4. Demand Supply Chakra leading to Boom and Gloom Spirals in Market and Society

Metaphor of Economic Chapati making coupled with Dialectical chakras has EPS (Economic, Political and Social) significance for a nation as well as for the world as it has various implications for Economic policies, Political dynamics and Social harmony. In the age of globalization dialectical swastikas, chakras and spirals originating in one nation acquire a momentum of their own and influence other nations and the world because of global interconnectivity. In fact, impact of economic, political and social events in one nation can be felt across the globe as the 'dialectical intensities' get enhanced because of interconnectivity of various factors leading to a 'viral impact' across the globe. Hence, need for 'Holistic Globalization' and 'Harmonic Capitalism' as new vision for society. In Corporate context it implies moving towards 'Holistic Corporate Management' (HCM) based on the triad of Profit, CSR and Good Corporate Governance.

7.4 Towards a New India Vision

At different points of time in Indian narrative, different compelling visions for India have been articulated. For example, Mahatma Gandhi gave his vision of

Ram Rajya that was primarily based on Self (S) and Society (S) rooted in the idea of simple living and high thinking and a decentralized system. Pt. Nehru under the influence of Russian vision and leftist thinking adopted the vision of Socialism that was based on the primacy of the State over the Self (Spiritual) and Society (People) with roots in centralized approach. He also rejected Gandhi's vision that provided primacy to Self and Society in contrast to State. In Nehruvian vision, Political (P) in the form of Centralized top down approach played a greater role in structuring the society. In 1991, under the influence of rightist thinking, a new vision of LPG (Liberalization, Privatization, Globalization) was advocated and adopted by Narsimha Rao and Manmohan Singh. It was based on primacy of Market / Economics (E) over the State (Political), Society (People) and Self (Spiritual). This vision rejected both Gandhian and Nehruvian visions and focused on top down model of Capitalism. It ignored capillary action dimension of development. Around 2000, Former President A.P.J. Kalam articulated his vision of 'Developed India'. This vision was largely inspired by primacy of Technology (T) though he recognized significance of the Spiritual. Thus, different visions originated depending upon thinker's experiences and inspirations.

Given the experience of above articulations about India's vision, a new 'Integral vision' is needed that will integrate and not reject, Gandhi (Self and Society: S, S), Nehru (Political: P), Narsimha Rao and Manmohan Singh (Economic: E) and A.P.J. Kalam (Technology: T). This new integral vision based on a Holistic integration of various visions of India since the time of Gandhi leads us to the idea of 'Development STEPS': Social (S), Technological (T), Economic (E), Political (P) and Spiritual (S), development of the nation. Transition from socialistic to capitalistic to holistic vision based on STEPS model is the need of the hour for Holistic Development and Management (HDM). We can hear the echoes of this 'integral vision' in the vision of our Prime Minister, Shri Narendra Modi who envisaged the idea of 'collective development' through 'collective energy' for benefit of everyone. Table 7.1 provides us an overview of these different visions emerging from India's development experiences.

Table 7.1. India Visions – An Overview

Ram Rajya	**Socialistic Vision**	**Capitalistic Vision**	**Developed India**	**Holistic Vision**
Gandhi Pre 1947	Nehru 1947	Narsimha Rao 1991	APJ Kalam 2000	Narendra Modi 2014
People Driven	State driven	Market driven	Technology driven	Holism driven
Spiritual (Self) & Social	Political (P)	Economic (E)	Technological (T)	Integration

This holistic vision of 'Holistic India' represented by Holistic Development and Management (HDM) in contrast to socialistic and capitalistic visions, is rooted in balancing four fundamental forces represented by four forces swastika and its balancing through economic chapati making and moderation of 'dialectical intensities' within a nation. Using heart metaphor, Fig. 7.5 presents this vision in the form of a 'Heart Vision of India' for nation's holistic and 'Harmonic Development' with a view to create a harmonic society for benefit of every citizen.

Figure 7.5. Heart Vision of India – Towards Holistic India: A Framework for HDM (Holistic Development & Management)

This heart vision of India as 'Holistic India', envisages Prosperity, Justice and Peace (PJP) for all. It also represents a ' new Idea of India'. For this vision to become reality, policy makers, strategy thinkers, professionals and common people need to ask following three fundamental questions almost on daily basis with respect to their visioning-envisioning, policy making, decision making and problem solving:

1. Is policy making and strategic thinking leading to Prosperity for all? (Is there proper economic chapati making?)
2. Is policy making and strategic thinking leading to Justice for all? (Are social dialectical chakras properly managed?)
3. Is policy making and strategic thinking , taking the society in direction of Peace for all? (Is there class harmony, community harmony, gender harmony etc. across all the classes?)

India in 2014 moved in the direction of a new vision represented by Holistic Development Management (HDM). HDM aims at Prosperity, Justice and Peace for all human beings to create Happiness for everyone. For Corporates, it implies movement towards Holistic Corporate Management (HCM) based on three pillars of Profit, CSR and Good Corporate Governance.

❑

Part III

New Models and New Mantras

CHAPTER 8

The 'BEST' Model of Strategic Management*

In this chapter we provide the concept of "BEST" managers and also the "BEST" model as a strategic management framework. In this framework the idea of BEST Managers is decoded from the word BEST itself.

8.1 Four BEST Factors

The 'BEST' concept is essentially a holistic concept of managers and management wherein the following four factors are considered as essential components of the decision making process (Sharma, 1996, 1998):

B : Behavioral

E : Economic

S : Strategic

T : Technical

B *i.e.*, Behavioral dimension refers to the labour management or the management of human resources. E *i.e.*, Economic dimension refers to the management of financial resources. S *i.e.*, Strategic dimension refers to gearing towards the product markets for marketing the product. It takes into consideration the quality dimension also. T *i.e.*, Technical dimension refers to the Technical aspects.

Thus, the 'BEST' suitable managers combine the four aspects of management in a harmonic way to create the necessary synergy and success. It may also be indicated that BEST model also represents an equivalence of four factors of creation *viz.*, 'men', money, management and machine. B factor represents 'men'

*From Factors of Production to Factors of Creation: 'BEST' Model as Strategic Management Framework, Subhash Sharma, Abhigyan, Journal of FORE School of Management, New Delhi, Oct.–Dec. 1998, 16:4, pp. 43–47.

or labour, E factor represents money or capital, S factor represents management or 'managerial capacity' and 'entrepreneurial capacity' of risk taking, T factor represents machine or technology.

Figure 8.1 presents the 'BEST' framework in a diagrammatic form of a steering wheel to represent the dynamic nature of organizations.

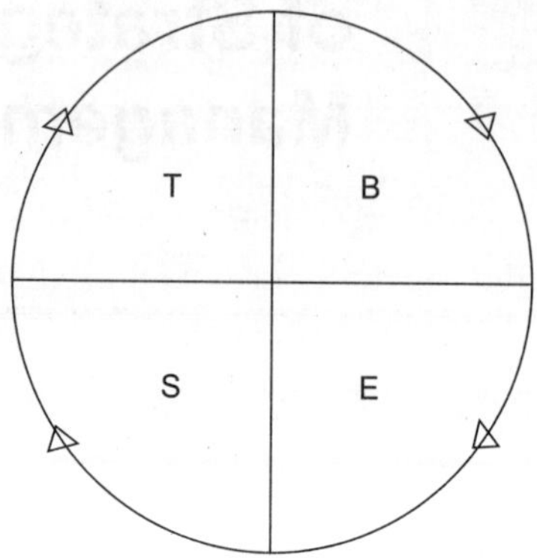

Figure 8.1. 'BEST' Model As a Steering Wheel Model

The relevance of the 'BEST' framework can be more easily seen in the context of the changing competitive scenario in the wake of liberalization and globalization. This is because there is a shift from the production driven approach to the market driven approach to the economic activities. Indeed the BEST model refers to the following four types of markets:

B refers to Labour markets

E refers to Capital markets

S refers to Product markets

T refers to Technological markets

The four markets *viz.*, labour markets, capital markets, technological markets and the product markets influence the business organizations as well as individual producers. A manager has to deal and co-ordinate the inter-linkages between these markets. Figure 8.2 presents this framework.

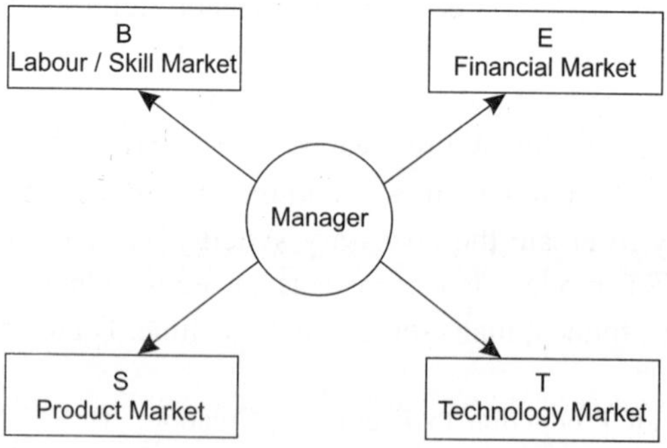

Figure 8.2. Manager as Markets Coordinator

For getting manpower, manager has to understand the changes happening in the labour or skills market. For getting finances, he or she has to understand the nature of capital markets. For getting suitable technology the manager has to access the technology market and for selling the product, manager should have understanding of the product market. Since, all these markets are external to managers / organizations, the role of the managers is to co-ordinate the relevant factors from these markets with a view to co-align and coalesce them for achieving the goals and objectives of his / her organization. Thus, managers have to not only take care of internal 'BEST' but also co-ordinate the external 'BEST'. Figure 8.3 presents this model of manager's role.

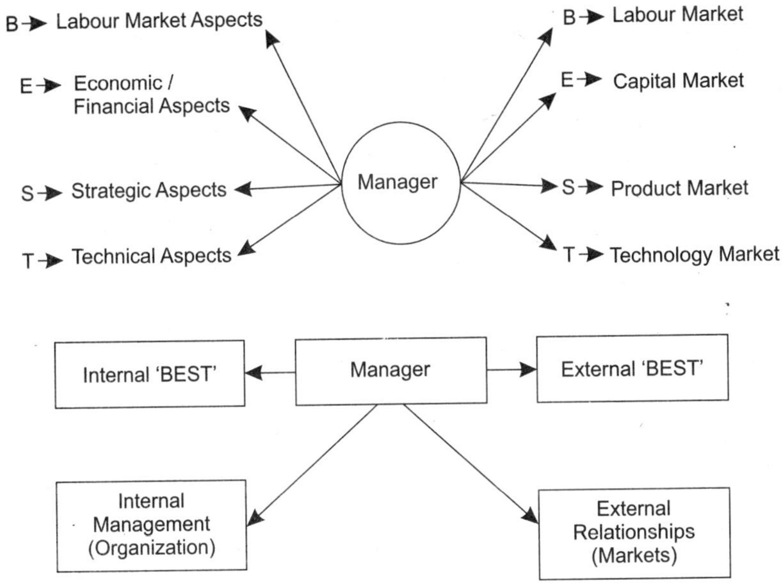

Figure 8.3. Internal External Linkages Between Organizations and Markets

With liberalization and globalization, a number of changes are taking place. We can identify the following types of changes:

1. Incremental change
2. Radical change
3. Sea change

Earner the 'BEST' factors used to be relatively static, however, because of radical and sea changes in the complexion of competition, the 'BEST' factors are becoming complex, dynamic, fluid, fuzzy and chaotic. Thus, industries can be analyzed along the competition spectrum presented in Fig. 8.4:

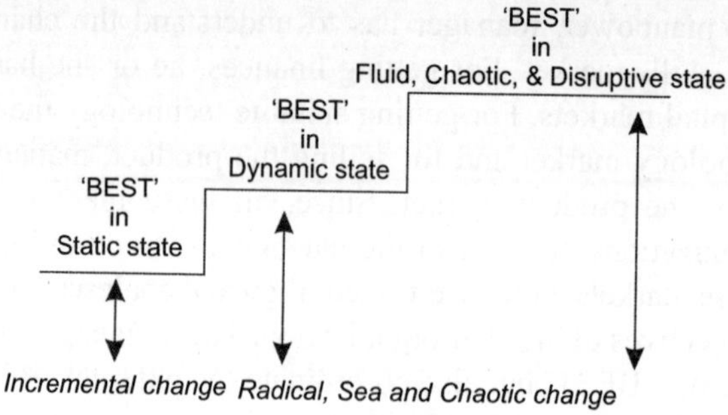

Figure 8.4. Nature of 'BEST' Factors and Their Inter-relationship with Change

While some industries are still operating on the static side of the market competition spectrum others have already moved towards the fuzzy, chaotic and disruptive side of the competition spectrum. For example, software industry is on the fuzzy, chaotic and disruptive side of the change spectrum. Labour skills shortage and increasing wages indicate that labour markets or skills markets are no more static as they used to be in the past. Indeed the impact of changes in the B, E, S and T factors is already influencing the fortunes and future of India Inc. Only the best suitable managers would create a new road to performance', because they combine in an efficient and effective manner the B, E, S and T components of economic activities.

It may be indicated that the 'BEST' model also identifies four types of managers and their managerial styles. 'B' oriented managers emphasize the behavioral aspect, 'E' oriented managers concern themselves primarily with the cost controls and bottom lines, 'S' oriented managers look for new opportunities for the organization and 'T' oriented managers are mostly technology driven. However, for a holistic perspective a balanced approach is required and BEST managers and BEST leaders should aim at developing their 'BEST competencies'.

8.2 'BEST' Model as a Strategic Management Framework

Transition from a very generic 'concept of strategy' to formulation of specific models of strategic management is a relatively recent phenomenon. Now the well known models of strategic management that have become part of the 'received knowledge' include, BCG model, Porter's five forces model and Prahlad and Hamel's core competency model etc. The BCG model is known as Boston matrix uses interesting metaphors like 'dogs', 'question marks', 'stars' and 'cash cows' to classify the businesses and products on the basis of market shares and market growth. One is reminded of equivalent business folklore metaphors of Kamdhenu and Kalpataru which some Indian businessmen have been using for their products and lines of business. Another model is Porter's five forces model wherein five forces impinging upon an industry are analyzed in terms of suppliers, buyers, potential entrants, competitors and 'substitutes'. This model leads to a better understanding of the industry dynamics. With the arrival of Prahlad and Hamel's core competency concept, another model was added to the field of strategic management. Currently these three models *viz*., the BCG model, Porter's five forces model and Prahlad and Hamel's core competency model are part of the received knowledge in strategic management and are included in the standard management text books.

'BEST' model suggested here can provide some additional Insights which can complement and supplement the existing frameworks. Thus, BCG model can be further analyzed in terms of 'BEST' factors for each type of businesses and products to know more about 'best' stars and 'best' cash cows. Industry-dynamics can also be analyzed in terms of 'BEST' factors to get further insights into nature of Porter's five forces analysis. 'BEST' model can also be integrated with Prahlad and Hamel's core competencies to arrive at the 'BEST' competencies / 'BEST' 'basket of competencies'. Thus the 'BEST' model can supplement the existing frameworks of strategic management.

'BEST' model can be used to analyze changes in industry scenario through BEST Analysis of the industry. As an illustration, we provide in the discussion below, an indicative analysis of changing nature of 'BEST' factors in Indian Tea industry during recent years.

B factor or the behavioral dimension is undergoing a change in terms of attitudes of workers towards work. Further, today's plantation workers are far more aware about their own work environment because of education and spread of electronic media.

E factor is reflected in increasing cost of production and plateau levels of productivity.

S factor is production manifesting itself in environmental consciousness on the part of consumers and need for new products on the part of organizations.

T factors changes can be seen in the form of new clones as well as other bio-technology innovations.

The nature of change in the B, E, S, T factors in Indian Tea industry is moving from a relatively static state to a more dynamic state wherein interplay of B, E, S & T factors is becoming more complex. A detailed BEST Analysis of the nature of changes in B, E, S & T factors would reveal the industry dynamic and would thereby help in outlining proper strategies for enhancing competitive advantage of an organization.

Taking a clue from the plant life we can develop a matrix similar to BCG matrix. In this matrix the products and businesses can be classified according to two criteria *viz*., growth rate, (slow or fast) and value addition (high or low). Figure 8.5 presents this matrix. Accordingly the products or businesses could be classified as 'glomerita' (slow growth, low value addition), 'sandalwood' (slow growth, high value addition) and 'grass' (fast growth, low value addition) and 'Eucalyptus (fast growth, high value addition). The portfolio mix of the products and businesses can be analyzed using these metaphors. It may be indicated that these metaphors are easy to understand and accordingly this matrix is useful as an analytical tool.

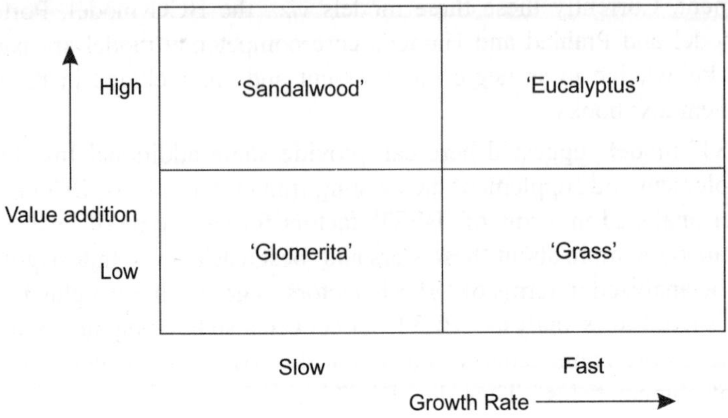

Figure 8.5. Value Addition Matrix as a Strategic Management Framework

Though no revision had been made in the BCG matrix since its development in the 70s, the model presented here could be viewed as a revision, an extension of the same or an addition to the current strategic management literature. In comparison to the BCG model, this model also presents the idea of risk, though implicitly. We have called our model as a 'new age strategic management framework' because our metaphors are drawn from nature and encompass both growth and risk.

To improve their competitive advantage, organizations should focus on their 'BEST Competencies' and for this they need to focus on competition and competitiveness analysis.

It may be indicated that focus of PEST analysis is on external environment. This can be supplemented through BEST analysis which can be used for both external environment as well as organizational analysis.

8.3 The BEST Strategy Cube[1]

The BEST strategy cube focuses our attention on Competition, Competitiveness and Performance. Following three questions are important for this purpose:

1. How to compete and beat competition
2. How to grow and improve competitiveness
3. How to improve performance

[1]'Managerial Approach to Sectoral Analysis: Managing in a Global Mandi', Subhash Sharma, *Sankalpa: The Journal for Management Development & Application*, Utkal University, July–December 2001, 9:2, pp. 12–23.

Accordingly focus of BEST strategy is on the following three:

1. Competition Analysis
2. Competitiveness Analysis
3. Performance Analysis

An analogy from sports field is useful. In every sport, competition, competitiveness and performance are the key parameters. In case of industry analysis also these three are important aspects of analyzing industry and organizations within it.

1. **Competition Analysis:** In competition analysis, we need to focus on nature of competitive forces, nature of industry in terms of sunrise, mid-noon, sunset etc. As the focus is on Market, an analysis of Opportunities and Threat (OT) is critical. Further, Michael Porter's five force model is also useful in this respect. In this framework, Porter identifies five competitive forces as, force fields and these include, bargaining power of buyers, bargaining power of suppliers, the rivalry among existing firms, entry of new competitors and threat of substitutes. This framework focuses our attention on Buyers, Suppliers, Rivals and Threats (BSRT) and is essentially rooted in Demand-Supply-Threats (DST) framework wherein Demand-Supply framework is extended to include threat analysis and intensity of competition ('rivalry').

   Output side of an industry represents buyers and their bargaining power and input side represents the suppliers and their bargaining power. Rivalry among the existing firm is represented by current key players in the industry. Threats are represented by threat of new entrants and threat of substitute products and services. These five forces can also be presented in the form of a see-saw diagram, wherein one side represents the buyers side and the other suppliers side and fulcrum represents the key players and two threats are represented by two sides of a hinge supporting the see saw. It may be indicated that Buyers, Suppliers and Rivals are internal to the industry, hence, they represent internal forces and threats of new entrants and threat of substitutes are external forces influencing an industry or sector. Figure 8.6 presents this framework. In this diagram, we have also shown the opportunities as part of the framework.

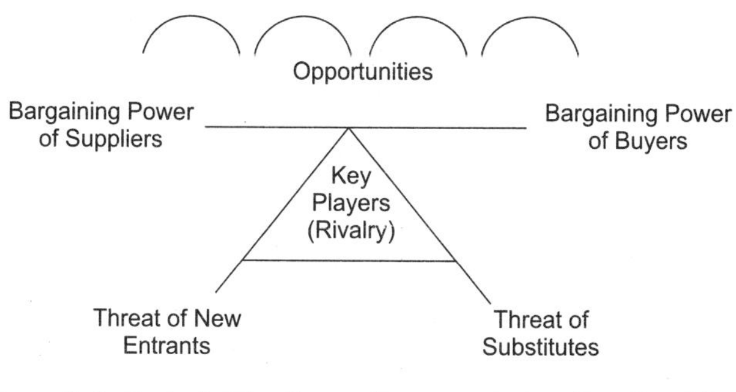

Figure 8.6. Porter's Five Forces Framework As a See-Saw Model

It is widely recognized that in competition analysis focus should be on opportunities and threats. While opportunities lead to growth, threats may lead to crisis and thereby inhibit growth. Both growth management and crisis management are critical to competition analysis. In view of the same, we can analyze an industry / sector in terms of Demand - Supply and Opportunities – Threats (DS-OT) viewpoint. This framework links the markets and the production structure of the industry through opportunities and threats analysis.

It may be indicated that foundations of Porter's framework are rooted in competition and threats view of the world. His mind was preoccupied with rivals and threats, and all the inhibiting forces, hence his framework reflected the same and in his framework he did not focus on opportunities and facilitating forces. Further, during recent years there has been a shift in the direction of cooperation *e.g.*, cooperation between rivals and also looking for blue ocean opportunities. This calls for a new framework of analysis.

As the Space and Pace of Opportunities and Threats are continuously changing in the Market, we need to incorporate SPOT (Space, Pace, Opportunities, Threats) analysis in our thinking. Further, Space and Pace of Demand and Supply are also changing, hence in the new framework of analysis we should incorporate following elements:

1. Demand-Supply (DS)
2. Opportunities-Threats (OT)
3. Space and Pace (SP) at which DS and OT are changing

Happenings at the market place are influenced by the above three vectors of market leading to lot of energy at the market place. Figure 8.7 presents this market energy framework wherein energy at the market place arises from interactions between above three market vectors.

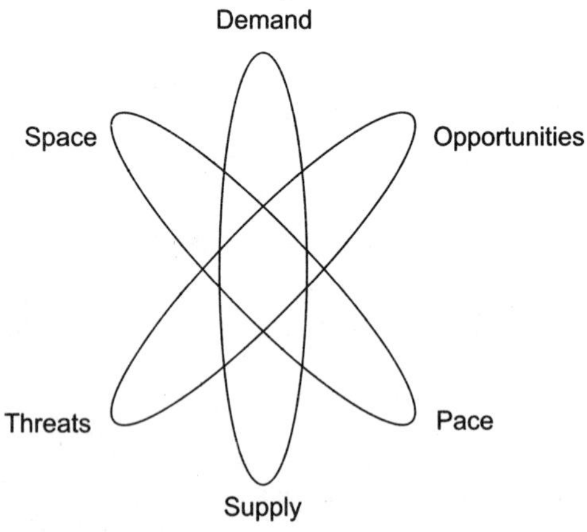

Figure 8.7. Market Energy Framework

This framework is helpful in analyzing whether market energy is going up or coming down or static. One can also get a subjective feel of the market energy arising from Demand-Supply, Opportunities –Threats and Space and Pace of change, as one visits the market place. It may be indicated that 'Forward Engineering' Tools Presented in this book, are useful for analysing competition.

2. **Competitiveness Analysis:** The focus of competitiveness analysis is on the Organization and its Strengths and Weaknesses. C.K. Prahlad's framework of core competencies is useful for this purpose. Elements of 'competition vector' may include, productivity, quality, cost of production, value addition capabilities and risks. For competitiveness analysis, an Index of Competitive Advantage (ICA) should be calculated for the sector and its business units. While the 'law of comparative advantage' draws our attention to the cost, we also need to look at the 'comparative advantages' in a holistic sense to determine the overall competitiveness. Through Organization Development & Management (ODM), we can focus on improving organization's competitiveness.

3. **Performance Analysis:** Performance of sector and business entities operating in the sector should be analyzed in terms of production, productivity, quality, cost of production, market shares, profitability etc. Sumantra Ghoshal's framework of Radical Performance Improvement is useful for improving the performance of the sector and its business units. While benchmarking studies are helpful for industries operating in stable environment, the approach of Radical Performance Improvement is more suitable in conditions of unexpected and unpredictable changes. Hence, both benchmarking as well as radical change management approaches are required for better performance. Various tools of Enterprise Performance Improvement Systems (EPIS) can be useful in focusing on Performance.

By integrating the three approaches focusing on Competition (Market), Competitiveness (Organization) and Performance, we can arrive at a three dimensional framework for competitive analysis. In this framework, Ideas given by Porter, Prahlad and Ghosal are integrated to arrive at a 'Strategy Cube'. This integrated framework is presented in Fig. 8.8.

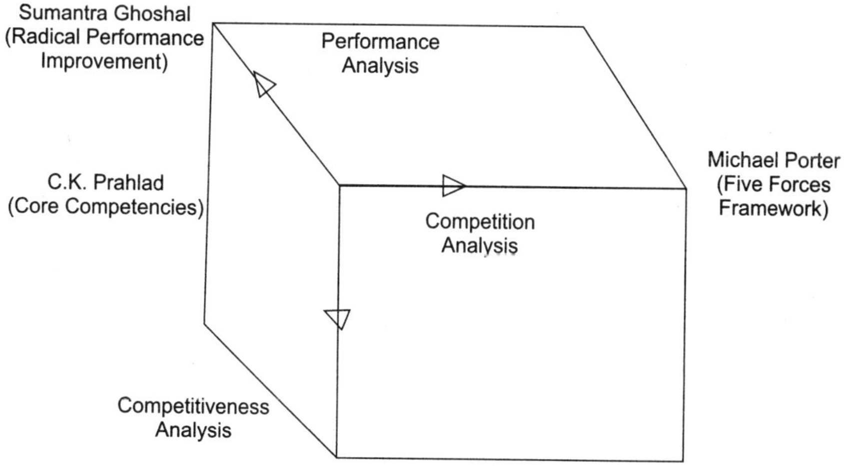

Figure 8.8. Three Dimensional Framework for Competitive Analysis

In sectoral analysis, changes in the BEST factors can be analyzed keeping in view the strategy cube presented here. In this analysis we need to focus on, how BEST factors are changing in Market, within the Organization and how these changes are reflected in the Performance of the organization?

8.4 Five Variables Model of Corporate Momentum: A Model for Competitive Advantage

The ultimate aim of competition analysis, competitiveness analysis and radical performance improvement is to 'Corporate wheel' into constant motion to endure competitive advantage on a continuing basis. The critical spokes in the corporate wheel include productivity, quality, cost, value addition and risks (p, q, c, v, r). If these spokes are in order, the wheel will move forward with ease. BEST leaders and managers help in ensuring that the spokes of the wheel are not broken and the corporate wheel moves forward to ensure optimal utilization of resources, required Return On Investment (ROI) and to achieve the goals and objectives articulated through the vision, mission and core values. Figure 8.9 presents the concept of corporate wheel wherein five variables *viz.*, productivity, quality, cost, value addition and risks constitute the key elements of competitive advantage. This model can be referred to as wheel model of competitive advantage. As wheel also symbolizes momentum, we refer to this model as five variables model of corporate momentum.

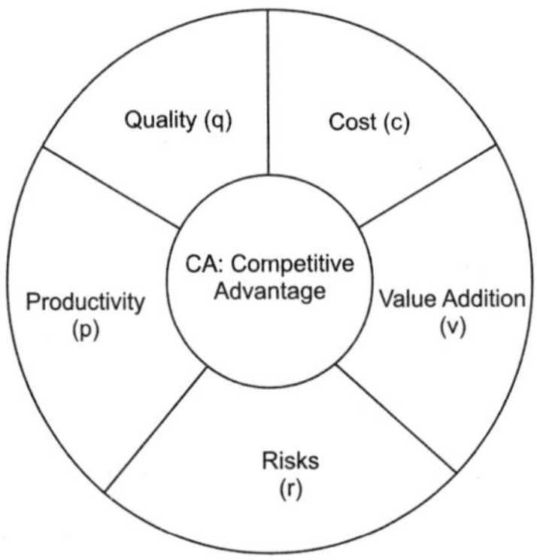

Figure 8.9. Five Variables Model of Corporate Momentum

8.5 Competitive Advantage and Stakeholders' Happiness

Ultimate objective of competitive advantage is to create happiness to the stakeholders of the business. The concept of customer satisfaction and customer delight has been highlighted in the recent management literature. Both customer satisfaction and delight could be achieved at the cost of other stakeholders. In fact, satisfaction and delight should be for all the stakeholders and not merely for the consumers or shareholders. Corporates can provide delight to their customers but pollute the rivers and environment. Such a delight could lead to social fights because holistic view has not been taken. This affects the long run competitive advantage or the 'sustainable competitive advantage'.

Figure 8.10 represents various stakeholders of an organization in a circle diagram. Objective of a business organization should be to delight all of them as they are all part of the extended family (Kutumb) of the organization. An organization should strive to make all members of the family happy.

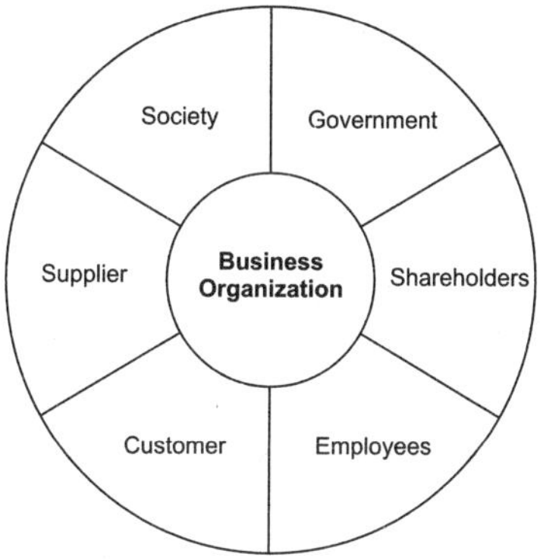

Figure 8.10. Delighting the Stakeholders

Each stakeholder group has its own requirements. Their '*aananda*' (happiness) comes from satisfaction of their needs. If the organization cares for the customers (provides products at the right price and right type of quality) then customers feel happy. Employees' happiness comes from the proper remunerations for their contributions. Suppliers feel happy if payments are made in time and there is transparency and honesty in the organization in dealing with suppliers. Society feels happy if organization is eco-friendly and is not polluting the environment. Government feels happy if organization pays its taxes honestly. Shareholders feel happy if they get 'proper' return on their capital. Thus, a good corporate citizen has to strive to keep every one associated with it in a blissful state.

Given above perspective, we can develop a Stakeholders Happiness Index (SHI) and rate corporates on the basis of this index. Table 8.1 provides a basis for developing this index:

Table 8.1. Indicative Parameters for Developing Stakeholders Happiness Index (SHI)

Stakeholder	Happiness Index	Parameters for Developing Happiness Index
Customer	SHI (C)	Quality, Price, Service, Complaints handling
Employees	SHI (E)	Job satisfaction, Career opportunities, ESOPs
Suppliers	SHI (Su)	Payment systems, Transparency and honesty in awarding contracts
Society	SHI (So)	Efforts taken to prevent pollution, Philanthropic contributions
Government	SHI (G)	Payment of taxes
Shareholders	SHI (Sh)	Fair return on capital invested

On the basis of the happiness index for individual stakeholders, we can develop a Total Stakeholders Happiness Index (TOSHI) through a multiplicative formula as given below:

$$TOSHI = SHI(C) * SHI(E) * SHI(Su) * SHI(So) * SHI(G) * SHI(Sh)$$

Corporates within the same industry can be rated on the basis of this index. Such information would induce a sense of accountability on the part of corporates. If Total Stakeholder Happiness Index (TOSHI) is to be improved, corporates should earn high points on a 'corporate reputation scale'. Balasubramanian and Kimber (2000) suggested a model of corporate reputation wherein four aspects of corporate reputation have been identified as Product / Service Reputation, Business Reputation, Credibility in Financial Markets and Social Reputation. In their framework, Product / Service reputation is based on "the way the products services provided by the organization are accepted in the market place". Business reputation is concerned with "relationship with suppliers, employees, government bodies and other members in the industry". Credibility in financial markets is indicative of the "strong fiscal reputation". Social reputation relates to the environmental and social concerns of the corporates.

In the final analysis objective of a business organization is not only to achieve competitive advantage but also to ensure happiness to all its stakeholders. This will ensure that the business organization evolves into a corporate citizen and a social institution.

In a concluding comment to this chapter it may be stated that while PEST analysis is useful for environmental analysis, BEST analysis is useful for both organizational analysis as well as environmental analysis. A manager or leader can use both to his/her advantage.

❑

CHAPTER 9

CINE Matrix: A Model for Strategic Scanning*

The concept of C I N E matrix is derived from management ideas in Arthashastra (Sharma, 1994). The following lines from the English version of Arthashastra provide us interesting insights that are useful to today's managers (Kangle, 1972, p.317 & 406). "Acts of human agency are good policy and bad policy; of nature's agency good fortune and bad fortune. For it is the act of the human agency and nature's agency that make the world go" (Book 6, Ch. 2, Sutra 6 & 7). When this concept is put in the analytical framework of a matrix, we get combinations that leads to, success, partial success and failures. The combination of good policy and good fortune *i.e.*, favorable conditions, leads to, success and the combination of bad policy and bad fortune *i.e.*, unfavorable conditions, lead to failures. Kautilya also states ...After ascertaining the strengths and weaknesses of powers, place, time...losses, expenses, gains...of himself and the opponent, the conqueror should march" (Book 9, Ch. 1, Sutra 1). Modern management technique of SWOT analysis has an interesting similarity to this concept. The above indicated Kautilyan ideas indicate that both internal and external factors influence a decision situation. In addition some of these factors could be within control while others could be non-controllable. These ideas lead us to a new analytical tool of "CINE" matrix for assisting us in strategic scanning and scenario building.

---

*CINE Matrix: A Model for Strategic Gearing, Subhash Sharma, Planters' Chronicle, 1997, 92:2, pp. 133–138, CINE Matrix for New Age Management: From the Black holes to the Nirvana Point, in Quantum Rope: Science, Mysticism & Management, Subhash Sharma, New Age International Publishers, New Delhi, 1999, pp. 109–114.

9.1 What is CINE Matrix?

CINE stands for four factors *viz.*, Controllable, Internal, Non-controllable, and External factors affecting a situation or influencing a group or an organization. Thus, the acronym CINE indicates the following:

C = Controllable

I = Internal

N = Non-Controllable

E = External

This information presented in a matrix or window form provides us a basis for analysis of a situation or problem. Figure 9.1 presents this conceptual framework. In this figure, X-axis is represented by Internal-External factors and Y-axis is represented by Controllable-Non- Controllable factors. Thus we get the following four cells of the matrix *viz.,*

Cell - I = Controllable - Internal ("CI")

Cell - II = Controllable - External

Cell - III = Non-Controllable - Internal

Cell - IV = Non-Controllable - External ("NE")

	Internal	External
Controllable	I ("CI")	II
Non-Controllable	III	IV ("NE")

Figure 9.1. CINE Matrix

While all the four cells are of importance to managers, cells I and IV representing the "CI" (Controllable - Internal) and "NE" (Non-controllable - External) factors are of particular relevance because much of management effort is directed in bringing Non-controllable - External factors within Controllable - Internal category.

9.2 Developing CINE Matrix

For developing CINE matrix, a small group that is thoroughly familiar with the situation, business or the activities of the organization, identifies the four types of factors *viz.*, controllable, non-controllable, internal and external. While many factors will fall neatly into the four cells, some may fall in the gray area. Once information is put into four cells, CINE matrix becomes a looking window to the problem situation one is facing. Different situations will have different configurations in the CINE matrix. Once configurations are known, it becomes easy to use them for the purpose of analysis.

In situations of diverse interests, CINE matrix can provide new insights as each interest group prepares a CINE matrix for itself and then presents its findings. This helps not only in an objective appreciation of others' view-points but also offers an opportunity for positive critique.

Multiple interests provide us multiple windows each representing its view-point. By putting this data together, we get a holistic view of the industry or organization as a whole. From this holistic view, emerges strategies and the scenarios as well as some possible solutions.

Figure 9.2 presents inter-relatedness of CINE matrices for an industry overview, comprising of CINE matrices for producers, regulating agencies, domestic traders and exporters.

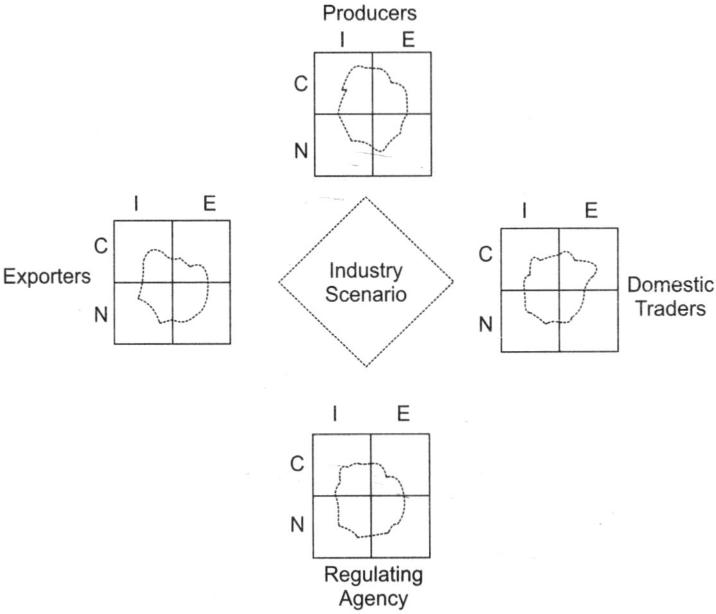

Figure 9.2. CINE Matrices for Industry Scenario

The methodology of CINE matrix for multi-window view includes the following steps:

Step 1 : Explanation of the concept.

Step 2 : Divide the entire group into the natural interest groups and each sub-group chooses its representative.

Step 3 : Each sub-group prepares a list of factors influencing the context and prepares a CINE matrix presenting classification of factors in terms of CINE matrix.

Step 4 : A group representative presents to the entire group the findings of the CINE analysis. Other interest groups make a critique.

Step 5 : Once presentation by all the sub-groups and the critique process is over, put all the windows together for the holistic perspective.

Step 6 : Group as a whole now is ready with multiple perspectives and can find possible solutions for the emerging scenarios.

This methodology has following broad aspects:

(*a*) Presentation of the conceptual framework.

(*b*) Assisting the groups in formulating CINE matrix.

(*c*) Summary of the key factors identified by various groups.

(*d*) Formulating scenarios and identifying possible solutions

9.3 Illustrative Configuration of CINE Matrix

Figure 9.3 indicates three illustrative configurations in which an individual manager or a department or an organization may operate.

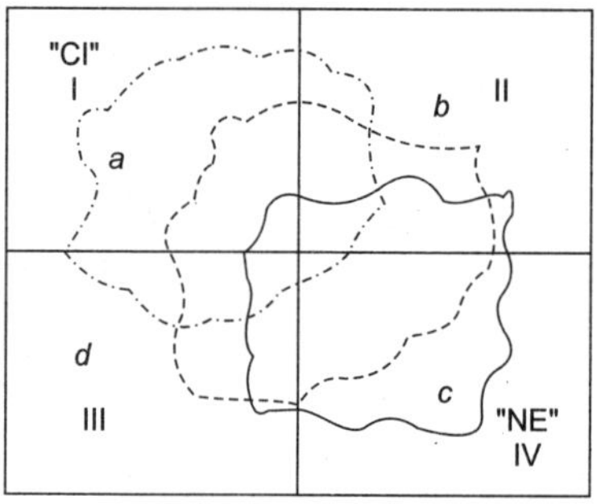

Figure 9.3. Situational Configurations

In configuration *a*, the manager is mostly operating in Controllable - Internal *i.e.*, "CI" situation. In configuration *b*, manager is operating nearly equally in all the four cells of the matrix. In configuration *c*, the manager is largely operating in Non-controllable - External *i.e.*, "NE" situation.

Once the matrix is prepared and factors are analyzed in terms of C-I-N-E, an action plan can be drawn up to bring the "NE" factors to CI-cell. In the action plan, attention is also paid to finding out better ways for monitoring the controllable - external (cell II) and non-controllable -Internal (cell III) factors.

CINE matrix can also be prepared by an individual manager, however, when it is used as a group-exercise, it leads to mind-pooling and group synergy. As a result, it helps in evolving new solutions to the problems managers face in their day-to-day situations.

9.4 Applications of CINE Matrix

CINE Matrix can be applied in variety of situations as presented further.

Mind Pooling Through CINE Matrix

CINE analysis, as envisaged here, is a group process in which each subgroup articulates its position on a rational and objective basis. Various positions are then aggregated and integrated to get a holistic perspective in which various pieces get combined like the work of art. It is conducted in an open ended session format to draw upon the group synergy. CINE analysis usually leads to formulation of new alternatives because many blind spots are removed when multiple windows are opened by the group itself. For all practical purposes, it is an analytical tool for mind-pooling, as It helps in pooling the ideas together.

CINE Matrix as a Problem Solving and Decision Making Tool

A number of factors can influence a problem or decision situation. When CINE matrix is used for analyzing a decision situation, it helps us in focusing our attention on factors that are controllable - internal, controllable - external, non-controllable - internal and non-controllable - external to the decision context. A weightage could also be assigned to various factors affecting the decision. Once the factors are identified and classified in terms of C-I-N-E factors, a better understanding of the decision situation emerges. As a group exercise it facilitates joint problem solving.

Once various factors influencing a decision situation are identified and put into CINE matrix format, further analysis of factors in terms of BEST analysis *i.e.*, Behavioral factors, Economic factors, Strategic factors and Technical factors can be undertaken. For example, Non-Controllable - External factors can be analyzed in terms of Behavioral, Economic, Strategic and Technical factors with a view to identify specific solutions.

CINE Matrix and the Change Process

CINE matrix is also useful in understanding the nature of change. Factors influencing a change process could be controllable or non-controllable. Further, they could be internal to the system or external to it. In addition, the configuration of change could undergo a new change thus pushing the configuration from one cell of the CINE matrix to another. The change strategy would involve converting the "NE" factors into "CI" factors, and ensuring that "CI" factors remain in the "CI" cell.

CINE Matrix for Joint Diagnostic Analysis

CINE matrix is not only a decision making tool, but also a generic analytic and diagnostic tool. It could be used for analyzing the factors affecting the productivity as well as quality. By bringing the "NE" factors into the "CI" cells, both productivity as well as quality could be improved. In addition, CINE matrix could also be used for conflict resolution. When conducted as a group exercise, it becomes useful for a joint diagnostic analysis of the problem situation.

CINE Matrix for Action Based Research

CINE matrix can also be used for action based research. It is particularly useful as a tool of qualitative research for exploratory and initial search for factors influencing a situation. On the basis of repeated CINE matrix exercises with groups familiar with the grass root problems / organization / industry, a list of critical factors in terms of CINE matrix could be drawn. Using a rating mechanism, the influence relativity of the factors could be judged. Thus CINE matrix could be useful as a research tool for industry analysis.

CINE Matrix as Integration of Control System and Strategic Management

It may be indicated that phrases such as internal and external are widely used in the context of SWOT analysis, risk management, change management and other managerial contexts. Further, the ideas of controllable and uncontrollable factors are also used in management control systems literature. The concept of CINE matrix integrates these ideas by integrating the control system and strategic management concepts.

CINE Matrix for Self Empowerment

The idea of internal and external locus of control has been known as an empowerment concept. The concept of the CINE matrix offers an analytical approach to identify the action plans for self-empowerment. Weiner (1977) extended the concept of internal and external locus of control by incorporating additional dimensions of nature of variability of the factors influencing the locus of control. He suggested that factors influencing the internality - externality could be stable or variable. Lewin suggested that the framework of force-field analysis wherein inhibiting and facilitating factors or the pressures are analyzed to understand the nature of change process. Once, these factors are further analyzed in terms of negative and positive impact, we get an analytical framework similar to CINE matrix. It may also be indicated that management theorists *e.g.*, Quinn and Rohrbaugh (1983) and Lindsay and Petrick (1997) use similar approaches for classification of competing management theories. It may be indicated that many managers unconsciously tend to use ideas / tools similar to CINE matrix in their day to day decision making in varying managerial contexts such as risk management, cost control, change management, *etc.*, CINE matrix by providing proper matrix format to such ideas and integrating them together in terms of locus and the focus, turns out to be a useful analytical tool for managerial decision making and problem solving.

9.5 Illustrative Applications of CINE Matrix

Two illustrative applications of CINE matrix analysis prepared by groups of senior managers in group exercise conducted by the author are presented here.

First illustration is a CINE matrix for a Tea Estate in Nilgiris. The second illustration provides a preliminary analysis of the plantation industry in terms of

C-I-N-E factors. The factors listed in various cells depend upon the situational context in which managers operate.

Illustration 1: The Unit of Analysis - A Tea Estate

The CINE matrix presented in Fig. 8.4, presents the observations made by a group of estate managers, in respect of the various factors having influence on the performance of an estate. As may be observed, the group identified a number of factors in the "NE" *i.e.*, Non-controllable - External cell. Discussion on these factors resulted in sharpening the attention on bringing the non-controllable factors into controllable situation.

	INTERNAL	EXTERNAL
CONTROLLABLE	* Labour absenteeism * Labour discipline * Labour welfare * Labour strike * Inconsistent intake of leaf * Plucking rounds * Replanting * Pesticide residue * Factory accidents * Factory hygiene * Quality control * Supply of made tea "CI"	* Labour availability * Dealing with Government Officials
NONCONTROLLABLE	* Inter union rivalry	* Labour wages * Expansion of plantation area * Cost of chemicals * Non availability and high cost of fertilizer * Law and order - outsiders affecting the movement of estate produce * Taxation * Encroachments * Power shortage and failure * Price fluctuation * Increase and decrease of demand "NE" * Influence of political leaders

Figure 9.4. An Illustrative CINE Matrix for a Tea Estate

Illustration 2:

This illustration emerged from the discussions of senior managers. It represents a preliminary and indicative analysis of the C-I-N-E factors for the plantation industry as a whole. The group also indicated tentative action plans as part of their analysis of the C-I-N-E factors. The group on the basis of their mind-pooling listed down the major problems and factors influencing the performance of the industry. The following is the list of problem areas and factors identified by the group, This analysis could be further refined on the basis of additional discussion.

1. Production: The focus should be on maximizing the production with the existing resources.
2. Research and Development: New thrust to Research & Development and adoption of best manufacturing practices.
3. Machinery: Need for proper maintenance and improved technology.
4. Public Relations: A public relation cell should be set up centrally which would co-ordinate with the Government organizations.
5. Warehousing: Central warehousing and maintenance need to be improved taking a futuristic view in reference to growth in production.
6. Health: Health awareness programs and regular check up for workers and others should be introduced.
7. Quality of Commodity: The focus needs to be on improving the quality. This could be done by adopting Total Quality Management (TQM) and ISO in a phased manner.
8. Timber Policies: Removal and Replanting of shade should be incorporated for better productivity. Timber cut from the plantations could be utilized for welfare purposes.
9. Water Management: Better water management practices are required. This would improve the productivity in plantations.
10. Labor availability: Labor should be mobilized from areas of unemployment and poverty into the industry.
11. Fertilizer: This should be made available when necessary through proper distribution.
12. Pesticides barriers and tolerance: Careful use of approved pesticides at recommended dosages should be implemented. Care should be taken in reference to residual effects as most of the plantation produce are for exports.
13. Infrastructure: Better roads and communication system should be adopted in co-ordination with the Government authorities.

14. Threat of free imports: Government should not encourage imports of agricultural items which is produced in our country. More encouragement should be given to small growers for better and modern systems.
15. Trade Unions: Trade union activities should be looked into for its positive approach on plantations, especially in respect to the survival of the industry.
16. Labor wages: The increase in wages should be based upon productivity.
17. Labor laws: Labor laws should be flexible and if not looked with proper perspective would lead to indiscipline on the property.
18. Land availability: There is no scope for further additional land and if available in the plantation area suitable for planting, it should be exempted from the Land Ceiling Act.
19. Tax Laws: Tax rates being extremely high to a tune of 65 per cent should be brought down on par with the other industries.
20. Port facilities: Better port facilities and quicker movement of the materials.
21. Finance: Availability of finance for development at lower rates of Interest.

After identifying the above factors and indicative suggestions, group classified these factors in terms of CINE matrix *i.e.*, Controllable - Internal ("CI"), Controllable - External, Non-controllable - Internal and Non-controllable - External ("NE") factors. During the presentation of these factors additional insights emerged from other participants of the discussions.

9.6 Experiential Learning

CINE matrix is not only an analytical tool for gaining insight into factors influencing a situation but is also a tool for experiential learning. Its usefulness as a diagnostic tool gets better appreciated, once a CINE matrix exercise is undertaken by the person himself/herself. As a diagnostic tool, it can also be used for self-analysis, with a view to identify factors influencing an individual in his/her individual context.

In various Management Development Programs, number of managers, representing middle and senior management levels have undertaken group exercises for preparation of CINE matrices conducted by this author. They have found it a useful analytical tool for managerial decisions. A few illustrative experiential responses from managers who participated in CINE matrix exercises during Management Development Programs, on the usefulness of the CINE matrix technique for team building, self-analysis, self-growth, problem analysis, problem solving, etc. are presented in Table 9.1.

Table 9.1. CINE Matrix Experiential Responses

CINE matrix has evolved excellent inner resource in me.
Group discussions on CINE matrix was useful in knowing the ideas from other members of the team.
The idea of CINE matrix is excellent. I will definitely use it in my day to day dealing with problems. CINE matrix is highly useful.
Put problems in CINE matrix and try to solve them.
CINE matrix model enables us to analyze the problems in a better way and plan strategies for their solving.
CINE matrix was especially an eye opener.
CINE matrix is extremely interesting and thought provoking.

"CINE" matrix has been found to be a useful analytical tool for analyzing nature of factors under which an individual is operating. It helps in a better understanding of a decision situation. It also helps in formulating action plans for better performance. As a framework for strategic scanning, it assists in scenario mapping and perception building on the basis of strategic factors influencing an organization. As a group exercise, it facilitates team building and joint problem solving.

CINE Matrix is also useful as a research tool. Maruthi Suresh (2010) has used it in his research in analyzing strategies followed by a Cooperative Milk Federation.

As a tool for problem solving and decision making, CINE matrix is useful both at an individual level as well as organizational level. It may be indicated that a periodic exercise of C-I-N-E factors provides dynamic view of changing situations. Kautilya had observed that "it is the acts of human agency and nature's agency that make the world go". CINE matrix helps us in analyzing the combined effect of the human agency and nature's agency on decision situations.

❑

CHAPTER 10

Forward Engineering for Strategic Gearing*

With the advent of the Industrial Revolution and the factory as the dominant metaphor of economic activity, rationality emerged as the main paradigm of industrial management. However, with the arrival of the cyber revolution and the emergence of services as a major economic force, creativity is emerging as a new paradigm in organizing economic activities and creating new institutions and organizations. To compete effectively in the marketplace, a paradigm shift from rationality vs. creativity to a combination of rationality and creativity is needed. Forward engineering, based on this new paradigm of a fusion between rationality and creativity, combines the rational-analytic and the intuitive-creative approaches to find unique solutions. Strategic thinking in the context of Forward Engineering implies an integration and synthesis of critical thinking and creative thinking. Thus, both rationality and creativity are combined in an imaginative way.

Forward Engineering starts with visioning & envisioning exercise. It implies envisioning a future and coming back from the future and undertaking actions in the present to ensure that envisioned future is created. In general there are following two processes involved in thinking about future:

1. Predicting future on the basis of past data, past performance and past experiences. For this, a variety of analytical techniques can be used.

*Forward Engineering: A Conceptual Framework, Subhash Sharma, 2nd Annual Convention of Strategic Management Forum (SMF), IIM Bangalore, May 27–29, 1999, Forward Engineering for Strategic Gearing: The Indian Tea Industry, Subhash Sharma, Management Review, IIM Bangalore, June 2000, 12:2, pp. 57–65, New Managerial Tools for Strategic Analysis, Subhash Sharma, 9th SMF Convention, Indian Institute of Management (IIM), Khozikode, May 18–19, 2006.

2. Creating a mental picture of future on the basis of intuition and imagination. This requires intuitive creative approaches to visualization.

Forward engineering starts with projecting oneself into the future and then moving back in time. It involves creative imagining, envisioning, anticipatory witnessing and mind pooling for creative solutions. 'Visualize and actualize' represented by visualization of future and its actualization in the present is the essence of the forward engineering. This idea can also be captured through the phrase, 'Dream actualization'.

Forward engineering provides a foundational premise for the strategic gearing of an organisation keeping in view its existing and new capabilities with respect to current and anticipated challenges in a competitive environment as well as in envisioning a new future. In doing so, it can be supplemented by various other techniques of Management Improvement Systems with focus on performance improvement such as HRD & Talent Management, Re-engineering, TQM, Six Sigma, etc. This makes the framework of forward engineering a comprehensive one as well as an overarching construct.

The analytical tools of forward engineering, described below, may be applied at the enterprise level as well as at the industry level, and have been tested by initiating a forward engineering exercise at the policy level for the Indian tea industry and other settings such as institution building etc., in the context of the new challenges of liberalization and globalization.

10.1 Analytical Tools and the Conceptual Framework

In a forward engineering exercise, analytical tools and techniques such as BOW analysis, METRIC analysis, CINE matrix, FATE analysis, SPOT analysis, Anti-benchmarking etc. are used, which offer a new degree of refinement to the conventional SWOT analysis framework of strategic management and could be considered innovations in the repertoire of strategic management tools. These tools help in articulating organization's ViSA (Vision - Strategies and Action plan) document. Focus of ViSA is on Vision, Strategy and Action plan. Vision provides the foundation for Strategy and focus of Action plan is on implementation of Strategy. Thus, both strategy formulation and strategy implementation are rooted in Vision. Further, Vision, Strategy and Action plan are also linked with ground realities. This is the essence of the ViSA document of the organization. It may be indicated that ViSA concept also serves as a framework for strategic management, as it links both strategy formulation and implementation with shared vision.

Forward engineering begins with 'business backbone analysis' coupled with capabilities and competence analysis. The author in a conversation with an Indian business family, learnt the native catch phrase of '*reedh ki haddi*' or business backbone, as a reference to the core business strengths. When this concept is extended to the corporate context, one arrives at the idea of 'backbone analysis' that identifies then 'natural strategic advantage' that an organization has developed over a period of time.

In 'backbone analysis' the focus is on core strengths. This analysis can be further supported by capabilities and competence analysis wherein the focus is on organizational capabilities and people's competencies in terms of existing and new requirements. Existing capabilities and competencies and new ones are charted to identify the gaps in the 'Basket of Competencies'. SWAN (Strengths, Weaknesses, Achievements, Next step) analysis is helpful in focussing on the next step articulated through forward engineering.

Along with the backbone analysis BOW (Barriers, Obstacles and Weaknesses) analysis is another analytical tool of forward engineering. While in conventional SWOT analysis, the idea of 'W' indicating Weaknesses is given its due place, the concept of BOW represents a further refinement of the 'W' of SWOT.

10.2 'METRIC' Analysis[2]

'METRIC' analysis is a five dimensional framework for strategic analysis and it draws our attention to following five aspects for improving competitiveness:

M : Market

E : Economic basis (E),

T : Technology

R : Resources (R)

IC : Institutional Capacities or Competencies

Figure 10.1 presents the METRIC model representing five aspects of competitiveness, in a diagram form.

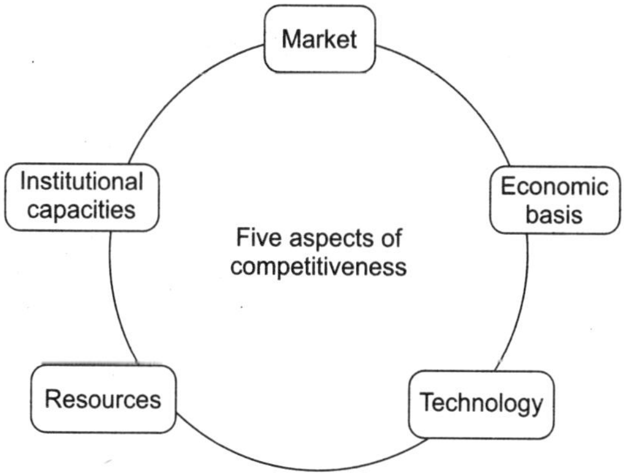

Figure 10.1. METRIC Model Representing Five Aspects of Competitiveness

First factor in METRIC analysis relates to Market (M). Market can be analyzed through following approaches:

---

[2]New Managerial Tools for Strategic Analysis, Subhash Sharma, SMF 9th Convention, held at, Indian Institute of Management (IIM), Khozikode, May 18–19, 2006.

I. Demand–Supply conditions

II. Product Market Matrix

III. Porter's Five Forces Model

IV. Space and Pace of Opportunities and Threats (SPOT)

V. Ethical Practices in the Market

In the subsequent discussion, we present METRIC analysis with illustration of the changes in Indian tea industry. India's tea sector has been experiencing many changes in the Market *e.g.*, changing tastes of customers, preference for branded products, demand for quality teas, etc. While the corporates have responded well to changes in the markets, the small grower section of the industry needs to sensitize itself to such changes in the markets.

Second factor relates to Economic (E) basis. Economics of tea production has been severely affected due to increase in cost of production. Further, Indian tea industry is known for bearing the social cost and this also affects the economics of tea production. While the industry has responded to the same through cost-cutting measures, however, there are always limits to cost cutting. Hence, the focus should be on value-addition to improve the economic basis of tea production.

The third factor *viz.*, Technology (T) plays a critical role in competitiveness. In tea industry, it implies modernization of processing factories. Industry has responded well to adoption of Information Technology (IT) to improve its competitiveness.

The fourth factor for improving competitiveness is the Resources (R) factor. Land, labor, capital and knowledge are the four critical resources. Hence, the need to focus on productivity of land, productivity of labor, productivity of capital and knowledge levels of workforce.

Fifth factor for competitive advantage is the 'Institutional Capacity' (IC) that includes 'basket of competencies' of the organization or sector. While corporates are well equipped with managerial capacity, capacity building initiatives are needed to improve the managerial capacity of the medium and small grower segment of the industry. This implies taking up 'capacity building' and HRD initiatives within the sector.

It may be observed that in 'METRIC' analysis, the first factor is 'Market'. Thus, it draws our attention to Market in contrast to many other mantras that tend to focus on production or the supply side. It may also be observed that in 'METRIC' analysis, the demand side is integrated with organizational and institutional factors.

Table 10.1 summarizes the above discussion on 'METRIC' analysis of Indian tea industry.

Table 10.1: Illustrative METRIC Analysis: Illustration form of Indian Tea Industry

Focus	Key Areas of Concern
M (Market)	Consumer preferences, Branding, Quality products, Niche Markets, Identity, USP (Unique Strategic Positioning) of Indian Tea, Demand position
E (Economic factors)	Cost of production, Supply, demand & price
T (Technology)	Technological upgradation, Modernization of Tea factories, Information Technology
R (Resources)	Productivity of land, Productivity of Labor, Productivity of Capital
IC (Institutional Capacity)	Capacity building of small & tiny growers, Strengthening Grass-root institutions

It may be indicated that METRIC analysis also draws our attention to different perspectives of Strategic Management (SM) that include, Market perspective, Economic perspective (*e.g.* differentiation based on cost advantage), Technology perspective (*e.g.* Technological innovations and disruptive technologies), Resources perspective (Resource based approach to SM), Institutional capacity (*e.g.* Capabilities based approach). Thus, METRIC analysis provides us an integrative view and an integrative approach to different perspectives of Strategic Management.

10.3 Scenario Mapping Tools

Following tools are useful for scenario mapping:

FATE Analysis

In forward engineering FATE refers to Future Anticipated Trends and Events. As Events impact an organization, it is important to undertake an Event Impact analysis and assessment. Idea of cause-effect geometry can be useful because events leave behind their shadows. Wishbone technique is useful in making a subjective assessment of the likely impact of FATE.

The FATE analysis can be coupled with capabilities and competence analysis for the purpose of anticipatory witnessing. FATE analysis can be facilitated by both analytical and intuitional approaches to trends and events. Intuitional approach may include wishbone analysis – a technique to make subjective assessment of a situation. Many times talking to industry experts and seeking their views can lead to an understanding of the anticipated trends and events. Since events create their short term and long term impact, Event Impact (Event: Significant, Non-significant, Impact: Short term, Long term) matrix may be used to facilitate FATE analysis.

CINE Matrix

CINE matrix is the most important analytical tool for forward engineering. CINE matrix stands for four factors affecting a decision: Controllable, Internal, Non-Controllable, External. The four cells of the matrix indicate the controllable-internal, controllable-external, non-controllable-internal and non-controllable-external factors. All the four cells are analysed and strategies for converting the 'NE' factors to 'CI' factors are drawn up.

In order to develop CINE matrix specific to the enterprise, a small group of individuals thoroughly familiar with the decision situations, business and activities of the organization identifies the factors influencing the unit / organization. The factors are then classified in the matrix format to arrive at the situational configuration that managers are facing with respect to these factors. If the situational configuration falls largely in the controllable-internal (CI) cell, managers have greater control over decision influencing factors. However, if the situational configuration largely falls in the non-controllable-external (NE) cell, managers are operating in a situation of difficulty and even adversity.

While drawing up CINE matrix for the industry, different interest groups such as producers, domestic traders, exporters and regulating agencies are involved in discussions and each interest group prepares its own CINE matrix. Information from all such group exercises is pooled together to get a CINE matrix overview of the industry. Groups also indicate the degrees of controllability and non-controllability of the factors in terms of high, medium and low. This helps in drawing up action plans to bring the NE factors to the CI cell.

SO-SO Window

In the *Arthashastra*, Kautilaya advises, 'after ascertaining the strengths or weaknesses of powers, place and time... losses, expenses, gains and troubles, of himself and of the enemy, the conqueror should march if superior in strength, otherwise stay quiet', He also articulates the concept of 'natural strategic advantage' in terms of the dog and crocodile metaphor. Extending this idea, CINE matrix analysis can be supported with SO-SO window. In the context of competitive situations, SO-SO window view is in terms of competition. Hence, other is viewed as competitor. In this context, SO-SO window provides an analysis of strengths and weaknesses of Self (S) and Other competitors (O). In analysing strengths, due attention should be paid to natural and acquired strategic advantages.

SPOT Analysis

Closely connected to FATE analysis, is the concept of SPOT – Space and Pace of Opportunities and Threats. As against SWOT, in SPOT analysis the pace of change gets due importance. SPOT analysis focuses our attention on a continuous assessment of the changes in the market in terms of space and pace of changes in the opportunities and threats. Figure 10.2 presents in a matrix format the SPOT analysis framework wherein the symbols of flying birds are indicative of the dynamic nature of opportunities and threats in a competitive situation. When an organisation's or nation's 'Basket of Competencies' is strong, it can not only create new opportunities but can also convert threats into opportunities.

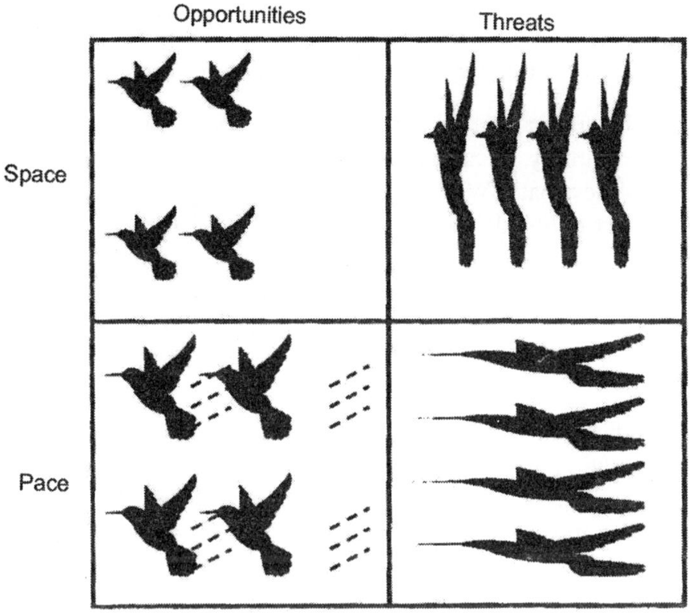

Figure 10.2. Framework for SPOT Analysis

10.4 Anti-benchmarking*

While the concept of benchmarking is being widely talked about, forward engineering encourages anti-benchmarking. The path of benchmarking is one of imitation and replication. The path of anti-benchmarking is that of creativity because it forces us to seek new ways. While we can certainly learn from benchmarking, this path is one of imitation and replication. The path of anti-benchmarking however, is that of creativity because it forces us to seek new ways, leading to a new competitive advantage. The concepts of anti-benchmarking and benchmarking are presented in Fig. 10.3. If organization B follows organization A along the path of benchmarking, it would remain behind particularly if the gap between A and B is large. Hence B takes an anti-benchmarking path and turns out a winner. The essence of anti-benchmarking lies in thinking, discovering and competing through a new path. It also represents the idea of 'new road taken' representing the 'road not taken by others'.

---

*New Mantras in Creativity & Innovation, Subhash Sharma, First International Conference on Igniting the Genius within, Indian School of Business, Hyderabad, Oct. 23–26, 2008.

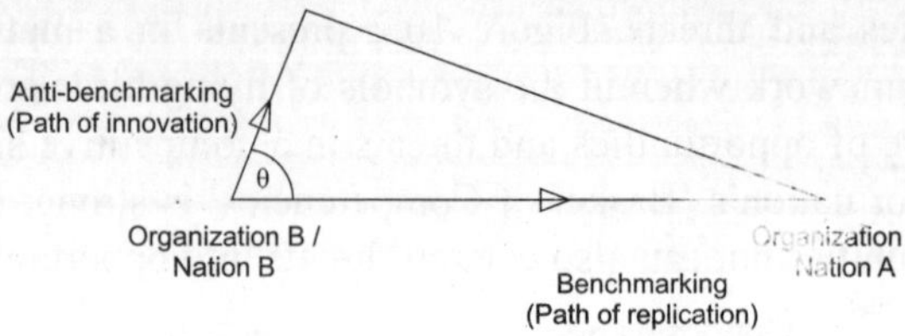

Figure 10.3. Benchmarking and Anti-benchmarking

Thus, anti-benchmarking is a technique for identifying the new path through innovation and creativity. It can also be referred to as Tan θ approach wherein θ is indicative of new path. While benchmarking and thereby the best practices approach suggests we should follow the leaders and try to bridge the benchmarking gap, the concept of anti-benchmarking suggests that we should identify a new path. In the spirit of thesis-antithesis and synthesis, we can arrive at the concept of benchmarking - anti benchmarking - new benchmarking. Through this approach, organizations can create Unique Strategic Positioning (USP) through innovative strategies.

It may be indicated that forward engineering is a creative search that goes far beyond standardisation and is fundamental to strategic gearing and re-innovation of institutions and organisations for forward movement in the competitive environment. It is not just a case of 'old wine in new bottles' but is a 'refined wine in a refined bottle'. The tools and techniques of forward engineering draws freely on both modern and ancient approaches to management especially Kautilya's *Arthashastra*.

10.5 Mind Pooling for Unique and Creative Solutions

When an arrow is set in motion an arrow of time also starts operating. Inherently, the arrow of time prevents a broken cup from coming back together again. But a new and beautiful piece of art can be created from the pieces. The art of reversing an organization's arrow of time is concerned with creating a new work of art with the help of forward engineering. There is no single standardised way of making the pieces combine. There are many creative solutions each unique in itself. In forward engineering the search is for those unique solutions that would enhance an organisation's proactive and strategic capacities. This search is facilitated through a mind-pooling exercise. Mind-pooling is a methodology for pooling collective intuitional wisdom leading to intuitional visioning. Group discussions in a CINE matrix exercise lead to pooling of ideas. The strategic tip of an organization has three components: technology, information and people. Together they make the organization unique. Hence, forward engineering for an organization is tailor-made to its requirements. Just as Zen gives cues for creative directions, forward engineering leads to creative solutions.

Table 10.2: Analytical Tools for Forward Engineering

Forward Engineering Tool	Explanation
FATE Analysis	An analysis of Future Anticipated Trends and Events.
ViSA	Vision - Strategies and Action plans.
METRIC analysis	Market, Economic, Technological, Resources, Institutional capacity.
SWAN analysis	Strengths, Weaknesses, Achievements, Next step.
BOW Analysis	An analysis of the Barriers, Obstacles and Weaknesses.
CINE Matrix	A matrix of Controllable Internal Non-controllable External factors influencing a decision situation.
SO-SO Window	An analytical window to compare one's strengths and weaknesses with that of competitors.
SPOT Analysis	Space and Pace of Opportunities and Threats.
Wishbone Analysis	A subjective method of assessing impact intensity.
Mind-Pooling	A methodology for pooling collective intuitional wisdom leading to intuitional visioning.

Illustrations of BOW analysis and CINE matrix are presented in Exhibits - 10.1, 10.2, 10.3 and 10.4. Illustrations related to tea industry have been prepared by estate managers during the training programmes. Illustrations related to software industry have been prepared by author's students on the basis of published data and discussions with the software professionals.

10.6 An Integrative Framework of Forward Engineering

The ideas presented so far can be complemented through various other techniques of Management Improvement Systems such as HRD, Re-engineering and TQM. This makes the framework of forward engineering a comprehensive framework as well as an overarching construct. Forward engineering is driven by the reach-out concept. Strategies for reaching out to the current and future customers is an essential aspect of forward engineering. When information on backbone analysis, CINE matrix, SO-SO window, FATE analysis and SWAN & SPOT analysis are combined together, we get a holistic view of the strategic gearing capacity of an organization. By combining these approaches together we get a comprehensive framework of forward engineering. A conceptual framework of forward engineering incorporating the various analytical tools is presented in Fig. 10.4.

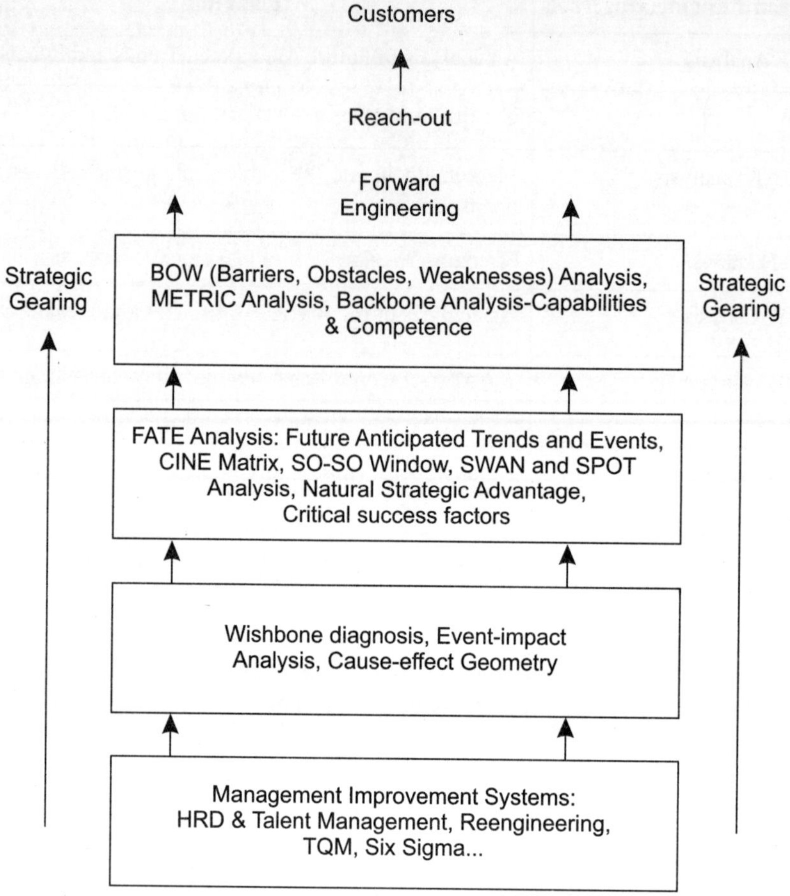

Figure 10.4. An Integrative Framework of Forward Engineering

10.7 Managerial SAW (Science, Art and Wisdom) for Forward Engineering

Hamel and Prahlad (1994) suggest the idea of 'reinventing' an industry. Michael Hammer (1993) suggests the idea of 'reengineering the corporation' wherein reengineering implied 'the radical redesign of business processes for dramatic improvement'. Thus, it was a tool for radical change management. However, Hamel and Prahlad's idea of 'reinventing' took us beyond reengineering for preparedness to 'compete for the future' and 'compete in the future'. When these ideas are correlated with the management control systems framework suggested by Anthony & Govindrajan (1994), we arrive at an integrative 3 Rs framework of forward engineering. At the policy / strategic level, reinventing the industry / organization implies creation of new opportunities. At the managerial level, restructuring the organization in consonance with reinventing would ensure preparedness of organizations to new opportunities. At the operational level, re-engineering of business process would lead to alignment of operational aspects of business to the new situation. Ghoshal *et al.* (2000) suggest the need for radical change management to make organizations responsive to the radical changes in social, political and business environment. 3 Rs framework is helpful in radical change management. Table 10.3 presents a summary of this discussion for creating strategic response to coping with changes and for initiating a forward engineering process.

Table 10.3: Three Rs Framework of Forward Engineering

Level	Strategic Option
Policy / Strategy Level	'Reinventing the industry'
Managerial Level	Restructuring the enterprises in alignment with its reinventing
Operational Level	Reengineering business processes

It may be noted from Table 10.3 that different Rs are required at different levels. However, there should be a proper alignment between the 3 Rs for rejuvenating an enterprise or nation. For change management, the three 3 Rs should be guided by the idea of "continuous creative constructions" wherein organizations undergo a continuing process of reinventing, restructuring and reengineering. This makes the organizations respond effectively to the radical changes taking place in the market. The idea of 'forward engineering' is rooted in the idea of 'continuous creative constructions' through creative envisioning by moving back from the future. This requires application of science, art and wisdom to arrive at appropriate strategies for radical change management through forward engineering.

It may be indicated that focus of reinventing is on innovation. Reinventing is essentially leadership function, as the aim is to create new dreams in consonance with the vision of the organization. It requires wisdom. In restructuring, the aim is to improve effectiveness by providing flexibility by restructuring the institutional structures and businesses. Hence art of management is needed. In re-engineering the focus is on efficiency, hence science of management is needed. Essence of forward engineering lies in aligning these three processes and it requires Managerial SAW (Science, Art & Wisdom) as well as Leadership SAW (Science, Art & Wisdom) to achieve the same.

Exhibit 10.1 BOW Analysis for Forward Engineering: Case of Tea Industry in North East

Barriers	Obstacles
* Inadequate land * Different climatic conditions * Unskilled labour * Lack of mechanization * Inadequate R & D and HRD * Lack of Infrastructural facilities in terms of power * Erratic supply of inputs such as fertilizers, gas, etc. * No control over price realization	* Terrorism * Government interference * Poor communication facilities * Low level of professionalism * Trade unionism * Export bottlenecks * Plantation Labour Acts * Dastoors * Law and order problems * Environmental degradation - floods and soil erosion
Weaknesses	
* Antiquated market system * Antiquated machines * Low level of ploughing back of profits * Lack of vision * Low level of motivation of staff * Inadequacy of health care * Poor health of work force * High fixed cost * Debility of soil after use of 100 years or so * Low productivity levels * Lack of career advancement * The R & D transfer too slow	

Exhibit 10.2 Illustrative CINE Matrix of a Tea Estate in North East

	I	E
C	• Admission • Productivity • Quality control • Land encroachment by labor • Sanitation & Hygiene • Proper planning • Proper communication of instructions • Working team spirit • Use of stores / machines • Production and quality • Habitual absenteeism • Labor welfare • Cattle trespass • Ineffective spraying • High cost of production • High labour ratio • Soil erosion • Labour health • Wages • Labour deployment ratio • Data generation for head office • Fertilizer application	• Wage fixation • Extremist menace • Communication / telephone & roads • Power crisis • Land purchase • Cattle trespass • Damage /destruction of properties • Destruction of power supply • Land encroachment • Financial stringency • Menace of wild animals • Housing finance • Forest degradation • Political interference • Alcoholism • Problem of residence of non workers • Sales policy • Borrowings • Head office expenses • Input / material purchasing
N	• Attitude of workers • Semi-literacy among workers • Population increase • Trade union activities • Topographical imbalance • Geological conditions • Transportation of green leaf / other inputs • Location of garden • Absenteeism • Low productivity of labor • Medical expenditure • Cattle trespass • Power & fuel consumption • Rent & taxes • Legal expenses	• Taxation • Natural calamities • Price fluctuations / auctions • Cost increase of inputs • Social & political disturbances • Fire hazards • Riots / extremist activities • Bundhs / strikes – local & outside • Wild elephant menace • Blockage of drain outlets • Climatic changes • Power & fuel supply

Exhibit 10.3 Illustrative CINE Matrix of Software Industry

	I	E
C	• Productivity & Manufacturing • Product Mix • Project Quality • Investment in Infrastructure • Employee Productivity	• Customer Base • Alliances • Virus / Bugs • Customer Relationships • Communication Systems • Educational Institutions
N	• Employee Turnover • Obsolescence of skills & Technology • Brain drain	• Changes in Technology • Government Policy • Laws, Rules & Regulations • Hackers • Software Piracy • Competitors • Buyers / Sellers • New Entrants • Substitutes • Hardware Availability

CONTROLLABLE - INTERNAL FACTORS

Productivity & Manufacturing: The productivity of a company in software is difficult to measure due to growing and dynamic environment. But still productivity is a factor that can be enhanced and increased over time. This can be seen in the performance of Indian software industry.

Product Mix: The choice of product mix has direct implications for profitability of any firm. Product development is a costly exercise requiring high investment.

Project Quality: The projects undertaken by the company is a good indication of how the company is currently doing and direction of its growth.

Investment in Infrastructure: Investment and resource mobilization is a factor of critical importance to the software industry with initial investment required being quite high.

Employee Productivity: The importance of skilled personnel cannot be over emphasized for the success of any software company. The training provided to employees and the professional satisfaction derived by the employees from the work assigned to them form a major factor contributing to the success and growth of firm.

CONTROLLABLE - EXTERNAL FACTORS

Customer Base: A study of the customer base of the company is also indicative of its reputation in world market.

Alliances: IT companies have shifted gears and are actively looking out for acquisition and mergers with IT companies of the West. Acquisition also facilitate entry of strong management.

Virus / Bugs: The highest threat from any source which is faced by a software company are the virus and bugs which make a software non-functional or in-operative.

Customer Relationships: For IS users in India, who had always been deprived of adequate service and maintenance, the concept of customer relationship management comes as manna and has become a popular buzz word.

Communication Systems: In today's era of mobility and quick access, communication is an essential peripheral of any industry and more so in software industry.

Educational Institutions: IT companies are looking at distance learning as a major opportunity with new computer education institutes coming up every day.

NON-CONTROLLABLE - INTERNAL FACTORS

Employee Turnover: The growth pace of software industry is exceptional, therefore leading to a high employee turnover.

Obsolescence of Skills and Technology: Heady pace of the industry's growth makes skills and technology obsolete very quickly, hence, an update is needed every now and then.

Brain Drain: India produces top quality IT professionals and due to good compensation given by foreign companies, many migrate creating a dearth of knowledge workers.

NON-CONTROLLABLE - EXTERNAL FACTORS

Changes in Technology: Technology is of supreme importance to the software industry. Industry changes very quickly, with PLC (Product Life Cycle) being leptokurtik in nature.

Government Policy: The Government acts as a promoter or obstacle in the path of an industry. During recent years, Government is playing a facilitator's role.

Hackers: In the terms and terminology of internet, hacking is the greatest problems faced by the net users.

Software Piracy: Every person who owns a PC would not essentially buy the original software packages. A lot of fake copies are available arising from software piracy.

Competitors: Competitors tend to influence strategies of the company in one form or other.

Buyers / Sellers: Strong linkages are required with buyers and sellers.

New Entrants: The industry due to its high level of knowledge requirement, investment and technology, poses an obstacle to new entrants.

Substitutes: There are many firms supplying almost similar products leading to easy substitutability.

Hardware Availability: With new developments in software, hardware compatibility is essential.

Exhibit 10.4 BOW Analysis of Software Industry

Barriers	Obstacles
• High Investment • Funds Mobilization • Acceptability • New Entrant Barriers due to MNCs • Heady Pace of Change • Costly R & D	• Established Brands • High Compensation • Hackers & Pirates • Small Customer Base • Substitutes • Cultural Division within the Company • Decline in Foreign Market
Weaknesses	
• Incompatibility • Lack of Vision • Obsolescence of Skills & Techniques • Misuse of Technology	

BARRIERS

High Investment: The initial investment requirement is high, creating a problem for small and new firms to enter the industry.

Funds Mobilization: Funds are very difficult to find as it is a high risk business.

Acceptability: The consumer base is small, therefore there are less number of people who are ready to buy the products available in the market.

New Entrant Barriers Due to MNCs: The MNC software companies are well established and thus have wider base which have to be seen while entering the industry.

Heady Pace of Change: The growth pace is very high, thus giving rise to shorter product life cycle.

Costly R & D: R & D of new softwares and products is costly.

OBSTACLES

Established Brands: In this industry there is a greater emphasis on brands, as people prefer to buy established brands only, giving a lot of difficulty to new players.

High Compensation: The employees due to their level of skill, demand high pay packets which are not in the scope of newly established companies.

Hackers & Pirates: Hackers & pirates act as deterrents to the company.

Small Customer Base: The customers base needs expansion.

Substitutes: A large number of substitutes are available for any one kind of application.

Cultural Division within the Company: A software company presents the most culturally diverse employee force than any other industry.

Decline in Foreign Market: There has been a decline in the software and hardware market in the foreign market.

WEAKNESSES

Incompatibility: With new software being developed every other day, there arises a question of compatible hardware. Even some new versions need a different configuration of hardware.

Lack of Vision: Everything becomes outdated very quickly, therefore a clear vision is needed and it needs to be followed thoroughly.

Obsolesce of Skills and Techniques: Skills and techniques are also become obsolete, needing a quick upgradation and regular training of employees.

Misuse of Technology: A firm creates a software or product with best intention at heart, but they may be used by people for unsocial purposes.

❑

CHAPTER 11 Enterprise Performance Improvement Systems (EPIS)*

This chapter provides a framework for EPIS (Enterprise Performance Management System) linking management control system concepts and 'forward engineering' tools. In management control system, the emphasis is on 'performance improvement'. This is achieved by setting a system based on the concept of 'control cycle', wherein a comparison is made with standards of performance and the reasons for the difference between the standards and actual performance are analyzed with a view to control and improve the performance. Further, continuous performance monitoring is an important aspect of the control cycle.

11.1 Foundational Framework for Designing EPIS

A framework of management control system was initially suggested by Anthony and Dearden (1981). They identified three levels of decision making and control *viz.*, strategic planning, management control and operational control. This framework was subsequently refined by Anthony and Govindrajan (1994) who suggested that boundaries of management control are bounded by strategy formulation and task control. Strategy formulation activity is concerned with goals, strategies and policies within the framework of vision, mission and values, and task control relates to efficient and effective performance of individual tasks. The three levels of control system framework can also be viewed in terms of Strategic thinking, Management planning & control and Operations management. These three levels also broadly correspond to the leadership functions, managerial functions and

*Enterprise Performance Improvement Systems (EPIS): Value Chain Matrix and Forward Engineering Tools for Performance Improvement, Subhash Sharma, *Sankalpa: The Journal of Management Development and Application*, Utkal University, Bhubaneswar, Jan. – June 2000, 8:1, pp. 81– 94.

operational functions within the organizations. Based on these three levels, an integrated strategic, managerial and operational planning and control framework is presented in Fig. 11.1 which integrates following aspects of an organization:

1. Vision, Mission and Values
2. Managerial Actions
3. Monitoring & Follow up

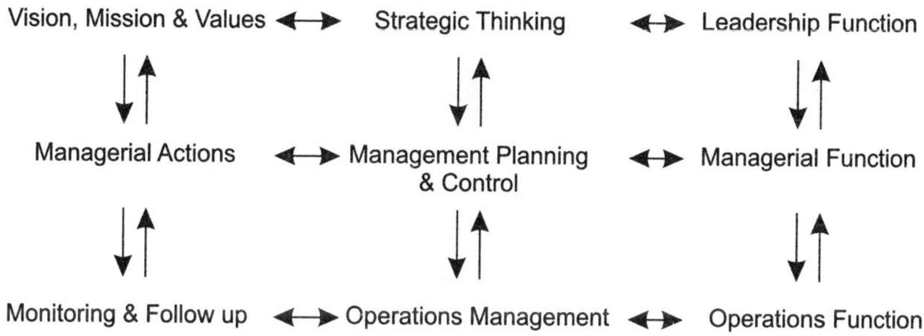

Figure 11.1. An Integrated Strategic Management and Operational Control Systems Framework

From Fig. 11.1, it may be noticed that the relationship between three levels is interactive in nature. It also implies that an organization's ViSA (Vision, Strategy and Action plan) should be supported with proper monitoring and follow up system.

It may be indicated that the traditional literature on management control system had emphasized the top down approach because of its 'command and control' philosophy. New thinking in control systems is rooted in interactive approach rather than command and control approach. Hence the diagram in Fig. 11.1 shows interlinking upward and downward arrows indicating that there is a continuous interaction between three levels. In designing Enterprise Performance Improvement Systems (EPIS), due consideration is given to all three levels as performance of an enterprise is influenced by decision making, problem solving and solution finding at all three levels.

Following three processes are critical to achieving an alignment between three levels of organizations:

1. Visioning and envisioning
2. Decision making
3. Problem solving

A manager has to integrate these three processes in order to be effective. Visioning and envisioning requires a manager to be creative, hence, strong in conceptual skills. Decision making particularly in unstructured situations requires intuition and creativity in addition to rationality. In structured situations, rationality works well, while in unstructured situations, there may be need to break the 'rationality wall' that managers may build around then. Problem solving at the operational level requires analytical and behavioral approach. Through visioning envisioning at the strategic level, decision making and problem solving at strategic, managerial and operational level, an organization can gear itself for 'vision actualization'. Figure 11.2 provides a framework of three managerial roles of a manager and leader.

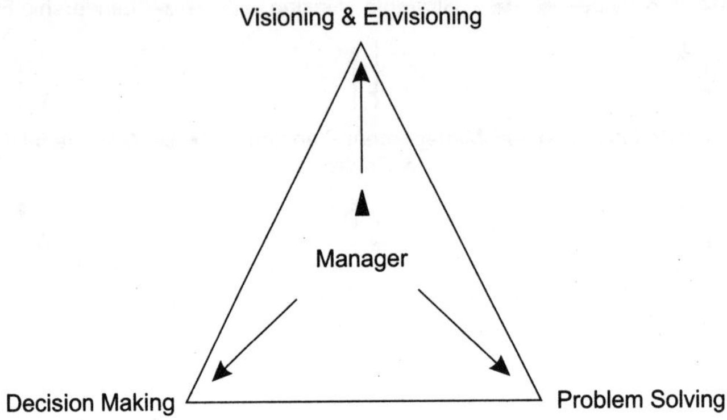

Figure 11.2. Three Managerial Roles of a Manager

These three managerial roles call for strategic thinking based on integration and synthesis of critical thinking and creative thinking wherein rationality and creativity are combined to arrive at holistic solutions. This implies an integrative approach wherein left brain (rationality) and right brain (creative) thinking are combined. It may be indicated that this approach to strategic thinking is rooted in wisdom equation, W = R + I, Wisdom = Reason + Intuition. It suggests that strategic thinking requires a wisdom approach to visioning and envisioning.

11.2 Tools of Forward Engineering for Designing EPIS

An organization operates within the context of competitive pressures and changes in environment. Hence, its all three levels *viz*., strategic, managerial and operations, should pay attention to the following four aspects of business context:

1. Changes in Environment
2. Competition
3. Opportunities & Threats
4. Enterprise Competencies

Figure 11.3 presents these four dimensions that influence the design of Enterprise Performance Improvement Systems (EPIS) in the form of an 'Arrow diagram'. Based on these four dimensions a ViSA (Vision, Strategies, Action plan) document can be prepared to guide managerial actions and to ensure good performance.

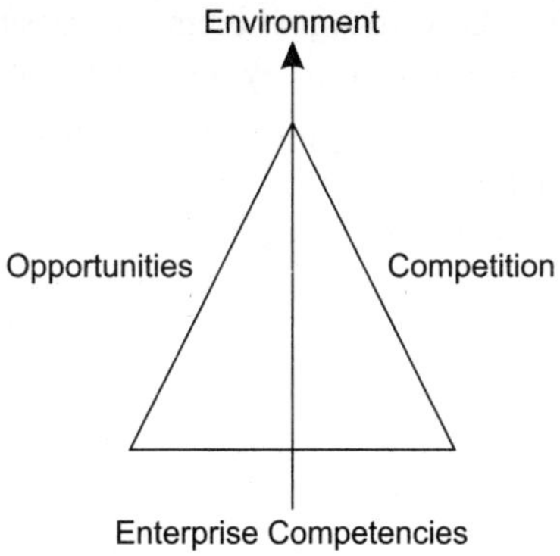

Figure 11.3. Arrow Diagram for Competitive Analysis

In order to deal with the above four factors, the following 'mental models' as tools of 'forward engineering' that have been empirically tested in the enterprise context, can be used by managers to improve their organization's performance:

1. FATE Analysis
2. BOW Analysis
3. SWAN and SPOT Analysis
4. SO-SO Window
5. CINE Matrix

The 'mental model' of FATE analysis focuses on changes in environment. In FATE analysis, our focus is on Future Anticipated Trends & Events.

BOW indicates deficiencies in competencies of organization, as its focus is on Barriers, Obstacles and Weaknesses. Managers have to face them in order to 'drive the FATE'.

SWAN Analysis focus is on Strengths, Weaknesses, Achievements and Next step. SPOT Analysis draws our attention to Space and pace of Opportunities and Threats. As against SWOT, in SPOT analysis the pace of change gets a due importance. SPOT analysis focuses our attention on a continuous assessment of the changes in the market space and pace. The following can be considered as a refinement of the SWOT analysis:

SWOT Analysis = SWAN Analysis + SPOT Analysis

In making an assessment of changes in opportunities and threats both analytical and intuitive methodologies are useful. For subjective assessment 'wishbone' that focuses on diagnosis through 'market feel' is a useful tool. Wishbone diagnosis of the space and pace of opportunities and threats can be supplemented with the popular Japanese technique of 'fishbone analysis' for analysis of cause and effect.

SO-SO window focuses our attention to competition and what others are doing to create and face competition. Both SWAN analysis and SPOT analysis can also be viewed through the SO-SO window, wherein an assessment is made about the way SWAN and SPOT are being viewed by the organization and its competitors.

CINE matrix provides us insights into Controllable, Non-controllable, Internal and External factors that influence decision making. In case of an organization, having corporate office and divisions, CINE matrix can be prepared at the corporate level as well as at the division levels. Within divisions, it can be prepared at the responsibility unit be it revenue center, cost center or profit center. CINE matrix can also be prepared for various links within the business value chain. CINE matrix when prepared for various components of the value chain, could provide solutions for strengthening the value chain links. CINE matrix is useful in integrating the three levels of decision making *viz.*, strategy formulation, management control and operations control, across the enterprise.

The ultimate objective of Enterprise Performance Improvement Systems (EPIS) is to 'drive the FATE'. Accordingly the above identified 'mental models' can be integrated in the form of a conceptual framework in consonance with the arrow diagram of an enterprise presented earlier. This 'Forward Engineering' framework can be used for articulating Enterprise Performance Improvement Strategies, and can referred to as 'Driving the FATE'. The framework is presented in Fig. 11.4.

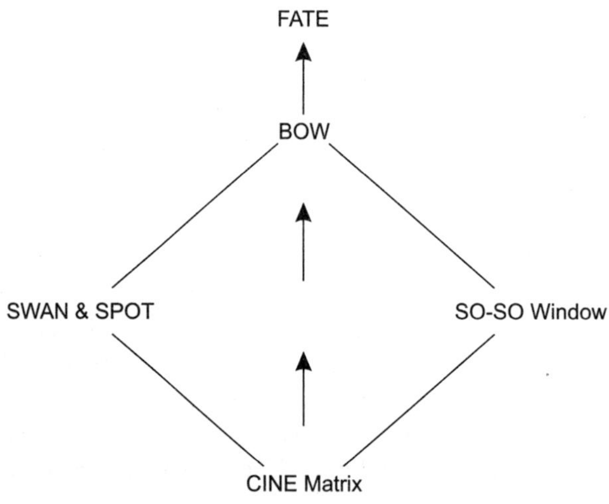

Figure 11.4. Forward Engineering Framework for Enterprise Performance Improvement Strategies

11.3 Managerial SPSS Strengths, Problems, Solutions and Strategies

Earlier we discussed about the visioning-envisioning, decision making and problem solving roles of managers. To facilitate these roles with a view to improve performance of the organization, the concept of Managerial SPSS analysis is very useful. Managerial SPSS draws our attention to Strengths, Problems, Solutions & Strategies'. It not only draws attention to Strengths and Problems (Pain points) but also focuses attention on Solutions & Strategies. Many times strengths provide answers to the problems managers are facing and as a result creative solutions emerge by focusing on strengths.

In order to undertake Managerial SPSS Analysis, a group exercise / brainstorming exercise can be taken up, wherein managers identify their organization's / Department's Strengths and Problems and brain storm to find out Solutions to the Problems and also long term Strategies to take care of the problems they face. It may be indicated that this SPSS exercise is not just a brain storming exercise but is also a mind pooling exercise because discussions lead to creative solutions because many different ideas are pooled together in the process of finding solutions. It may be indicated that for developing a system for performance improvement, it is important to highlight the strengths and problems of the enterprise and its business units / performance units. Undertaking SPSS analysis also helps in setting up 'decision circles' at managerial level and 'problem solving circles' at operational level.

It may be indicated that in contrast to SWOT analysis, focus of SPSS is on problem solving and deriving strategies by focusing on strengths and by finding solutions for the problems.

Table 11.1 presents an illustration of Managerial Analysis undertaken by a group of managers from a Tea Company in Assam during an interactive session with the author during Management Development Program. Managers identified strengths and problem and also identified solutions / suggestions and strategies. Solutions and strategies are not presented in Table 10.1 as they became part of confidential document of the company. It may be indicated that Managerial SPSS can also be used as a tool for analyzing Key Result Areas (KRAs).

Table 11.1. Managerial SPSS Analysis of a Tea Company by its Managers

Strengths	Problems	Solutions & Strategies*
Excellent tea estate/good location	High cost of teas	
Renowned brand & Ownership changes	Company goodwill ruined the morale of people	
Large quantities of the teas being produced	Low productivity of the age old bushes	
Professional Management talent	Militancy	
Good quality of tea	Theft of green leaf	

*Not indicated here as they became part of the confidential document of the company.

Good field practices	Too much interference of Government officials	
Good team work	Poor roads	
Good leadership & Absenteeism	Will to take the company further unemployed youth on estates	
Good health management at all levels of workforce	Distance of labor lines from plantations	
Work culture	No uprooting, replanting programs	
Having good skilled & Rising production cost	Semi-skilled work force	
Workers by & large Peace loving	Infrastructure at the estates needs improvement	
Fairly modern facilities	Quality inconsistent in some gardens	
Good coordination between headquarters and garden operations	Manufacturing policy not clear. Frequent transfer of executives	

In SPSS, focus is on strengths as well as on problems and solutions. Problems could be at the strategic level, managerial level or operational level and solutions could be strategic, managerial or operational in nature. Once problems are identified in terms of these three fold classification, it becomes easier to identify the solutions.

It may also be indicated that problems could be classified in terms of Behavioral, Economic, Strategic and Technical (BEST) factors and solutions could also be in terms of these factors. This further analysis helps managers in identifying nature of problems in terms of B, E, S, T problems and solutions in terms of B, E, S, T. Problems can also be classified in terms of level of decision making *viz.*, strategic, managerial and operational. This helps in addressing the problems at appropriate levels.

The essence of SPSS lies in evolving strategies from the strengths of the organization, keeping in view its problems and the solutions to the problems. Because of its focus on solutions and strategies, this tool also develops a problem solving orientation among managers and makes them optimists. It may also be mentioned that this tool also has a linkage with Lewin's Facilitating–Inhibiting factors concept, as strengths represent facilitating factors and problems represent performance inhibiting factors. Through solutions and strategies we overcome limitations imposed by performance inhibiting factors and thereby focus on performance improvement.

11.4 Resources, Sources and Forces

While conducting Managerial SPSS analysis, attention may be paid to Resources, Sources and Forces (RSF) influencing a manager in performing his/her tasks. A manager operates with certain human and other resources on his/her hand that include factors of creation such as knowledge, power, capital. Some of these resources are locally available, and some others are procured from other places. Thus, sources of the resources is of critical importance to the manager. In addition, he / she operates under several forces that impinge upon his / her work and role. These could be natural, man-made, political, market *etc.*, For example, PEST analysis is used to analyze Political, Economic, Social and Technology forces influencing an organization.

The resources, sources and forces analysis helps in identifying the areas of contracting out *i.e.*, the activities that can be contracted out in order to improve performance. In the era of globalization, the sources of resources could be from any part of the world. The movement of knowledge resources, capital and people is now taking place across the globe and is not restricted to local levels only. Further, the global changes are influencing the managers. Porter's five force analysis and METRIC analysis are useful force fields frameworks in analyzing the underlying changes. The framework of Resources, Sources and Forces, helps the managers in focusing their attention on strategic changes.

11.5 Parameters of Performance

It is important that parameters of performance are well articulated. If parameters of performance are vague, it becomes difficult to measure performance. Usually the critical variables would be identified for each responsibility area and periodic monitoring is undertaken to ensure the achievement of targets. It may be indicated that the focus should be on key parameters of performance. Information on too many variables could lead to "analysis paralysis" and unnecessary details. The magic number seven is a useful guide. Another magic number is nine. Usually seven to nine key parameters of performance are sufficient to measure the performance of a business unit or manager heading the responsibility center. These parameters could relate to productivity, quality, cost of production, profitability, value addition, customer satisfaction, training and development *etc.*,

Analysis of the resources, sources and forces and identification of parameters of performance, lead us to key performance areas and key problem areas. The key performance areas and the key problem areas may be inter-linked. Indeed some of the key problems may be affecting more than one key performance areas. In the Enterprise Performance Improvement (EPI) exercise, the inter-linkage between the two needs to be identified clearly.

For analysis of key problems, the analytical tool of CINE matrix discussed earlier is useful not only for problem identification but also for finding solutions. Further, a BOW analysis is conducted. Since in BOW analysis focus is on Barriers,

Obstacles and Weaknesses, it helps in identifying the solutions to overcome them so that the implementation of the identified solutions for performance improvement becomes easy.

11.6 Analysis of Change: Changing the Change and Changing with Change

Managers should be prepared to change with change and change the change. Therefore, an analysis of major changes in the last few years as well as analysis of anticipated changes is useful with a view to analyze the impact of changes on the performance. Analysis of change could include the following:

- Changes due to policies
- Changes in manpower composition
- Changes in ownership, if any
- Changes due to environmental factors
- Changes due to market conditions
- Any other significant change

In addition to above, Future Anticipated Trends and Events (FATE) should be projected to be prepared for 'future shocks' and 'future surprises' arising from anticipated changes.

Using the EPIS concepts a manager prepares a report on performance improvement of his/her unit/responsibility area. Wherever necessary the report is presented to the corporate headquarters with a view to identify the extent of corporate support required by the unit manager. Through EPI exercise managers can identify the support required to bridge the gap between the current status and the targets. Every time an EPI exercise is taken up a new base for growth is created. Hence, the idea of "quantum - jump budgeting" is fundamental to the EPIS concept. The focus of the quantum - jump budgeting or 'new base budgeting' is to make quantum jumps in performance and create a new base with every new jump in performance.

11.7 Managerial Scorecard (MSc)

EPI (Enterprise Performance Improvement) report is also useful for Performance Review, as it draws attention to Key Performance Areas, Key Problem Areas, Barriers, Obstacles and Weaknesses, CI (Controllable Internal) and NE (Non-Controllable External) factors. For any review, actual performance should be measured against the targets and reasons for non-achievement of targets should be identified.

It may be indicated that performance review process is facilitated through performance indicators. A set of indicators that includes the financial as well as non-financial parameters of performance could be drawn up, specific to the needs of the business unit. As indicated earlier, the magic numbers seven and nine are useful guide in identifying critical variables for performance measurement. The chart containing seven to nine indicators for performance measurement can be referred to as Managerial Scorecard (MSc). It could also be used as a comparison card by comparing the indicators of performance across similar business units. Thus, it could become a basis for Performance Ranking. Reward systems could be instituted for quantum jumps in performance as reflected through the performance indicators. During recent years, the concept of "Balanced Scorecard" has also been used to achieve goal congruence between corporate goals and business unit performance. Managerial Scorecard, when linked with strategic variables could also indicate whether there is proper goal congruence between managerial performance and organizational strategies.

11.8 Action Plan: Preparing an EPI Report

Managers making the self-assessment of their business unit could use the following format for writing the EPI (Enterprise Performance Improvement) report for their organization/Division/Department:

1. History & Profile of the Business Unit
2. Parameters of Performance
3. Organization's ViSA
4. FATE, SWAN & SPOT Analysis
5. BOW (Barriers, Obstacles & Weaknesses) Analysis
6. Resources, Sources & Forces
7. Key Performance Areas
8. Key Problem Areas
9. CINE Matrix
10. Managerial SPSS (Strengths, Problems, Solutions & Strategies)
11. Suggested Solutions
12. Recommendations for Performance Improvement

It may be indicated that EPI report preparation would be facilitated if the entire business unit management team is involved in doing this exercise. An EPI report would also help in preparing a comprehensive Business Development Program/Business Development Report which could form a basis for making quantum - jump in performance improvement. The EPI framework can also be useful for creating organizational turnarounds because of its focus on performance improvement.

The 'mental models', concepts and ideas suggested in this chapter are useful in designing and developing performance improvement systems. The tool of Managerial SPSS is particularly useful to leaders and managers in arriving at creative solutions to the problems they face in their managerial responsibilities. EPI (Enterprise Performance Improvement) through Managerial SPSS and other Forward Engineering tools, is the keynote of EPIS.

❑

CHAPTER 12 Organization Development and Management (ODM)*

Modern corporations are founded on four pillars of creation *viz.*, Knowledge, Power, Capital and Labour (KPCL). Accordingly in Organization Development & Management (ODM), all the four factors acquire importance.

12.1 KPCL Model

Harmony between four factors of creation represented by Knowledge, Power, Capital and Labour (KPCL), creates conditions for the growth and development of the organization. If there is no harmony, growth and development get adversely affected. During different periods of human history, different metaphors have been used to depict nature of relationship between these four factors of creation. During ancient times this relationship was represented through the metaphor of human being – Head/mind representing Knowledge, Hands representing Power, Backbone representing Capital and Legs support representing Labour. During industrial era, the metaphor of 'factory' evolved to describe the four factors of creation, wherein factors KPC (Knowledge, Power, Capital) represented the top of the building and L (Labour) represented the foundation. In the knowledge era, the metaphor of chakra / cycle evolved and the cycle is driven by Knowledge (K).

Thus, we have three metaphorical models representing relationship between four factors of creation. Figure 12.1 presents the three models and the changing metaphors in a diagrammatic form.

*Organization Development & Management (ODM): Total Capital Approach, in New Mantras in Corporate Corridors: From Ancient Roots to Global Routes, Subhash Sharma, New Age International Publishers, New Delhi, 2007, pp. 389–403.

In consonance with these four factors of creation, an organization needs to focus on four dimensions of management *viz.*, Knowledge management, Power (Relationships) management, Capital (Money, Finance) management and Labour management. Thus, KPCL model provides us a conceptual foundation for understanding four fundamental managerial functions in organizations, *viz.*, managing knowledge that includes Innovations, R & D and technology, managing power that includes relationships, network building, resource allocations processes *etc.*, managing capital that includes managing working capital, long term finances, risk management *etc.*, and managing labour or the human resources. It may be indicated that several new tools and techniques have been developed to manage each factor of creation. This has led to development of the field of management as a distinct field of study.

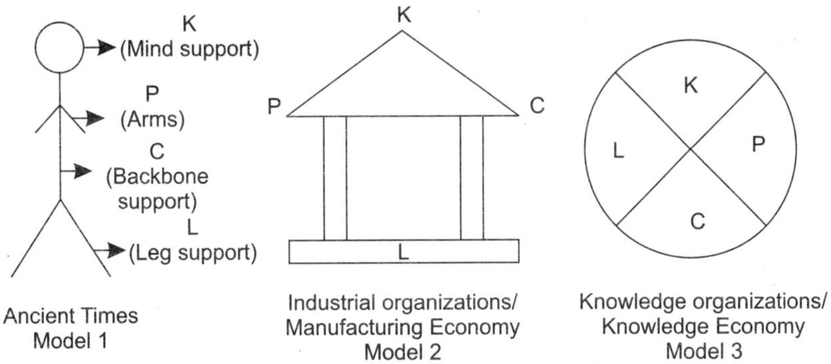

Figure 12.1. Changing Metaphors of the 'Factors of Creation'

It may also be noted that KPCL concept is applicable not only at the organization level but also at the level of society and nation. A society and nation should effectively manage knowledge, power, capital and labor resources to become competitive and developed. KPCL Analysis of a Nation implies, analyzing a nation's institutional structures in terms of Knowledge (K) systems (*e.g.*, education system, R & D organizations *etc.*,), Power (P) systems (*e.g.*, political institutions, bureaucracy, judiciary *etc.*,), Capital (C) systems (*e.g.*, wealth creation through corporate and small businesses, capital markets *etc.*,) and Labour (L) system (*e.g.*, labour markets, skill development, HR, Talent Management *etc.*,). To emerge as a super power, a nation should co-align and harmonize its KPCL systems. In Organization Development & Management (ODM) context, CEO and Board, should focus on co-aligning KPCL systems of the organization for its strategic gearing.

12.2 VSP Yantra for ODM

While KPCL analysis provides us a basis for four pillars of the organization, we need to integrate following three vectors to ensure growth and development of the organization:

1. V vector: Vision, Vistas, Values
2. S vector: Strategy, Structure, Systems
3. P vector: Purpose, Process, People

In the past, management concepts were heavily influenced by S vector representing Strategy, Structure and Systems. Management thought of the past was largely centered around the same. Later, well known Management Guru, Sumantra Ghoshal suggested the need for shift towards P vector representing Purpose, Process and People. During recent years, V vector in the form of Vision, Vistas and Values (core values), has been evolving and has entered the academic literature in the field of management and leadership. Now there is a need to integrate these approaches and in VSP Yantra, these three vectors are combined.

VSP yantra model can be viewed as a new model for study of organizations wherein nine dimensions (Vision, Vistas, Values, Strategy, Structure, Systems, Purpose, Process, People) represented by VSP vectors are given due attention and their interconnectivity is emphasized. Figure 12.2 presents the VSP Yantra as a basic framework for ODM.

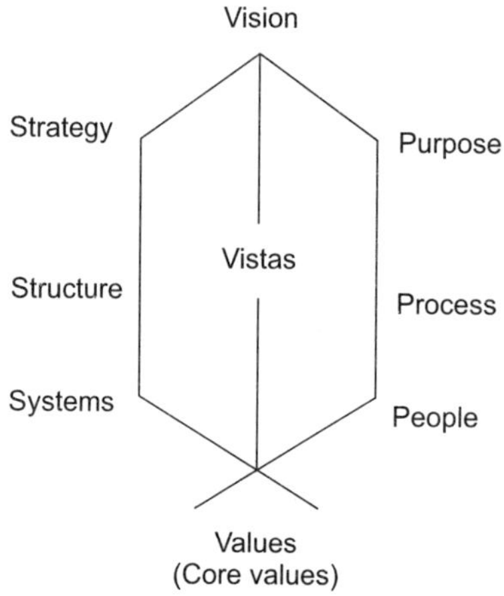

Figure 12.2. VSP Yantra as ODM Framework

VSP yantra presented in Fig. 12.2 can be compared with human brain, wherein S vector on the left side of the diagram, represents the left side of the brain and left brain approach to ODM, P vector on the right side of the diagram represents the right side of the brain and right brain approach and V vector in the center represented the center connecting line of the two sides of the brain and integrates the left brain and right brain approaches through Vision, Vistas and Values. Thus, in this model hard side of the organization represented by S vector is combined with soft side represented by P vector and hard and soft sides of the organization are connected through V vector.

Role of the CEO is to create a proper alignment between the nine elements of the VSP yantra and thereby drive the organization to its full potential. If these elements are not properly aligned, organization's performance will get affected.

It may be indicated that VSP yantra takes us beyond Mckinsey's 7 S framework (Strategy, Structure, Systems, Staff, Skills, Styles, Shared vision). In Mckinsey framework also there is a connectivity between hard and soft side of organization through shared vision that connects the hard side (represented by strategy, structure, systems) with soft side (represented by staff, skills, styles).

VSP yantra is not only useful for ODM but can also be used as a framework for developing case studies of organizations, institutions and movements to learn about the methods of achieving alignments between nine critical elements of the organizations.

It may be indicated that a new ABC of Management & Leadership is required to ensure harmony between various VSP vectors. This ABC implies 'Alignment, Balancing & Coordinating' (ABC) as three foundational ideas for management & leadership in the new age.

12.3 VSP Yantra and Institution Building

While VSP yantra is not only useful for organizational analysis and change management, but also has usefulness for institution building. This understanding is particularly needed because corporates are emerging as social institutions.

Following five elements can be identified as a basis for a framework ODM for institution building:

1. Shared vision or collective vision defining the strategic frame of the organization
2. Core values defining the way of business
3. Resources
4. Relationships
5. Structures, Systems & Processes

Collective vision represents the 'shared vision' along with strategies and action plans expressed in the form of a ViSA (Vision Strategy Action plan) document. Shared vision may be rooted in Dream that organization wants to convert into reality. Strategy formulation is linked with Vision and Action plan represents the plan for strategy implementation. Thus, in ViSA both strategy formulation and strategy implementation are part of the management process. Purpose of ViSA document is to ensure 'vision actualization'. The vision is supported by 'core values' which indicate the way business is done in the organization. They constitute the cornerstone of 'principles of business'. Resources of the organization include knowledge resources, human resources and capital. Relationships include relationships with stakeholders *viz.*, customers, employees, shareholders, society and Government. Structures, systems and processes include governance structures to ensure good governance, monitoring and performance measurement systems through scorecards. Accountability and transparency are part of internal processes.

Structures, systems and processes should be designed to facilitate achievement of results. This framework of ODM and institution building is presented in Fig. 12.3.

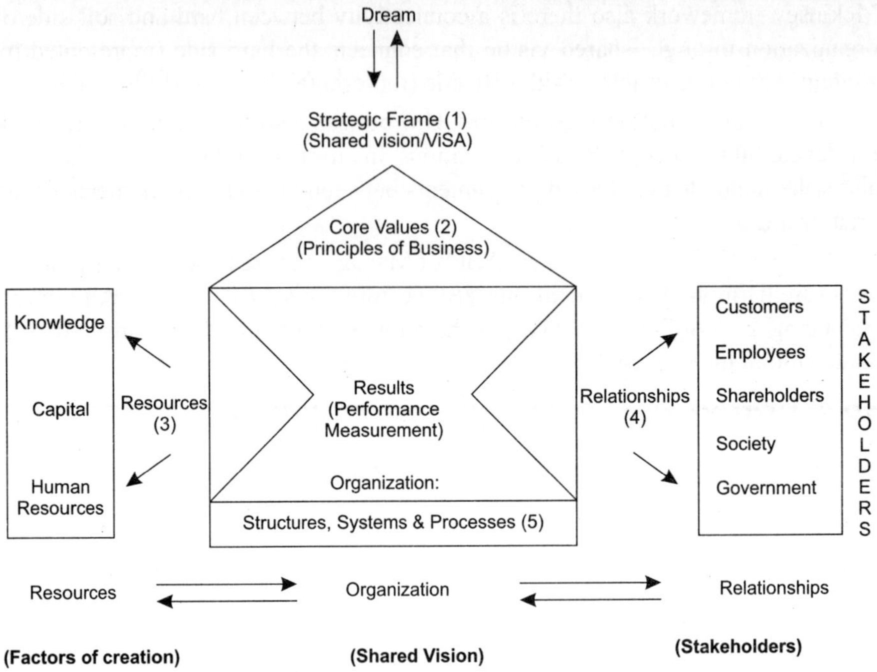

Figure 12.3. A Framework for ODM & Institution Building

It may be indicated that this framework has a linkage with KPCL (Knowledge, Power, Capital and Labour) factors of creation and various stakeholders. While Knowledge (K), Capital (C) and Labour (L), represent knowledge resources, capital and human resources, Power (P) represents the relationships with various stakeholders and is indicative of the Leadership factor.

This model draws upon various elements of the VSP yantra and links them with Resources (factors of creation), Relationships (with Stakeholders) and Results (Organizational Performance). Further, essence of this model lies in highlighting connectivity of the factors of creation and stakeholders through shared vision & core values as well as through organizational performance. Model indicates that essence of institution building lies in 'vision actualization'.

In this book, we presented a framework of managerial requirements and decision styles in terms of three processes *viz.*, visioning & envisioning, decision making and problems solving. It may be indicated that ODM and institution building is facilitated by these processes. Table 12.1 provides a summary of various tools that are presented in this book and are useful in visioning & envisioning, decision making and problem solving.

Table 12.1. A Summary of ODM & Institution Building Tools

Level	Managerial Requirement	Tools
Strategic level / Policy level	Visioning & Envisioning	ViSA, Wishbone analysis, Mind-pooling, SWAN & SPOT analysis, Omega circle perspective
Managerial level	Decision Making	CINE matrix, Anti-benchmarking, Non-liner thinking, Decision circles
Operational level	Problem Solving	Managerial SPSS, Problem solving circles

12.4 VSP Yantra, ODM and Radical Change Management[3]

Nature of organizations has been changing over a period of time. At one point of time, paradigm of pyramid provided the basis for creation and development of organizations. 'Design of Organizations' was based on the pyramid metaphor rooted in the ideas of rigid structures and command & control mindset. Researchers developed theories and concepts and empirically tested them sitting inside the pyramid. However, in due course a new paradigm evolved. Pyramid gave way to a matrix. Matrix organizations became the buzzword originating from the project management approach to creation and development of organizations. Empiricists provided new formulations of hypotheses for 'Design of Organizations', this time sitting inside a cell of the matrix and sometimes looking at the organizations from outside the boundaries of the matrix. With the advent of Information Technology, a new concept and a new metaphor for 'Design of Organizations' evolved. The metaphor of Network/Wired Network provided the basis for creation and development of organizations. Now organizations are experiencing chaos. As a result, the metaphor of chaos is emerging as a new metaphor leading to 'dissipative structures' and 'amoeba structures' as a basis for organizations to operate in chaotic environment. This calls for flexible structures, team work and trust. Figure 12.4 captures this transition in thinking about creation and development of organizations from pyramids to 'dissipative structures'. The metaphor of 'dissipative structures' captures the essence of ever changing organization because not only 'dissipative structures' dissipate to give way to new structures as per new requirements but also constantly change shapes like 'amoebae'. Maira (2002) suggests the metaphor of 'perfect storm' arising from interaction of various forces of change leading to unpredictability. Perhaps a better metaphor could be 'imperfect storm' rather than a 'perfect storm'.

[3]'Radical Change Management: From Managing Pyramid to Managing in Chaos' Subhash Shrama, *Paradigm*, The Journal of IMT, Ghaziabad, January–June 2002, 6:1, pp. 1–9.

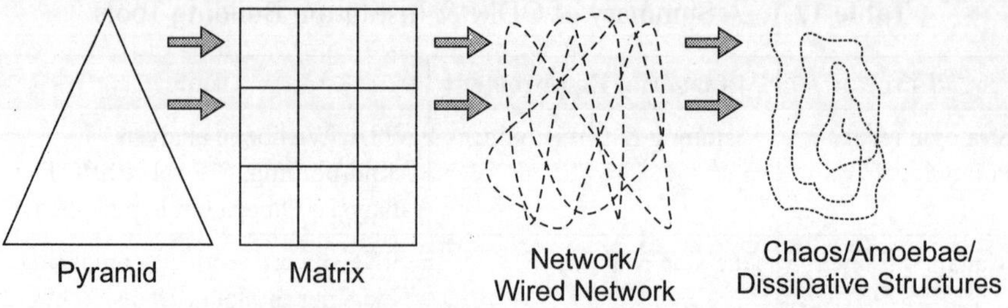

Figure 12.4. Changing Metaphors for Design of Organizations

Thus, there is a paradigm shift from managing pyramids to managing dissipative structures. It may be indicated that literature on Change Management has been growing in view of the need for managing an ever-changing organization. In general, the literature focuses on nature of change, forces of change, types and models of change, mantras of change, *etc.*, For example, Harigopal (2001) and others provide discussion on these themes dealing with change management.

In consonance with above indicated organization structures, there are four types of managers; 1. Pyramid Managers who feel comfortable in a structured and bureaucratic set up. They want to convert the organization or their department into a pyramid. 2. Matrix Managers: They achieve their tasks through better co-ordination and co-operation without caring for bureaucracy within the organization. 3. Network Managers: They act like nodes and see their role as facilitators and 'obstacle removers'. 4. Amoeba Managers: They display high tolerance for ambiguity. Being creative and innovative, they shape their organizations through futuristic vision. Within organizations, there is a constant struggle between these four types of individuals / managers. Organizations are increasingly realizing the need for network and amoeba managers, if they have to survive in today's complex business environment.

Above indicated typology of managers has a correspondence with the Rowe's (1987) decision styles typology. Pyramid managers are directive, authoritarian and power oriented. Matrix managers tend to use analytical decision style and are analysis oriented. Network managers rely on behavioral style to build networks and are relationship oriented. Amoeba managers are creative and intuitive and tend to use the conceptual style and are innovation oriented. They are most effective in situations of complexity, chaos and uncertainty. Table 12.2 summarizes this discussion.

Table 12.2. Structures and Decision Styles of Managers & Leaders

Nature of Structure	Primary Orientation	Decision Style
Pyramid 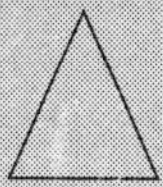	Power	Directive, Authoritarian, Bureaucratic
Matrix 	Analysis	Analytical
Network 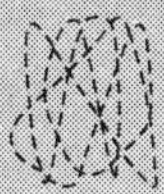	Relationship	Behavioral
Chaos 	Innovation	Conceptual

There are many theories of change. Newton's laws describe change in terms of force, momentum, action-reaction, *etc.*, Second law of thermodynamics explains change in terms of 'entropy theory'. Big bang theory of origin of universe, describes change in terms of 'singularities', where laws of physics fail. Accordingly, big bang theory of change in organizational context describes sudden emergence of new organizations through a big bang birth. Darwin's theory of change describes change in terms of random mutation and adaptation. Rebellion and revolutionary theories of change describe change in terms of 'quantitative change leading to qualitative change'. Challenge and Response (CR) theory of change, advocated by Arnold J Toynbee in the context of History, views change in terms of response to the new challenges. Lewin's theory of change describes change in terms of facilitating and inhibiting forces. Confucian and other Eastern theories of change, consider change as a cyclical process. Chaos theory of change views change in terms of 'butterfly effect' and transformation of caterpillar into a butterfly. Thus, there are a large number of theories of change. Lewin's change model of unfreezing - moving - refreezing has been a popular model of OD interventions for change management. However, it is linear in nature with simplistic assumptions about nature of change and is unsuitable for non-linear changes occurring in chaotic contexts. While it had utility in the context of pyramid and matrix organizations operating in relatively stable environment, its utility for Radical Change Management in the context of 'dissipative structures' and complex environments is limited. Hence, need for a new framework.

Ghoshal *et al.*, (2000) draw upon the well known metaphor of change, 'from a caterpillar to a butterfly', and apply it to the context of radical change in the context of business enterprises. They also suggest the metaphor of "valley of death". According to them, "transformational change is a journey through the valley of death". Using the ideas from chaos theory, we suggest the metaphor of the 'valley of depth'. It is a positive metaphor in contrast to Ghoshal's 'valley of death'. Transformational change implies exploring the depths / opportunities that nobody has explored before.

In organizations and society, change can occur because of manifestation of internal or external dialectical tensions and dialectical intensities, which can take varying forms such as see-saw form, swastika form, dialectical chakra form resulting in positive and negative energy spirals. Figure 12.5 presents four change initiating processes that could be referred to as 'chakra' theory of change because they create a variety of dialectical chakras within organizations.

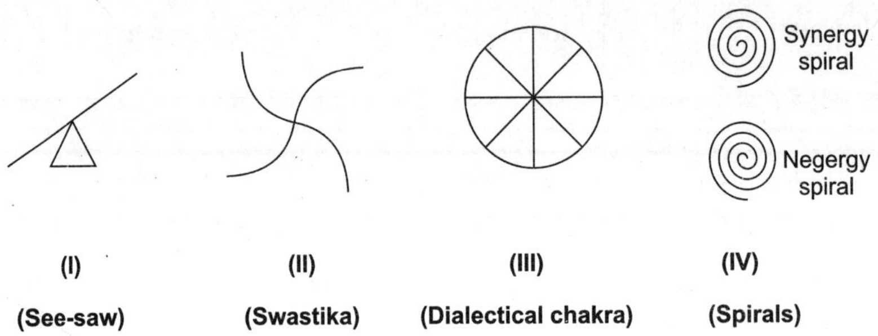

Figure 12.5. Organizational Metaphors of Change and Change Process

As a result of internal and external turbulence, contemporary organizations operate in dynamic and chaotic state. Hence, need for continuous innovation and creativity to create positive propelling energy for the organizations.

Radical change management can be implemented through 3Rs framework of Reinventing, Restructuring and Re-engineering the organization at the strategic, managerial and operational levels. At the strategic level the concept of reinventing has been advocated by many management gurus. The restructuring at the managerial level should be in alignment with reinventing. Further, re-engineering of processes and activities at the operational level should be in alignment with both reinventing and restructuring.

VSP Yantra can help us in understanding the change processes within organizations because VSP vectors get influenced in variety of ways because of new changes and challenges.

12.5 A New Organizational Model

It may also be indicated that a new organizational model has also emerged during recent times. This model from the knowledge era is distinct from the earlier models from 'kingdom era' and 'industrial revolution era'. Various models of organizations such as bureaucratic model from kingdom era / colonial era, 'input-output' or mechanistic model from industrial era and closed matrix model of project management, *etc.*, are being replaced by 'network' / open matrix model from knowledge era. In the new model of 'new age organizations' or 'knowledge organizations', organizations are seen as value creating and values enhancing companies. They do so by reaching out to all its stakeholders. The Chief Executive Officer, is hermit / sage & counselor unlike the CEO of the Industrial era. He / she is a 'Corporate Rishi' who is Rishi like, bubbling with 'silent energy' and is Creative, Enlightened & Organic (CEO) leader (Sharma 2007). Such a person is strong on Heart Skills (Kapadia, 2009).

In new age organizations / knowledge organizations, CEO's role is inspirational rather than merely motivational, accordingly team building and norm setting are his / her key tasks. Focus of CEO and his / her team is on 'dream actualization' and 'vision actualization' at the collective level and not merely 'self-actualization' at the individual level.

Employees in such organizations are 'knowledge units' and not merely worker or a mere 'factor of production' or input. As 'knowledge units' they should be allowed to grow to manifest their full potential. 'Contribution to Value Creation' is a major performance criterion for employee performance assessment.

Decision making process in such an organization is rooted in 'Quality circles' at operational level, 'Decision Circles' at managerial level and 'Omega circle' approach at strategic level. Decision circles is a democratic and consultative process and control and coordination systems are based on decentralization of performance units. Omega circle approach refers to integration of multiple perspectives of the issues and problems a leader is facing. It implies a 360 degree approach to strategic thinking, decision making and problem solving. This is facilitated through 3D (Discussion, Dialogue, Discourse) approach to creative solution finding.

Management theory in such organizations is a combination of Theory X, Theory Y, Theory Z represented by Theory K and Leadership theory is Theory T, represented by T = T1 + T2 + T3, wherein T1 (Transactional), T2 (Transformational) and T3 (Transcendental) approaches wherein a 'Touch of Transcendence' is given to every sphere of human activity. Theory T identifies three types of leaders *viz.*, T1, T2 and T3 types. T3 types provide a touch of transcendence through HOPE - Higher Order Purpose of Existence. This is also reflected in the cultural symbols of the organization. Cultural symbolism in such organizations has an inspirational value and they serve as symbols of Inspirational Motivation for the stakeholders.

Sumantra Ghoshal (2000) talks about 'smell of the place'. Extending this idea further, sight and sounds of the place are equally important. These three ideas when combined together lead to the 'spell of the place' and 'feel of the place'. We can represent this idea in terms of a spell equation, Spell = S^3 ($S \times S \times S$) (Sight, Sounds, Smell). It is important that an organization should make their workplaces so attractive that workplaces exhibit their own spell. Many workplaces now provide soft music at the workplace. This was unthinkable in factory context where sounds of machines dominated the environment. Extending these ideas further, culture, particularly in the context of a nation, can be represented by C (Culture) = S^3T^2 (Sight, Sound, Smell, Touch, Taste). 'Feel of the place' is captured through this formula. In case of nations, this feel may get reflected in terms of music, dance, cuisine, national consciousness and other aspects of the soft power of a nation. This formula can also serve as a framework for creating an inspiring organization culture in corporate context. It may be indicated that this approach provides us another perspective on culture taking us beyond Hofstede's and other frameworks on culture that emphasize the hard power approach.

Open matrix nature of such an organization allows it to synergize with new continuities arising out of new opportunities. Hamel & Prahlad (1994) suggest the need for "a deep understanding of potential discontinuities". In essence, a discontinuity should be converted into a new continuity or a new opportunity as part of the strategic approach. Prahlad describes this concept through the metaphor of 'Strategy as a discovery'. Management and leadership in open matrix organizations are rooted in the ABC (Aligning, Balancing, Coordinating) approach.

Table 12.3 provides a summary of these characteristics of New Age Organizations.

Table 12.3: Guiding Concepts of New Age Open Matrix Organizations

Dimension of the New Age Organizational Model	Guiding Concept
Organization	Value creating and Values enhancing companies, Reach-out to its stakeholders
Structure	Open Matrix, Network
CEO	The Hermit & The Counselor, Corporate Sage, Corporate Rishi, Creative Enlightened & Organic (CEO) leader who uses ABC (Aligning, Balancing, Coordinating) approach to management & leadership
CEO's Mode of Operation	Inspirational rather than motivational, Team Building & Norm Setting, Focus on 'dream actualization' and 'vision actualization'
Employees	Knowledge Units (allow knowledge units to grow), 'Contribution to Value Creation' as performance criteria, Knowledge Circles
Decision Making Process	Quality circles at operational level, Decision circles at managerial level and Omega circle approach at strategic level
Control Systems Functioning	Based on Decentralization and Value-flow Analysis rooted in Revenues flows - Cost flows matrix, Value Chain Matrix
Nature of Capital	Physical, Human, Knowledge, Social & Spiritual Capital (Five Forms of Capital)
Management & Leadership Theory	Theory K and Theory T (T = T1 + T2 + T3), A Touch of Transcendence
Cultural Symbols of the Organization	Inspirational symbols for Inspirational Motivation

There is a need to transform the bureaucratic and mechanistic organizations to this new model. This would happen when organizations are transformed to knowledge organizations and bureaucrats are transformed into CEOs of the new age variety. It may also be indicated that Sumantra Ghoshal, Gita Piramal & C. Bartlett (2000) in their book, *Managing Radical Change*, suggested the metaphor of "Company As a University". This is the most appropriate metaphor for 'new age organizations' and our discussion on the guiding concepts of new age organizations is also in consonance with this metaphor.

VSP yantra as an ODM tool, provides a framework for finding new co-alignments for the nine elements of the VSP yantra in the context of new organizational changes and challenges and the emerging new organizational model.

12.6 Role of Inspirational Motivation in ODM

Idea of Inspirational Motivation is very useful for Organization Development & Management (ODM). Transformational leader use Inspirational Motivation as an important idea in motivating stakeholders towards transformation of the organization to meet new challenges.

Sharma (1996 & 2006) provides a 'holistic model of inspirational motivation' with roots in karma-yoga leadership and in this model he identifies three factors of motivation *viz.*, Abiotic (A), Biotic (B) and Inspirational (I), (Western Windows Eastern Doors: WWED, p. 119). Abiotic factors include the physical facilities, while biotic factors include those aspects which induct the life force into organization such as trusting organization culture that makes the organization as a 'living entity'. As per Wikipedia, "In ecology and biology, **abiotic components** or **abiotic factors** are those non-living chemical and physical parts of the environment that affect ecosystems". In case of organizations, it refers to the physical infrastructure and hygiene factors at the workplace. Vision, mission and values in combination with ViSA (Vision, Strategies & Action plans) document, provide the Inspirational force to the organization. Motivational climate in organizations is influenced through these IBA factors. It may be indicated that under Inspiration people perform in spite of lack of Resources (*e.g.*, Hygiene factors). India's freedom struggle under the inspirational force of Mahatma Gandhi is an illustration of the same. Gandhi took the route of 'spiritual awakening' to create right conditions for inspiration and motivation for liberation of a nation. In general, there are three approaches to create change *viz.*, autocratic, democratic and spiritual awakening. Choice of a particular approach depends upon the mindset of the leader.

IBA/ABI, three factors model of motivation can be contrasted with Hertzberg's Two Factor theory wherein Hygiene and Motivators are identified as foundation for employee motivation. After the development of the idea of Transformational Leadership, role of Inspirational Motivation is well recognized. IBA model integrates this insight and thereby provides a new approach to motivation theory that takes us beyond Hertzberg. If we retain the phrases used by Hertzberg, we may refer to IBA/ABI model as HMI model of inspirational motivation representing three factors as Hygiene factors, Motivators and Inspirational force (s).

It may be indicated that above discussed three factors theory referred to as ABI/IBA model of inspirational motivation has an equivalence in Theory T (T = T1 + T2 +T3). Abiotic / Hygiene factors have equivalence in T1 (Transactional) approach to motivation, Biotic / Motivators have equivalence in T2 (Transformational) approach to motivation and Inspiration originates from T3 (Transcendental) approach to motivation. It may be indicated that there is an element of 'psycho-spiritual awakening' in T3 approach to motivation. This is also reflected through HOPE (Higher Order Purpose of Existence) that a leader generates. Thus, Theory T can be considered as a Theory of Inspirational Motivation as well as a conceptual model for Transcendental Management & Leadership (TML).

In new age open matrix organizations, IBA model of inspirational motivation and thereby Theory T provides us a useful tool for ODM because it draws managerial attention to not only hygiene and motivators but also to inspirational factors and thereby inspirational symbols within organization.

12.7 Grounded Praxis Approach (GPA) to Strategic Management

In Grounded Praxis Approach (GPA) to management and leadership, there is a strong linkage between macro perspectives and ground realities *i.e.*, between vision and action. The attempt is to narrow down ViSA (Vision- Strategy-Action) gaps. In grounded praxis approach to Strategic Management, Strategic Thinking, Management and Leadership processes are integrated and due attention is given to ground realities. Thus, Management and Leadership processes in the organization are not only linked with Strategic Thinking but also with the ground realities. In the context of a nation, such an approach leads to good governance because Management & Leadership processes are not only aligned with Strategic Thinking but also with ground realities. Figure 12.6 provides this framework of Strategic Management (SM), wherein fundamental processes of SM in organizations *viz.*, Strategic Thinking, Management and Leadership are interconnected and are also linked with ground realities.

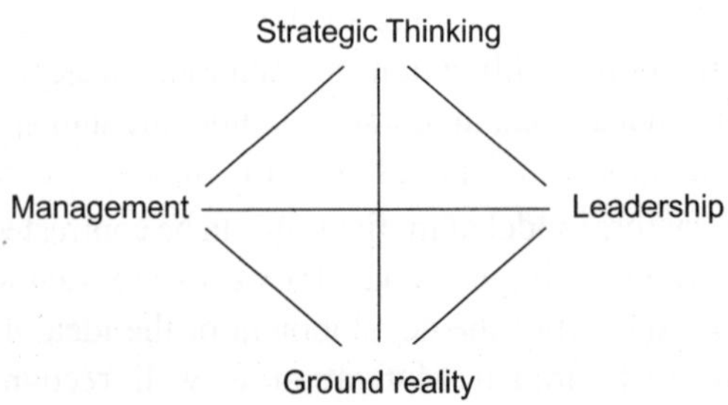

Figure 12.6. Grounded Praxis Framework of Strategic Management

Forward Engineering provides a foundational premise for strategic gearing of an organization keeping in view its existing and new capabilities with respect to changes and challenges in competitive environment. It has futuristic orientation and a futuristic perspective reflected in visioning and envisioning of future. Its focus is on Strategic Thinking. Enterprise Performance Improvement System (EPIS) has performance orientation / perspective and Organization Development & Management (ODM) has growth & development orientation / perspective. The two are also interrelated because performance improvement leads to growth & development of the organization. Grounded Praxis approach integrates Forward Engineering, EPIS and ODM with ground realities and thus has ground realities orientation / perspective. Figure 12.7 which also echoes the idea of inter-linkages between Strategic Thinking, Management and Leadership, provides this framework of grounded praxis approach to strategic management in terms of four orientations / perspectives discussed above.

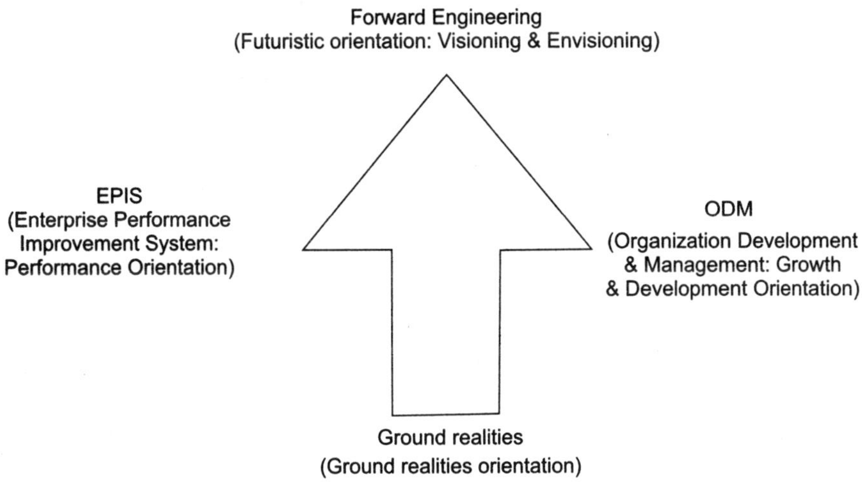

Figure 12.7. Grounded Praxis Approach to Strategic Management

Role of CEO and top management team is to integrate Forward Engineering (Visioning and envisioning), EPIS (Performance improvement) and ODM (Growth & Development) keeping in view the ground realities with reality check. This is the essence of the grounded praxis approach to strategic management. Grounded praxis approach can also be applied in the context of Nation, wherein the processes of visioning & envisioning, performance improvement, growth & development with an understanding of ground realities / reality check, are important for the policy makers for advancement of a Nation.

It may be indicated that various tools of analysis presented earlier in various chapters of this book, such as METRIC analysis, Managerial SPSS, VSP yantra, CINE Matrix, SWAN & SPOT analysis *etc.*, are useful in facilitating the grounded praxis approach to strategic management of organizations.

❑

Part IV

Ethical Foundations

CHAPTER 13

Ethical Foundations of the New Corporate Model*

Corporates have been undergoing a fundamental change in their response to new social requirements. In the earlier model of corporates, bottom line or the profit approach was the only guiding factor. However, during the recent years, social responsibility of the corporates has also assumed new significance. Further, the need for good governance has also been realized. Thus, a new corporate model of an 'ideal corporate' is emerging wherein a corporate is built on a new triad of profit, social responsibility and good governance. Such a corporate is based on a new philosophy of 'wealth generation with grace and values' coupled with social, environmental and spiritual responsibility. Ethical foundations of this new corporate model are based on a new balance between teleological, deontological and virtue-ethics approaches to business ethics.

13.1 TCP Model & Yantra

TCP model presented below provides us the intellectual foundations for the new corporate model. TCP model defines three fundamental principles and corresponding equations about a holistic view of life, nature and human beings.

Principle 1 - T Principle: T principle refers to Total (T) view of life in terms of Transactional (T1), Transformational (T2) and Transcendental (T3) approaches to relationships of human beings with others including nature. This view of life is represented by the following equation:

*Towards A New Age Corporate Model: A Holistic Approach to Corporate Development, 6th SMF Convention, Xavier Labor Research Institute (XLRI), Jamshedpur, April 24–26, 2003, Ethical Foundations of New Corporate Model: Implications for Strategy and Leadership, Subhash Sharma, 10th SMF Convention, Indian Institute of Technology (IIT), Mumbai, May 10–12, 2007.

$$T = T1 + T2 + T3$$

Principle 2 - C Principle: C principle refers to the Complete (C) view of nature in terms of Competition (C1), Co-operation (C2) and Connectivity (C3). Connectivity (C3) represents the inter-connectivity of human beings with everything *viz.*, with other human beings, with plant and animal life and with cosmos in general. This view of nature is represented by the following equation:

$$C = C1 + C2 + C3$$

Principle 3 - P Principle: P principle refers to Personality (P) view of human beings in terms of three levels of self *viz.*, lower self (P1), middle self (P2) and higher self (P3). Lower self is reflected in terms of selfish interest and self interest, middle self is reflected in terms of enlightened self interest, and higher self is reflected in terms of enlightened collective interest and altruism. In Indian thought, it is also displayed through three gunas *viz.*, Tamas, Rajas and Sattava. The Personality equation or the P equation is as follows:

$$P = P1 + P2 + P3$$

When these three TCP principles / equations are combined, we arrive at a comprehensive view of life, nature and human beings and thereby human society and its institutions. This view in a matrix format can be referred to as TCP matrix and is presented in Fig. 13.1. This matrix in its geometrical form of three triangles is referred to as TCP yantra.

T	C	P	
T3	C3	P3	T3 C3 P3
T2	C2	P2	T2 C2 P2
T1	C1	P1	T1 C1 P1

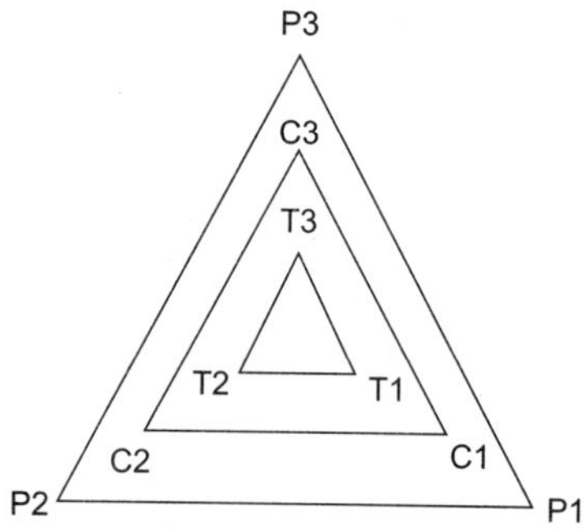

Figure 13.1. A Holistic Worldview as a Foundation for A New Corporate Model

It may be indicated that T1 C1 P1 describes the situation in which every dimension of life is transactionalized. This worldview is competitive and in it lower self finds its manifestation in terms of competition, greed and self-interest. T2 C2 P2 describes the situation in which humanism prevails, human relationships are in transformational mode. Co-operation prevails and the middle self moderates the lower self and transforms it into co-operative and transformational modes. T3 C3 P3 describes the situation in which spiritualism prevails. Human relationships are in transcendental mode. There is touch of altruism, harmony and connectivity.

It may be emphasized that while T1 worldview is driven by C1P1, T2 worldview is driven C2P2 and T3 worldview is driven by C3P3. T principle in terms of T1, T2 and T3 can be referred to as Theory T, in the context of Leadership. In fact, it can be considered as a general theory as it is applicable not only in the context of Management and Leadership, but also in the context of human consciousness. It also represents an integrative and holistic approach to human existence. Its extension in the form of TCP matrix / TCP yantra also represents the TCP vision for the new corporate model. Theory T and its extension in the form of TCP matrix / TCP yantra, provides conceptual foundations for Holistic Management in general and Holistic Corporate Management (HCM) in particular, wherein Transactional (T1), Transformational (T2) and Transcendental (T3) approaches are combined in making the organization an institution of significance to the society, nation and the world.

It may be useful to connect above discussion with changing metaphors about organizations and societies *viz.*, metaphors of Darwinian jungle, neurons and nirvana. Darwinian metaphor of jungle focuses on competition and survival of the fittest, metaphors of neurons, emerging from neuro sciences emphasizes cooperation and connectivity and metaphor of nirvana emphasizes spirituality. These three metaphors also broadly correspond to Body, Mind, Spirit view of human existence and can be used to classify and categorize management ideas by tracing their roots to these metaphors. Now new management thinking is emerging from the neuron and nirvana metaphors that emphasize cooperation, connectivity, symbiosis, synergy and ethical behavior.

13.2 Ethical Foundations of Organizations

TCP Vision presented above leads us to an understanding of the ethical foundations of organizations. Three streams of ethical approaches that take us beyond the traditional "Commandment approach" are as follows:

1. Teleological; 2. Deontological; 3. Virtue Ethics.

These approaches are now part of the 'received knowledge' in the field of ethics. For example, Hartman (2002) provides a discussion on these perspectives in business ethics.

While 'commandment approach' was rooted in theology, the above three approaches are part of 'ethicotarian' worldview. Thus, in the field of ethics, there is a transition from 'theology' to 'ethicotarian' view, wherein focus is on 'scientific' approach to ethics and values. There is further evolution towards 'inner search' *i.e.*, inner exploration of higher consciousness that gets reflected in human and spiritual values. This is in consonance with transition from Religion to Science to Spirituality and thereby to a New Age.

The three approaches to ethics broadly correspond to the TCP matrix. T1 C1 P1 corresponds to teleological worldview and T2 C2 P2 corresponds to deontological worldview, T3 C3 P3 corresponds to virtue ethics worldview. Thus, in TCP matrix, all the three approaches to ethical decision making find an appropriate place. We can represent the above discussion through E (Ethics) diagram as presented in Fig. 13.2.

- T3C3P3: Virtue ethics worldview
- T2C2P2: Deontological worldview
- T1C1P1: Teleological worldview

Figure 13.2. Ethics (E) Diagram for a New Corporate Model

Ethics diagram presented in Fig. 12.2 represents a framework of 'typology of ethics' in terms of market values, social values and spiritual values as T1C1P1, T2C2P2 and T3C3P3 represent imperatives of Market, Society and Self. In corporate context, Teleological view (T1C1P1) provides justification for profit approach, Deontological view (T2C2P2) provides a rationale for corporate social responsibility and virtue-ethics view (T3C3P3) provides philosophical foundations for good corporate governance. Thus, TCP yantra represents the essence of the new corporate model, wherein corporates are concerned not only with teleological view *i.e.*, profit maximization but are also concerned with corporate social responsibility *i.e.*, deontological worldview and good governance *i.e.*, virtue ethics worldview.

Teleological approach is primarily concerned with consequences of actions and is reflected in terms of 'utilitarian vision' and utilitarian approach to life reflected by 'cost-benefit' calculus and economistic view of the world: In corporate context, it gets manifested in terms of bottom line oriented approach and primacy of profit approach. Deontological approach emphasizes the duty orientation view of life and can be referred to as 'goodness ethics' as its focus is on doing good for the benefit of others. Virtue ethics view takes an 'idealistic' perspective of values. In corporate context deontological view is reflected in terms of an organization's duty towards society and gets operationalized in terms of CSR (Corporate Social Responsibility) activates and virtue ethics view foundations for good governance. These three approaches are part of the 'ethicotarian' worldview, wherein teleological, deontological and virtue ethics approaches find a balance.

It may be indicated that ancient Indian literature *viz*., Ramayana, Mahabharata and Gita and Arthashastra provide us equivalences with respect to virtue ethics, deontological and teleological approaches. Ramayana is virtue ethics oriented as it is the story of the ideal king who is best human being (Maryada Purushottam), Mahabharata and Gita are deontological in nature because of their focus on dharma and Arthashastra is teleological in its approach. From these equivalences we also get a perspective on management and leadership styles *e.g.*, Tripathi (2009) provides a discussion on essentials of effective management from Gita to develop a framework of human values oriented ethical management. It may be indicated that conceptual roots of Theory T can also be traced to these sources. Being teleological, Arthashastra is T1 (Transactional) oriented, Mahabharata and Gita are deontological in nature and thereby T2 (Transformational) in their approach and Ramayana is virtue ethics oriented and thereby has T3 (Transcendental) touch. It may be indicated that Indian Guna theory with its roots in ancient Indian literature, identifies four types of expressions of Self in terms of Tamas, Rajas-Tamas, Rajas-Sattava and Sattva. It can be considered as a Grand Theory of Management, Leadership and Ethics, because it provides a framework for a meta synthesis of existing theories of management, leadership, ethics and human development originating from different parts of the world.

While focus of Virtue Ethics leadership is on virtuous and ethical actions, focus of Deontological approach is on duty/*dharma* and responsibility orientated view, to management and focus of Utilitarian approach is on getting the things done without much concern for deontological view or virtue ethics. Thus, according to this view there are three leadership models *viz.*, virtue ethics leadership, duty/*dharma* driven leadership and utilitarian model of leadership. Virtue ethics approach leads to good governance, which Mahatma Gandhi captured through the evocative phrase of Ramrajya. Extending this idea further, Sharma (1999, 2007) suggested the idea of sacro-civic society. Deontological view creates a concern for society that gets reflected in social responsibility and utilitarian view focuses only on ends without caring for means employed to achieve the ends. These three models of leadership correspond to T3 (Transcendental), T2 (Transformational) and T1 (Transactional) models of leadership as defined in Theory T.

Leaders with higher consciousness are driven by self-saffronization *i.e.*, ability to self sacrifice for the benefit of society, nation and the world. Such enlightened leaders combine self-actualization with self saffronization and self realization. In India, saffron colour stands for sacrifice, leading us to the concept of self saffronization. It also stands for spirituality and thereby self realization.

Figure 13.3 provides the linkage between various schools of ethical thinking and their reflection in the new corporate model based on integration of profit, social responsibility and good governance requirements. Thus, the new corporate model has its conceptual foundations in 'ethicotarian' philosophy of a balance between teleological, deontological and virtue ethics world views reflected in terms of efficiency, equity and ethics.

Figure 13.3. Towards a New Corporate Model

To get further understanding of the above discussion, we can decode the world ETHICS to reflect underlying ideas for the new corporate model. Explanation of ETHICS acronym and corresponding equations are presented in Table 13.1.

Table 13.1. ETHICS Foundations of New Corporate Model

ETHICS Equations	Teleological	Deontological	Virtue Ethics
E = E1+E2+E3 T = T1+T2+T3 H = H1+H2+H3 I = I1+I2+I3 C = C1+C2+C3 S = S1+S2+S3	Efficiency (E1) Transactional (T1) Hedonism (H1) Indulgence (I1) Competition (C1) Self-interest (S1)	Equity (E2) Transformational (T2) Helping others (H2) Idealism (I2) Co-operation (C2) Self-Sacrifice (S2)	Ethics (E3) Transcendental (T3) Harmony (H3) Integrity (I3) Connectivity (C3) Self-realization
Indicative colours	Green	Red	Saffron
Philosophical Roots	Utilitarian	Ecotarian	Ethicotarian
Key Note	Survival of the fittest	Empowerment of the weakest and duty of the fittest	Arrival of the best to lead the rest
Key Phrase	Management Thought	Social Discourse	Spiritual Concerns

In general, management thought and thereby management education is primarily rooted in the teleological worldview. For holistic development of management professionals, it is necessary to expand the horizons of management thought and management education beyond the teleological worldview. Herein lies the relevance of the new corporate model and six 'ETHICS' equations for management education.

The traditional corporate model was rooted in the philosophy of maximizing the shareholders wealth. Subsequently this model evolved into multiple stakeholder models. In their third stage of evolution, the corporates have been conceptualized as corporate citizens. Hence, the expectation of ethical and environmental concerns has gained importance. Corporates are expected to follow the 'principles of ethical business' and not merely, 'principles of business'. In their fourth stage of evolution, corporates are emerging as 'social institutions' with considerable influence on society and lives of people. Hence, people's expectations from the corporates are changing. In this stage of their evolution corporates are expected to achieve a new balance between efficiency, equity and ethics. This balance is also reflected in terms of new concepts such as triple bottom line and 'profit, people and planet' view of the role of corporates. New catch phrases such as Corporate Social Responsibility (CSR) and good governance also capture the essence of this thinking.

13.3 Towards an Integrative Vision of Market, Society and Self

The discussion presented in this chapter leads us to an integrative vision of Market, Society and Self presented in Fig. 13.4.

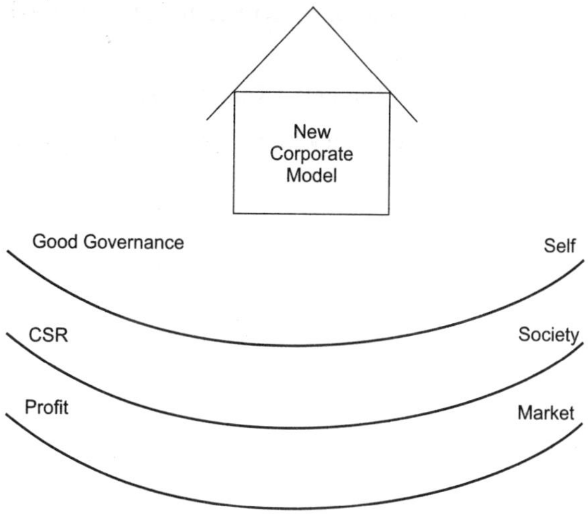

Figure 13.4. An Integrative Vision of Market, Society & Self

TCP Model presented earlier provides intellectual and conceptual foundations for this integration. Corresponding to Market, Society and Self, a corporate has three responsibilities *viz.*, Profit responsibility, Corporate Social Responsibility and Good Governance Responsibility. This is the essence of the new corporate model. TCP model also provides us a new vision of society that could constitute a new 'political manifesto' for nations as it provides us a direction for creating a sacro-civic society wherein Market, Social Responsibility and Good Governance constitute three key ideas for building a society leading to Prosperity, Justice and Peace (PJP) for the nations and the world.

Realization of above indicated vision of integrating market, society and self, is facilitated through KTG yantra wherein Management, Leadership and Spirituality are combined in the organization context providing us a framework for ethical management and leadership. This yantra is represented by three triangles related to Theory K of Management, Theory T of Leadership and Theory G (Guna) of Spirituality. Sharma (2007) defines these 'theories' in terms of following equations:

I. Theory K: $K = X^{a} * Y^{b} * Z^{c}$

X, Y , Z refer to Theory X, Theory Y and Theory Z of Management and a, b, c represent the intensities with which X, Y and Z styles are used.

II. Theory T: $T = T1^{a} * T2^{b} * T3^{c}$

T1, T2, T3 refer to Transactional, Transformational and Transcendental approaches to Leadership and a, b, c refer to intensities with which these styles are used.

III. Theory G (Guna): $G = (\text{Tamas})^{a} * (\text{Rajas})^{b} * (\text{Sattava})^{c}$

a, b, c represent the intensities with which Tamas, Rajas and Sattava approaches are used.

Tamas, Rajas and Sattava (TRS-तरस) refer to 'levels of consciousness'. Theory G implies that managerial and leadership processes should operate from 'higher level of consciousness, *i.e.*, from Rajas and Sattava levels of consciousness. This is the essence of HQD (Human Quality Development). It also implies moving beyond Greed (G1) to Goodness (G2) and Godness (G3). Thus, Theory G can also be expressed in terms of G1, G2 and G3 hierarchy of actions, as a 3G model of ethics.

Knowledge (K), Power (P) and Money (M) can be used either for Greed (G1) or for Goodness (G2). When used for Goodness, we arrive at KPMG model for creating ethical synergy in society.

Above discussed KTG yantra provides us a conceptual foundation for implementation of ethical practices in corporates to ensure that corporates not only create wealth but do so in a responsible manner and fulfill their social, environmental, ethical, moral and spiritual responsibility to various stakeholders.

In the Harmonic Globalization framework presented in this book, it was indicated that there is a need to achieve a balance between four fundamental forces *viz.*, Market, State, People and Self. Force of Self could be in terms of Tamas, Rajas-Tamas, Rajas-Sattava and Sattava, and these four aspects of Self find varying expressions in Market, State and Society. Self qualities of leaders in terms of above indicated four types of actions and styles, lead to different configurations of societies and organizations. A proper balance is achieved when force of Self as a spiritual force is used in leadership and decision making. This dimension of significance of Self has been largely missing in the Strategic Management literature. Time has come to fill this missing gap in Policy making and Strategic Management. This also implies a shift towards Holistic Corporate Management (HCM).

❑

CHAPTER 14

Character Competence of the Corporation*

"Whatever a great person does is followed by others,
Whatever standards the person sets, people follow the same."
(Gita, 3-21)

The idea of ethical philosophy is both ancient and modern. The above sloka from Gita presents the concept of 'ethical benchmarking' in a very clear manner. In the popular consciousness, this concept is also known as *Yatha Raja, Tatha Praja i.e.*, citizens and the leaders are the mirror image of each other. Hence, the emphasis on high ethical standards on the part of the leaders. When this Gita sloka is interpreted in corporate context, it implies that expression CEO should in essence stand for Chief Ethical Officer. The above sloka of Gita is also applicable to corporates, we have to just substitute the expression 'great person' by 'great corporate'. With this substitution, the sloka acquires a new corporate meaning *viz.*,

"Whatever a great corporate does is followed by others,
Whatever standards the corporate sets, others follow the same."

During ancient times the concept of ethics in business or 'business ethics' was expressed by the expression, *shubh-labh i.e.*, ethical profits or the profit earned through ethical means. This idea remains valid even today even though the nature of production system, organizational forms and technology has undergone many changes. The idea of *shubh-labh* also sums up the essence of the ethical philosophy of the corporations.

---

*Character Competence of the Corporation, Subhash Sharma, 3rd SMF Convention, Perspectives on Strategic Challenges and Imperatives, held at Indian Institute of Management (IIM), Calcutta, Kolkata, May 4–6, 2000. Character Competence of the Corporation, Subhash Sharma, *Journal of Human Values*, July–Dec, 2002, 8:2, 107–118.

14.1 Why Concern for Ethics?

Why a sudden concern with ethics? One reason is the vast gap between the Ideal and the Real we witness today. There is a gap between the 'statement of values and the state of values'. Though the ideal of *shubh-labh* is known, the phenomenon of unethical means to earn profit is also a stark reality. Hence, the need for ethical sensitivity to narrow down the gap between the ideal and the real, between the statement of values and the state of values, between the thought, speech and action (Manas-Vaach-Karma). In Gita (Sloka 4-7 and 4-8) we find the dynamics of ethics being manifested through the arrival of ethical leadership to correct the social imbalance caused by *adharma* or the unethical practices.

> "As and when goodness declines and wickedness shows its rise,
> O! Bharata in such situations, I myself arise." (4-7)

> "For the protection of the good and destruction of evil,
> I am born in every age for establishing goodwill." (4-8)

There are many developments that are part of the current global reality and are indicative of the rise in 'social entropy' or negergy (negative energy). Justice V.R. Krishna Iyer (1996), prefers the expression 'ethical entropy' to refer to the "developments which are seriously eroding our polity". The following are the eight developments contributing to social entropy in general:

1. Alienation of self from SELF
2. Environmental Degradation
3. Gender Insensitivity
4. Excessive Consumerism & Greed (ECG)
5. Corruption
6. Income Inequalities
7. Rise in Crime and Various Forms of Terrorism
8. False Consciousness

Along with the liberalization and globalization, these eight 'sins' of modernity (!) or negative forces have also been liberalized and globalized. Hence, the concern for restoring the ethical values in the society to prevent its ethical degeneration and increase in social entropy. The social entropy is a result of three ECGs *viz.*, Excessive Consumption and Greed, Excessive Consumerism and Greed and Excessive Competition and Greed. Therefore, we are seeing the emergence of the ECG generation widening the Ideal - Real gap. Hence, the need for a concern for ethics in public life and business.

14.2 Paradigms of Ethics

Traditionally, there have been three broad paradigms or conceptual lenses for the theoretical study of ethics *viz.*, the teleological, deontological and the virtue ethics.

They have also been referred to as 'theories' of ethics and schools of thought. The deontological approach is rooted in the concept of 'duty'. This approach is derived from the Greek word 'deontos' referring to duty and obligations. Thus, the focus is on the duties and obligations rather than consequences of action. We are reminded of the famous Gita's sloka, *Karmanye Vadika raste*; *ma phaleshu kadachan* - Your right is to do your duty and not be concerned about the fruits of your action.

The major conceptual / theoretical ideas in the deontological school come from Kant's idea of 'categorical imperative' - a 'command' (imperative) that is categorical (no exceptions). Categorical imperatives are like commandments, which must be followed without exception. "Kant characterized moral rules as imperatives that express what we ought to do categorically rather than hypothetically" (Boatright, p.55). Kantian ethics constitute the foundation of the deontological school. When applied to organizational context, an organization needs to identify its 'categorical imperatives' to resolve the ethical dilemmas it faces.

In sharp contrast to the deontological school, the teleological school is primarily concerned with the consequences of actions. 'Greatest good of greatest number' defines its ethical principle. Utilitarianism belongs to the teleological school of ethics. Since utilitarianism is based on the idea of maximum good of maximum number, it ignores the interest of those who are out of the pale of this maxim. In fact, it is precisely these 'left out' persons who may be most needy and who bear the consequences of the actions leading to the maximum good of maximum number. Environmentalists have observed that it is the poor people who bear the brunt of environmental damage, though they are not creator of the damage. Hence, instead of cost-benefit analysis, which utilitarianism advocates, it is more useful to conduct benefit-burden analysis to see the impact of actions on the last few. Gandhi advocated this perspective through his talisman. "Look at the poorest of the poor and see how your decisions are going to affect him". This is in sharp contrast to the utilitarianism.

Another non-utilitarian view comes from the idea of happiness for all and not merely maximum good of maximum number. "*Subjan hitay subjan sukhay*" instead of "*Bahujan hitay bahujan sukhay*". This idea has also been expressed in the famous sloka, "*Sarve bhavantu sukhina...*". Let there be happiness for all. Thus, survival of all is the ethical principle of existence, in contrast to utilitarianism, which ignores this ethical concept. Viewed in terms of the above discussion, environmentalists could also consider utilitarianism inherently anti-environment.

Virtue ethics theorists advocate 'virtue theory' rooted in Aristotle's ideas of virtue. "According to Aristotle, the values to be developed are best learned by studying the lives of heroic persons. Societies, where such virtues as honesty, fidelity, humanity and generosity are the norm point to great individuals as models that provide the guidance for individual moral action. Aristotle thinks all the virtues are communicated this way. Confused about honesty? Look at stories of honest behaviour in spite of the consequences, as related in sagas and epic poetry"

(Byham, 1996, p.47). The continuing popularity and relevance of Ramayana and Mahabharata in India, points to the deep influence of 'virtue theory' on common masses. In a way virtue theory is trans-temporal and is independent of the ideology, technology, production systems and forms of organizational structures.

In addition to these paradigms, another perspective has emerged from the conceptual and empirical work of Sorab Sadri and his associates - *Dastoor and Jayashree.* They call their 'school of thought' as Praxis school wherein the word Praxis they have borrowed from Marxist literature. According to them, "Praxis school suggests a kind of need for acceptance, in the corporate world. Its formulation was entirely based on the managerial responses from Indian industry and is born out of the empirical data at hand" (Sadri, *et al.*, 1999, p.126).

According to this school, "If the decision-maker can discuss his / her decision openly and freely within his / her peer group, then the decision is deemed to be an ethical one" (Sadri, *et al.*, 1999, p.93). It may be indicated the world is beyond the dichotomy of black and white and is full of gray and gray of different shades. The Praxis theory of ethics is most suitable to resolve ethical dilemmas falling in the gray area. Indeed most of the time managers are dealing with gray area. Herein lies the usefulness of this theory / approach. Some would argue that Praxis school essentially refers to the norm setting in the gray areas.

Within the Praxis school, there is a variation in views. While Sadri claims that praxis arises out of 'false consciousness' and the need to belong, Jayashree claims that this leads to curb on creativity and innovation. As a result, meritocracy goes out and mediocrity goes into the business paradigm (Sadri).

Thus, in the ethics literature, four distinct approaches could be identified *viz.*, teleological, deontological, virtue ethics and Praxis. The pioneering work of S. K. Chakraborty (1995) could be classified in the category of virtue theory rooted in Vedantic ethics. The work of another scholar *viz.,* Mathias (1994) also belongs to the virtue theory category. Even the idea of "spirituality-at-workplace in the land of dollar God" (Srinivas, 1998) could be considered belonging to virtue theory approach to ethics and ethical leadership. In contrast to the above, Sadri (2001) suggests that the literature on relevance of Indian Ethics to Management can be classified in three paradigms or streams *viz.*, Soul-based Thought (Chakraborty & Mathias), Mind-based Thought (Sadri & Jayashree) and Ideal-Real Dualistic Thought (Subhash Sharma).

Boatright (1997, p.47) observes "despite their differences, utilitarian and Kantian ethics both address the question, what actions are right? Virtue ethics asks instead, what kind of person should we be?" Virtuousness and virtuosity is at the heart of the virtue theory. The difficulty comes in practicing the virtuosity, because it demands a very high level of virtuousness on the part of individuals. Further it amounts to moralizing and contradictions can be observed even in the lives of those who advocate extreme form of virtue theory.

A practical formula, incorporating ideas from various theoretical sources could also be summed up as the JRD formula, wherein, J stands for Justice, R for

Rights and D for Duties. Justice is critical to ethics as is indicated by Rawls (1971) in his book *Theory of Justice*. The primary focus of his theory is on 'social justice', with an emphasis on 'equality of opportunities'. In his theory he identifies two 'principles of justice' that deal with distribution of utility among the members of the society and the equality of opportunities. According to Rawls, in utilitarianism adequate attention is not given to the way utility is distributed among members of the society. Hence, he proposes his principles of justice to create a new ideal of social justice in terms of a principle of utility distribution and a principle of equality of opportunities. Justice is also linked with rights and duties, which should go hand in hand.

Different schools of thinking also provide us an insight into different styles of leadership. Teleological leaders focus on ends without caring for the means. Deontological leaders focus on duty / *dharma* and virtue ethics leaders focus on virtuous and ethical dimension in life, living and leadership. These approaches have equivalence in Theory T of management and leadership which identifies three styles of leadership in terms of T1 (Transactional), T2 (Transformational) and T3 (Transcendental). Because of equivalences of T1, T2 and T3 with teleological, deontological and virtue ethics approaches, Theory T can also be considered as General Theory of Leadership and Ethics. In practice, managers and leaders use a mix of T1, T2 and T3 approaches in dealing with ethical issues. Hence, they use a 'grounded praxis approach to ethics'. Grounded praxis approach can be considered as an extension to Sadri *et al.* Praxis approach. Grounded praxis approach to ethics suggested by Sharma (2007) is rooted in achieving a balance between following three aspects of human existence:

1. Order-Disorder as two aspects of nature
2. Good and Evil coexist
3. There is space between Freewill and Determinism

Sharma (2012) suggests the concept of 'Mind Balancing Attitude' ('MBA') to strive for balance between above three aspects of human existence that have implications for individuals, nations and corporations.

14.3 Cracking the Ethical Dilemmas

Ethical dilemmas are part of organizational reality. What are the methods that may help us in dealing with this reality? The literature suggests following three approaches can help us in dealing with the ethical dilemmas:

1. **Dialectics:** The dialectical method is rooted in identifying the contradictions and uses the contradiction to clarify the situation of ethical dilemma. Its focus is on polarities and opposites. It can be viewed as a methodology of Position - Opposition - Proposition. In the traditional dialectical analysis, the focus is on change through articulation of opposite position. However, in the idea of Position - Opposition - Proposition, dialectics is combined with dialogue. It may also be indicated that deontologists tend to use dialectic to create a

dialectical or 'countervailing' forces to change the society. Earlier dialectics was viewed merely in the form of good and evil. It was an ancient idea, Hegel gave it a sharper focus and Marx applied it to social context.

In ethical dilemmas, we need to ease the 'dialectical tension' arising from the antagonism between opposing ideas (Schey, 1996). In such situations, the concept of the intensity of dialectics is a useful concept because it focuses on the intensity of the ethical dilemmas. Once we comprehend the intensity of dialectics, the answers to ethical dilemma could also flow easily.

2. **Dialogue:** The second approach to ethical dilemmas is resolving it through dialogue. In dialogue, there is an engagement with the issue and there is a continuing discussion. Thus, it is a democratic process wherein the dilemmas are looked from various perspectives and frameworks. The very process of dialogue leads to new solutions, because in dialogue approach, the focus is on "asking the right questions and raising the proper issues". Dialogue of Socrates narrated by Plato could be supplemented with the Indian Syadvad approach, wherein each problem or issue is looked at from various angles. Syadvad is metaphorically described by the well-known Indian story of the blindmen and the elephant.

3. **Commentary:** Commentary is an Indian tradition. A commentary is written to elaborate the viewpoint and provide a logical explanation. Metaphorical expressions could also be used to highlight various perspectives. Through commentary ideas are updated and brought to explain the current and future context. Further, through application of ideas to the contemporary context, ideas get updated and a continuity is maintained. The Chinese through works of Lao Tzu & Fahien adopted this Indian tradition but somewhere it got lost in folklore, magic and fictional ideation (Sadri).

In an eclectic approach to ethical dilemmas, all the three approaches *viz.*, the dialectics, dialogue and the commentary, could be used by managers in confronting and resolving the ethical dilemmas. All the three approaches can help in 'conscientization' - a term coined by Paulo Freire to refer to inner awakening to social contradictions.

14.4 Ethical Imperatives: Individual, Organization and Markets

Given the above background on theories and approaches to ethics, as well as methodologies of resolving ethical dilemmas, we now propose the IOM framework for business ethics. This framework has three components *viz.*, individual ethical function, organizational ethics and the market ethics which define the boundaries of the ethical imperatives for the corporates.

Individual's Ethical Function

An individual's ethical function can be expressed in the form of the following equation:

$$I = \varphi(C_1, C_2, C_3)$$

Wherein C_1 = Character

C_2 = Conduct

C_3 = Commitment to values

And $C_1 + C_2 + C_3$ = A rise in corporate ethical consciousness

In interpersonal interactions, the ethical functions of two individuals intersect leading to synergy or negergy between individuals. This in turn has an impact on the organizations and society.

Organizational Ethics

Organizational ethics or corporate ethics could be viewed in terms of an integral function of individual ethical functions of n decision-makers.

$$CE = \int^{n} I\, dc$$

The other way of defining the same idea is as follows:

$$CE = \int_{i=1}^{n} \Sigma I$$

Collective Ethics Function = ϕ (I_1, I_2, I_3,..........)

wherein I_1, I_2, I_3,.......... represent the ethical functions of the key decision-makers influencing the collective ethics function.

Market Ethics

Market ethics implies ethics of competition in the market place. From the days of Adam Smith, wherein invisible hand was dominating in the context of perfect competition, to the days of liberalization and globalization, wherein visible hand many times gets the upper hand in the market dynamics, there has been considerable change. The invisible hand could have eliminated the problem of ethics because market takes care of ethics through price determination and price discovery. According to Friedman "sole responsibility of business is profit maximization". And this is best achieved through free markets. A broader view is now gaining ground *viz.*, "firms have other social responsibilities in addition to profit maximization". Further, free markets exist only in textbooks. Today's market reality shows the manipulations by the visible hands in many forms. Monopolistic tendencies of the corporations, insider trading in the bourses, unethical advertising etc. point to the failure of the ethical basis of the markets. It is indeed interesting that many new phrases have found entry in the market lingo *e.g.*, phrases such as level field playing, terms of competition, corporate governance etc. have acquired common usage. They all have arisen out of the ethical concerns at the market turf, pointing to the need for ethical sensitivity and proper regulatory mechanisms. In essence, a paradigm shift is required from Greedonomics to Moral Economics or Ethical Economics at the market place.

14.5 IOM Framework: A Holistic View of Business Ethics

The discussion about individual ethical function, organizational ethics and the market ethics, can be integrated through the IOM framework of business ethics, which indicates that there is an interactive relationship between the I *i.e.*, Individual's ethics, O *i.e.*, Organizational ethics and M *i.e.*, Market ethics. This relationship can be expressed as follows:

$$BE = IE \times OE \times ME$$

wherein BE stands for business ethics, IE stands for Individual's ethics, OE stands for Organizational Ethics and ME stands for Market Ethics and the symbol × is a mathematical operator indicating the interactive relationship.

This interactive relationship takes place within the socio-culture system of the society as well as the political system. Figure 14.1 presents the IOM framework of business ethics.

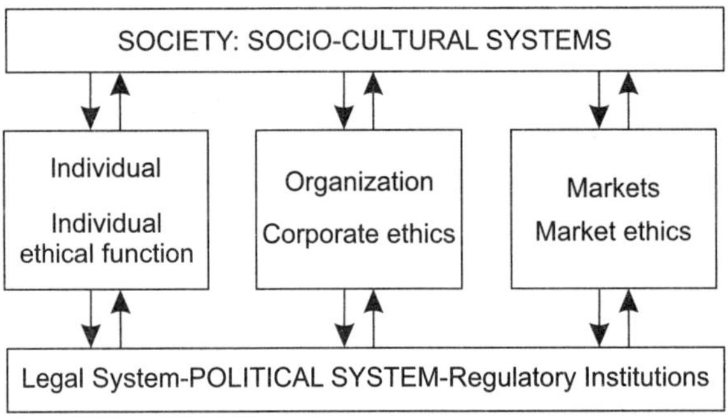

Figure 14.1. IOM Framework of Business Ethics

14.6 Towards Character Competence

Prahlad and Hamel (1990) popularized the idea of core competence. However, even more important than core competence is the idea of character competence. The difference between the core competence and character competence is like difference between skills and ethics. A person can be high on skills but low on ethics (skills strong, values weak) (Chakraborty, 1991). When a similar notion is extended to organizations, we can classify organizations in terms of a 2 × 2 matrix with high-low combinations on core competence and character competence. For example, Microsoft is known for its core competence but what about its character competence. Many would argue that its monopolistic tendencies are indicative of its low score on character competence. Figure 14.2 presents this core competence and character competence matrix for classification of organizations.

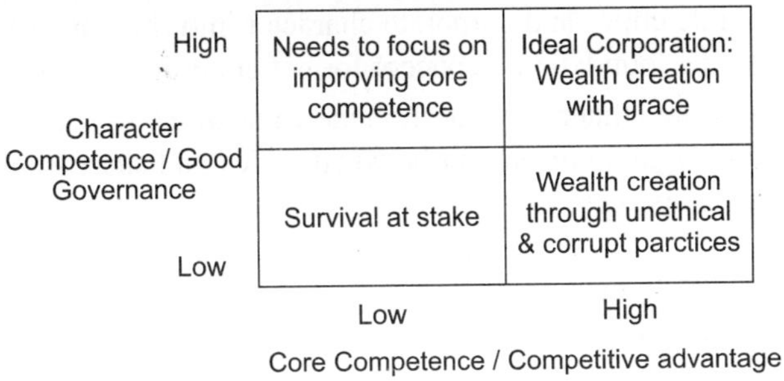

Figure 14.2. Core Competence & Character Competence Matrix

Thus there are four types of corporations:

1. Low on core competence / competitive advantage and low on character competence / good governance
2. Low on core competence / competitive advantage and high on character competence / good governance
3. High on core competence / competitive advantage and low on character competence / good governance
4. High on core competence / competitive advantage and high on character competence / good governance

Actions of a Corporate can be categorized in terms of VENUS (Virtuous, Ethical, Neutral to ethics, Unethical and Sinful) spectrum of deeds/actions. In VENUS model of 'typology of deeds'. VE also represents for Virtue Ethics school of thinking about business ethics. Wealth creation through unethical and corrupt practices leads to 'crony capitalism' with harmful effects on society. Ideal corporations are represented by high core competence and high character competence reflected through its virtuous and ethical approach to wealth creation. Such corporations create wealth with grace leading to 'Corporate shubh labh'. It may be indicated that expressions of VENUS actions can be seen in Market, State and Society in varying forms. When virtuous and ethical actions dominate, we move in the direction of Virtuous cycle leading to Virtuous State and Virtuous society. However, in modern societies, we find interplay of all five types of actions and therefore presence of corruption etc.

It may also be indicated that only by lifting the corporate veil, we can know about the character competence and most of the time it is not possible to pierce through the corporate veil. While corporates pay a lot of attention to core competence, many times they hardly pay much attention to character competence. Indeed the need for ethical business has become more urgent in the era of e-commerce, because e-technology has opened new scope for many new unethical practices. Hence, the need for the idea of character competence has also become critical. Sherosky (1999) also talks about a similar notion in the form of 'corporate character'. However, the idea of character competence brings the concept of corporate ethics and corporate character into sharper focus. It could as well be considered a foundational concept for better corporate governance.

It may be indicated that many question the value of ethics and value of values, because they don't find a correlation between ethics and success. Will character competence lead to success? For answering this question, we need to redefine the concept of success. Success should not be measured merely in terms of the bottom line but in terms of 'ethical bottom line'.

To operationalize the idea of character competence we need to develop an index of character competence. For this we can draw upon the stakeholder theory. Corporate's ethical behavior could be viewed in terms of its obligations towards shareholders, customers, suppliers, employees, community & environment and Government. Since there are contradictions in expectations of various stakeholders, rating of the corporation on these expectations should be done by the members belonging to the specific category only. Accordingly representatives from these six category of stakeholders could be asked to rate their corporate on a five point character competence scale with 1 indicating poor state of stakeholders interest, 2 Below the expected level (EL), 3 Expected level (EL), 4 Above expected level and 5 Extra-ordinary level.

These responses can then be aggregated to arrive at the character competence index. A further refinement in this index can be brought out by assigning weightages to the interests of the different stakeholders. Data in respect of the leading corporates within the same industry *e.g.*, IT industry could be collected through polling on the internet or otherwise. Corporates can then be ranked according to Character Competence Rating (CCR). Ratings on CCR could be made available to all the stakeholders as well as public at large. This would lead to improvement in Corporate Governance. It may be indicated that CCR can be used for ranking only within a particular sector, because enterprises within the sector operate in a similar environment. Comparing them across sectors would be like comparing the apples and oranges.

While difficulties in quantifying the character competence through a rating mechanism are understandable, it is not impossible to provide qualitative assessment on the character competence of the corporation. In absence of rating by an outside agency, corporates should include in their balance-sheets, a qualitative character competence report for the benefit of various stakeholders.

It may be indicated that we can also develop appropriate index to measure the character competence of the nation. Indeed, it may be easier to rank the nations on a character competence scale, because data on several surrogate measures is easily available. For example, data on corruption can provide us a measure on the character competence of a nation.

14.7 Improving Character Competence: Back to Basics

For improving the character competence of the corporation, we need to get back to basics. The following ideas could help us in this direction:

1. **Intention and Action or the Ethical Intent:** The essence of the ethics test lies in 'intentionality in action'. Intentionality in action could be classified in terms of three categories *viz.*, good, bad and malicious. In terms of Indian guna theory, the sattvik-rajasik combination belongs to the good category, tamasik with rajasik combination belongs to the bad category and the purely tamasik intentionality represents the ugly or the malicious category. In applying the intention and action ethics test, it is also important to focus on the purpose of action. Is it purely in the selfish interest or is it for the good of others? Selfish interest, enlightened self interest and enlightened collective interest correspond to the tamasik, rajasik and sattvik actions of guna theory. When actions are driven by purely selfish interest, they tend to be in the category of bad and malicious actions leading to high levels of social and corporate entropy. The essence of ethics test lies in the idea of ethical intent of individuals and organizations. Many times ethical intent could be more important than the 'strategic intent' concept of Prahlad and Hamel.

   In consonance with guna theory, we suggest 3G (Grabbing, Goodness, Godness) model of motivation wherein an individual is driven by three types of motives *viz.*, grabbing motive, giving motive and 'giving up' motive. A tamasik person displays grabbing motivation, rajasik person displays giving motivation (S.K. Chakraborty) reflected in the phrase, 'joy of giving'. A sattavik person displays 'giving up' motivation. It also means sacrificing (*tyag*) motivation and includes the idea of 'forgiving motivation'. It may be indicated that 3 G model is rooted in the Indian idea of 'Hierarchy of Deeds' that represents hierarchy of actions in terms of tamasik, rajasik and sattavik actions (Sharma 1996). While Maslow's hierarchy of needs concept focused on needs, focus of hierarchy of deeds is on human actions that get reflected in Market, State and Society in a variety of ways. It may be indicated that hierarchy of actions is also reflected in terms of NPS (Negergy/Negative energy, Positive energy, Synergy) model of consequences of tamas, rajas and sattava actions that we observe in organizations and scoiety.

2. **Individual and the Organization: The Ethics Matrix:** The ethical interface on various issues can be viewed in terms of an ethics matrix indicating the individual's and organization's ethical orientations. An individual's orientation could be viewed in terms of unethical practice OK and unethical practice Not OK. Similarly, organization's orientation could be viewed in terms of unethical practice OK and unethical practice Not OK. Thus, we have the following four situations presented in Table 14.1.

Table 14.1. The Individual - Organization Ethics Matrix

	Individual's View	Organization's View	Consequences/Solutions
1.	Unethical Practice Not OK	Unethical Practice Not OK	Ethical Synergy
2.	Unethical Practice Not OK	Unethical Practice OK	Whistle Blowing
3.	Unethical Practice OK	Unethical Practice Not OK	Moral Correction / Exit
4.	Unethical Practice OK	Unethical Practice OK	Public Interest Litigation

The ideal citizen and the ideal corporate citizen belong to the first category wherein the standards of ethics are very high. However, standards of ethics suffer either because of individuals or because of organizations or because of both. At least to some extent the situation can be corrected through norm setting and corporate governance. Unethical practices on the part of individuals can be checked through norm setting and standards of ethics for the organization could be raised through better corporate governance.

3. **Towards Ethical Professionalism:** Though the concept of ethics was inherent in the idea of professionalism, however, over the years we find an erosion in the meaning of professionalism. The word professional is today devoid of its ethical content. It simply refers to the skill acquisition. Hence, the needs for 'ethical professionalism' as an overarching construct to denote those highest ethical standards are maintained within a profession. It implies drawing up a code of conduct for the professionals. It also implies drawing up a code of conduct for the corporations. In fact, during recent years efforts have been on to draw a code of conduct for the corporation, but there are gaps as far as code of conduct for management professionals is concerned. It has been observed by many that management is the only profession wherein management graduates at the time of graduating don't take any oath! Even management teachers don't take any oath of ethical professionalism! Some even encourage unethical behavior in the name of pragmatism and 'smartness'. The reality out there is the jungle-raj of unethical behaviour, hence, 'survival of the fittest' is the only rule, thus goes the argument. There is no effort and initiative to convert a jungle-raj to a civilized-rajya.

   Sadri, Jayashree and Ajgaonkar (2002) provide a meaningful definition of professionalism. It implies the willingness and the ability to "make a promise, to deliver and to deliver as promised without compromising basic values".

4. **Towards A New Managerial Grid:** The idea of Blake and Mouton's managerial grid is a well-known idea. Concern for production and concern

for people, constitute the foundational pillars of this grid. However, this two dimensional grid needs to be extended to three-dimensional lattice, wherein concern for values is included as part of the grid. Another way of looking at the 'managerial lattice' is the metaphor of the picture frame or the string model of managerial grid, wherein the grid hangs on the string of values. Stronger the string of values, better is the character competence of the corporation.

The new managerial grid can make use of the idea of polarities for creating a transformation from negative values to positive values. Indian thought provides a number of polarities such as *asatya-satya* (falsity-truth), *anyaya-nyaya* (injustice-justice), *rajsatta-tyag* (power-renunciation of power), *lobh-sanyam* (greed-balance), *anachar-sadachar* (bad conduct good conduct), *etc.* These polarities provide us a 'theory of change' with emphasis on change from negative values to positive values. We can call this change theory as the HCL formula, wherein HCL stands for Harmony, Co-operation and Love. The essence of the HCL formula could be viewed as 'Transformational Ethics', wherein emphasis of individual, organizational and social transformation lies in transformation from negative values to positive values. Table 14.2 presents the essence of the HCL formula.

Table 14.2. Transformational Ethics through HCL

The HCL Formula	
From Acrimony To Harmony	From Oppression To Liberation
From Negergy To Synergy	From Tension To Tranquility
From Vicious Cycles To Virtuous Cycles	From Bitterness To Betterness
From Conflict To Co-operation	From Illwill To Goodwill

5. **Total Values Chain:** The idea of Total Value Chain has been around to improve the efficiency and effectiveness of the business operations. However, Total Value Chain should be viewed within the context of Total Values Chain *i.e.*, whether organization is contributing to enhancing the positive values both within the organization as well as in society. While Total Value Chain emphasizes the efficiency framework, Total Values Chain points to the ethical values framework within which the organization operates. It suggests that value addition should take place within the framework of values addition that includes the human and spiritual values. It also implies that ethical values should be practiced across the total value chain from the production to the marketing.
6. **Redefining Success:** In general, the idea of success needs to be redefined. Success has been narrowly defined in terms of financial parameters and numbers that are many times devoid of ethical content. Thus, bottom-line is emphasized rather than the 'ethical bottom-line'. Indeed, 'shubh-labh' or the ethically earned profit should be the new parameter for defining business

success. The extent to which the corporates fulfill their social responsibility should also be part of the definition of success. The idea of character competence suggests that the notion of corporate success should be redefined.

14.8 Inculcating Ethical Sensitivity

The ideas of ethics in business, managerial ethics, ethics and management etc. have become part of the management thought and management theory. Further, development in this field requires translating the theoretical frameworks into operational tools and concepts which managers can use in their day to day context. Hence, the need for ethics based management models. In our view, ethics based management models can be broadly classified in three categories *viz.*, 1. Relating to 'idealized' and 'idolized' state, 2. Relating to ground reality out there and 3. Bridging the gap between 'ideal' and 'real'. For developing ethical sensitivity, all the three approaches are required. It may be indicated that inculcating ethical sensitivity requires going beyond self-actualization (Maslow) to self-saffronization (sensitive to ethics) and self-realization (Raman Maharishi). Ethically sensitive leaders combine self-actualization with self-saffronization and self-realization.

Every profession is rooted in 4Ps *viz.*, Principles (P1), Practices (P2), Perspectives (P3) and Philosophy (P4). Following 4Ps equation defines an Enlightened Professional (EP).

$$EP = P1 + P2 + P3 + P4$$

An Enlightened Professional integrates Principles, Practices, Perspectives and Philosophy of her/his profession. This integration is achieved through her/his skills, values, wisdom & vision.

In conclusion, it may be stated that discourse and discussion on the ethics in business should continue through dialectics, dialogue and commentary, taking into consideration various paradigms in the form of deontological, teleological, praxis, practical spirituality and other approaches. They would all contribute in different ways in improving not only the character competence of the corporation but also the character competence of the nation.

❑

CHAPTER 15 Holistic Performance Scorecard of Corporations*

Performance scorecard is an important tool to measure performance of an organization. Earlier scorecard was largely focused on financial performance of the corporation. For example, Padta system followed by some Indian organizations was rooted in daily reporting of financial performance, particularly in terms of cash generation. Many monthly and quarterly reporting systems were also focused on financial performance as key determinant of organizational performance.

15.1 House of Business

For any performance measurement system we need a foundational framework. The metaphor of 'Business House' conceptualized in terms of following five key functions represented by SMFPHR, can serve as a conceptual model:

1. **S**: Strategy
2. **M**: Marketing
3. **F**: Finance
4. **P**: Production
5. **HR**: Human Resources

Metaphorically, the roof of such a business house is constituted by the Strategy, Marketing and Finance triangle. Its room represents the production function and

*Towards Holistic Performance Scorecard: A New Strategic Imperative, Subhash Sharma, 11th SMF (Strategic Management Forum) Convention, Indian Institute of Technology (IIT) Kanpur May 8–10, 2008, Towards Holistic Performance Scorecard: A New Strategic Imperative, *Vilakshan*, Vol. V, No. 2, Sept. 2008, pp. 33–45, Towards Holistic Performance Scorecard, Subhash Sharma, in 'Changing Ideas in Strategy', (Ed.) Arun Sinha, Narosa Publishing House, New Delhi, 2010, pp. 7–16.

its foundation is represented by Human Resources. Such a view of a business house gives us a conceptual basis for designing Business Success Performance Scorecard (BSPSc). Figure 15.1 represents this perspective to develop such a performance scorecard.

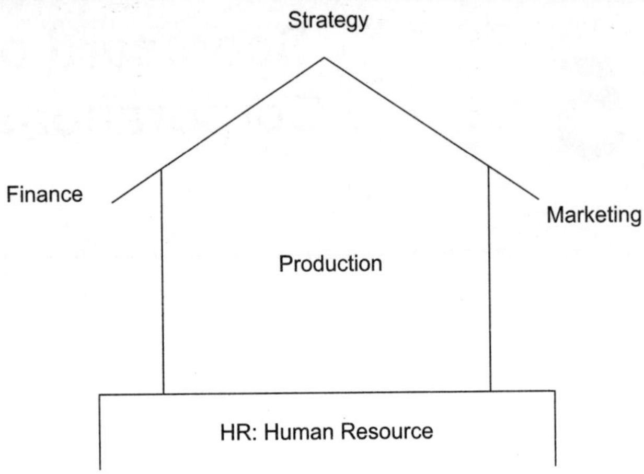

Figure 15.1. House of Business for Developing Performance Scorecard

When performance scorecard takes into consideration the performance of the entire business house, we obtain a better assessment. The performance scorecard should also consider SWAN analysis with respect to each function as well as the whole organization. The concept of SWAN analysis (Sharma, New Mantras in Corporate Corridors, 2009, 403) has the following elements:

S: Strengths

W: Weaknesses

A: Achievements

N: Next step/Next initiative

When SWAN analysis is conducted for each function and for the organization as a whole, it creates a linkage with organization's ViSA (Vision, Strategy and Action Plan). This is the essence of the scorecard based on the business house metaphor suggested above.

15.2 Balanced Scorecard and Beyond

Kaplan and Norton (1996) took another view and developed the concept of Balanced Scorecard. They suggested that vision and strategy of an organization should be linked with the following four perspectives: Customer Perspective, Financial Perspective, Internal Business Perspective, and Learning & Growth Perspective.

They elaborate on these perspectives in terms of following key ideas:

Customer perspective: To achieve our vision, how should we appear to customer?

Financial perspective: To succeed financially, how should we appear to our shareholders?

Internal business process: To satisfy shareholders and customers, what business processes must we excel at?

Learning and growth perspective: To achieve our vision, how will we sustain our ability to change and improve?

They argue that scorecard should focus on a balanced view of the organization in terms of the above indicated four perspectives and these four perspectives should be linked to vision and strategy. They also suggest that each perspective should be analyzed in terms of objectives, measures, targets and initiatives. This would ensure that the strategy is translated into operational terms. Figure 15.2 presents their model of Balanced Scorecard.

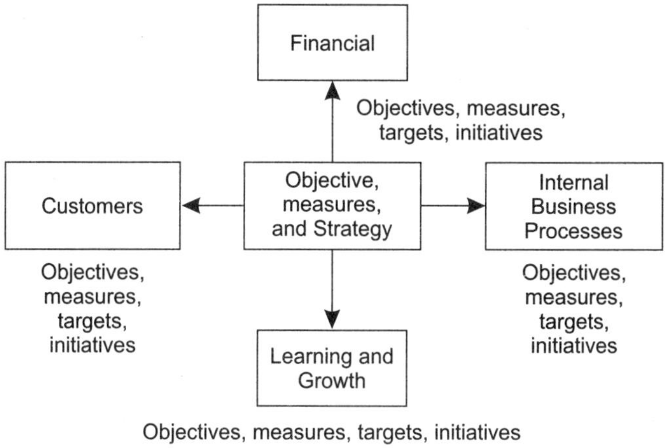

Figure 15.2. Kaplan & Norton (1996) Conceptual Framework for Balanced Scorecard

(**Source:** The Balanced Scorecard, Robert S Kaplan, David P Norton, Harvard Business School Press, Boston, Mass., 1996, p.9.)

Balanced Scorecard represented a breakthrough, because earlier scorecards were largely restricted to financial performance; they were not directly linked to the strategy of the organization.

It may be observed that the four perspectives suggested by Kaplan and Norton broadly correspond to SMFPHR framework of organizations presented in the form of 'Business House'. Customer perspective is captured in performance scorecard of the marketing function. Financial perspective is captured through the finance function. Internal business process to a large extent is captured by performance scorecard of the production and operations function of the organization. Learning and growth perspective is captured through performance scorecard of the Human Resource Development function. Thus, there is broad correspondence between the two frameworks. Managers of the 'Business House' are also interested in knowing how the house appears to customers, shareholders as well as other stakeholders. In their framework, Kaplan & Norton focus largely on customers and shareholders. When we use the metaphor of 'Business House', we get a better conceptual foundation as now the focus is on how the house appears not only to customers and shareholders but also to other stakeholders as well as society at large. Is this house creating pollution? Is it environmentally sound? Such questions are not answered by Kaplan and Norton's Balanced Scorecard. Hence, in true sense it is not properly balanced. In addition, their framework does not include concerns such as corporate social responsibility, ethical performance of the corporation. Thus, there is need to develop a new approach to scorecards wherein these dimensions are also taken into consideration while assessing the performance of the corporate. It implies a holistic view of performance and thereby we need to develop Holistic Performance Scorecard (HPSc). Thus, Business Success Performance Scorecard (BSPSc) as well as Balanced Scorecard should be expanded to measure performance on holistic basis.

It may be indicated that Michael Porter and Mark Kramer (2006) have expanded the traditional view of strategy by suggesting interdependency between business and society and thereby between society and strategy. However, Gustavsson (2007) suggests that there is a need to go beyond the 'extended strategy' concept of Porter and Karmer and move towards 'transcendent strategy' wherein strategy formulation and implementation takes a 'consciousness' view of the organization, so he points to the need for establishing a link between spirituality and strategy. These expanded views about strategy take us in the direction of Holistic Performance Scorecard.

For development of holistic performance scorecard, we also need to look at the evolution of a new corporate model as well as its new conceptual foundations. The discussion below provides an overview of the evolutionary journey of the new corporate model.

15.3 Four Stages Model of Corporate Evolution

Ackoff (1981) provides us an evolutionary view of changing concept of corporation. According to him, "The concept of corporation has evolved from one that was mechanistic to one that was organismic and from organismic to organization. Viewed as machine, it was taken to have no purpose of its own, but an instrument for use by its owners in pursuit of their profit objective. Viewed as organism the corporation was taken to have survival and growth as it principal purpose. Viewed as an organization, the corporation was seen to have responsibility to all its stakeholders and society, the larger system of which it is a part" (pp. 48–49). Ackoff further suggests that corporations should contribute to improve the quality of life of others. He suggests the need for developing measurement systems for the same. This is a pointer towards the idea of Holistic Performance Measurement Systems (HPMS).

Drawing on Ackoff and others, Sharma (2005, 2007) identifies four stages of evolutionary journey of corporations. These are as follows:

Stage I: Corporations and Shareholders: The primary objective of the corporate was to maximize the wealth of shareholders. Competition, efficiency and profit provided the basis foundation for this model.

Stage II: Corporations and Stakeholders: There are many stakeholders and there should be a proper balance between the interests of various stakeholders. For example, corporations can maximize the wealth of shareholders by polluting the rivers. Social movements have now put pressure on corporations to prevent this. Ackoff (1981) suggests that Corporation should have responsibility towards all stakeholders.

Stage III: Corporations and Society–Citizenship model: In this stage of their evolution, corporations have been conceptualized as corporate citizens. Hence, expectations on ethics and environmental concerns have gained importance. Corporations are expected to follow 'principles of ethical business' and not merely, 'principles of business'. It may also be indicated that Michael Porter and Mark Kramer (2006) have expanded traditional view of strategy by suggesting interdependency between strategy and society.

Stage IV: Corporations and Sustainable development–Corporations as social institutions: In this conceptualization, corporations are viewed as social institutions with dominant influence on society. Hence, there is need for a symbiotic relationship between society and the corporations. They are expected to contribute towards sustainable development of society. Their linkage with sustainable and holistic development needs strengthening. As social institutions corporations should achieve synergy between efficiency, social equity, ethics and environmental concerns.

While Stage I model was largely an efficiency model, in stage II model, social equity concerns were incorporated to some extent, and in stage III model, ethics were also considered important for conduct of business. Now in their stage IV evolution as social institutions, corporations are expected to achieve appropriate balance between efficiency, social equity and ethics and also be concerned with transcendental values of environment, women's equity, psycho-spiritual advancement *etc.*, This is a new age model wherein corporations are viewed as social institutions and not merely business entities, that is, in addition to the bottom line concerns, they have a social purpose, and they should be guided by sustainable and holistic development. Figure 15.3 presents the above discussed evolutionary perspective of the corporate model.

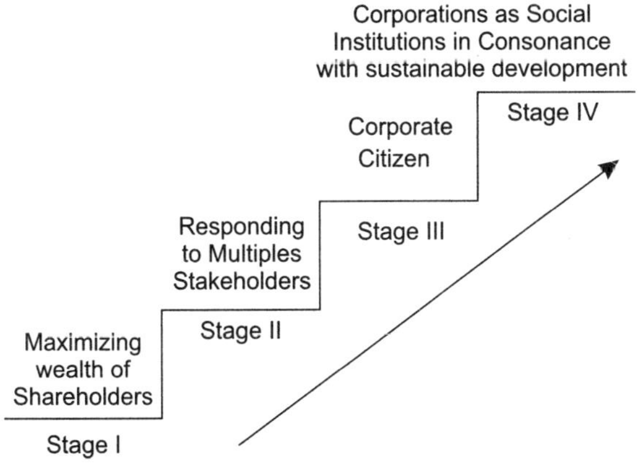

Figure 15.3. Four Stages Model of Corporate Evolution

15.4 Four Es Framework of Holistic Corporate Management (HCM)

Evolution of the new corporate model is also linked to new paradigms of development thinking. Evolution of development thinking from economic development to new paradigms of sustainable development and integrative holistic development has influenced the corporate world. Sharma (1996) suggested the 4 Es Swastika model of holistic development and management emphasizing the need for achieving a proper balance between following four *Es*:

1. Efficiency
2. Equity
3. Ethics
4. Ecology

Figure 15.4 presents this framework as a synergy model development. In this model, the 4 Es are in dynamic interaction and they are in proper harmony thereby synergy is created in society.

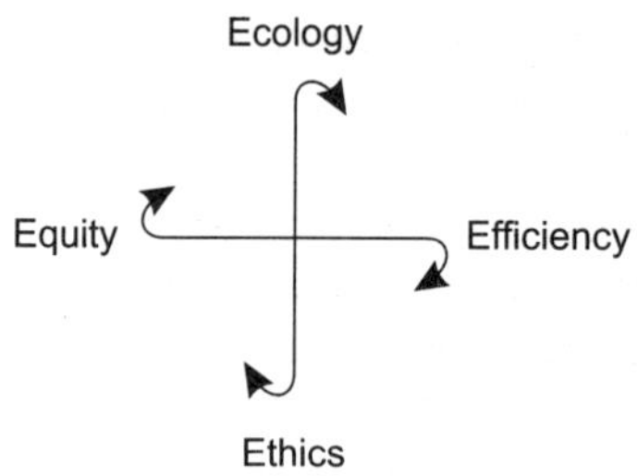

Figure 15.4. Four Es Framework for New Corporate Model

(**Source:** Management in New Age: Western Windows Eastern Doors, Subhash Sharma, 1996, p. 92)

When applied in corporate context, this model leads us to the concept of Holistic Corporate Management (HCM), wherein foundations of corporate management are based on the four pillars of efficiency, social equity, ethics and ecology. Efficiency implies bottom-line concerns. Social equity dimension is reflected to some extent by corporate social responsibility (CSR) and neighborhood concerns. Ethics dimension is reflected in good governance and the 'Character Competence of the Corporation' (Sharma, 2002). Ecology is reflected in terms of concern for environment and implementation of the concept of sustainable development in corporate context through 'environmental management systems'. Thus, in Holistic Corporate Management (HCM) all four dimensions of the 4 E model find integration.

It may be indicated that the 4 E model has equivalence in 3 Ps models of Profit, People and Planet. This model, also known as triple bottom line model, suggests that corporations in addition to profit should also focus on CSR and environmental concerns captured through the imaginative phrases, people and planet. In fact, corporate social responsibility, environmental concerns and good governance have become new strategic imperatives as well as "new mantras" for the corporate world. We can hear their echoes in the Board rooms and corporate corridors.

Prahlad and Hamel (1992) suggested the concept of Core Competence. This concept originated from the efficiency model of the corporates. However, for Holistic Corporate Management (HCM), we need to include 4Es framework. Hence, corporations as social institutions should focus on the following:

1. Core Competence and similar other strategic management tools in consonance with efficiency and competitive advantage paradigms.
2. Corporate Social Responsibility (CSR) towards society to meet social expectations of social equity paradigm. Corporate Social Dharma (CSD) is a more expansive idea to emphasize the idea of Corporation's duty (*dharma*) towards society.
3. Concern for environmental issues.
4. 'Character Competence of the Corporation' in consonance with ethics and good governance requirements.

These four ideas constitute a new conceptual foundation for designing Holistic Performance Scorecard.

15.5 From PEST to STEPS: Strategy and Spirituality Link–Guna Theory in Strategic Management

Philosophical foundations of the new corporate model can also be traced to some well-known Indian concepts such as Gandhi's Trusteeship model, concept of loksangraha (welfare of the society/stakeholders) and the concept of *shubh-labh*. Gandhi's trusteeship model is finding its expression in multiple stakeholders' concept of the corporates. The concept of *loksangraha* is expressed in the idea of Corporate Social Responsibility (CSR) and the concept of *shubh-labh* is finding its expression in ethical concerns as well as 'moral sentiments' of business as advocated by Adam Smith. In fact, the *shubh-labh* concept takes us beyond Adam Smith's 'moral sentiments' as it also suggests the need for a spiritual touch to business activities. It may be indicated that in the expression *shubh-labh, shubh* is indicative of the sacred dimension and *labh* is indicative of the economics dimension. Thus this concept has a linkage with the concept of "sacro-economic" view of business activities.

Charles Drekmeier (1962) mentions the phrase 'sacro-economic' in his seminal work, 'Kingship and Community in Early India' providing us an insight that the concept of sacro-economic view has been in existence in Indian civilization since ages. Sauvik Chakraverti (2000) observes that, "The expression (*Shubh-labh*) which translates roughly into 'auspicious profit' implies that ancients had unearthed the morality of the market and found its effect wealth generation through profit-

beneficial to society". While the idea of 'sacro-economic' has been in existence, its application in the field of management and in the corporate context is new. In corporate context, it implies that corporate is not merely an economic entity but should be viewed as 'sacro-economic' entity. Conventional literature on strategy is based on competitive advantage framework and ignores the 'moral sentiments' as well as 'sacro-economic' view of enterprises. Even, Kaplan and Norton's balanced Scorecard does not care for Adam Smith's 'moral sentiments'.

Above stated three ideas *viz.*, Trusteeship (from Gandhi), *loksangraha* (from Gita) and *shubh-labh* (from Indian business tradition) provide us a new conceptual foundation for the new corporate model wherein corporates are considered social institutions and not merely profit making machines at the cost of environment and social disruption. This framework can be referred to as 'House of *Shubh-labh*' and is sacro-economic in its strategic architecture. This is the essence of the 'sacro-economic' model of corporates.

New conceptual foundations suggested in our discussions require a shift from PEST analysis to STEPS analysis to incorporate the nature of spiritual environment in which organizations are functioning. Spiritual environment includes the ethical context of business. In PEST analysis, ethical dimension is not given due consideration. STEPS model suggested by Sharma (2001) in the context of a nation's development vision has following dimensions:

S: Social

T: Technological

E: Economic

P: Political

S: Spiritual

When applied in the context of environmental analysis and to the field of strategic management, it suggests a link between spirituality and strategy. It may be indicated that PEST is not a very positive metaphor. In contrast, STEPS is a positives metaphor. It may also be indicated that link between spirituality and strategy has not been explored. As indicated earlier, recent work by Gustavsson (2007) provides a broad indication for a need to explore this linkage. In general, an indirect linkage has been highlighted by many through the need for ethical concerns in the activities of the corporation. It may be observed that traditionally strategy literature was rooted in the competitive advantage framework and maximization of shareholders' wealth. However we do come across people who refuse to add certain types of business activities to their portfolio because of environmental, social, ethical and spiritual concerns. For example, many vegetarian business persons refuse to enter non-vegetarian business even though it may add to their competitive advantage. The recent concept of Socially Responsible Investments (SRI) is also an indicator in this direction. Ethical and spiritual concerns are also considered critical for good governance.

Drawing from Porter's 'extended strategy' and Gustavsson's 'transcendent strategy' concepts, we arrive at the **SSS** (Spirituality-Society-Strategy) model wherein strategy formulation and implementation is driven by spiritual values and spiritual concern including ethical concerns as well as social responsibility requirements. This is in consonance with Indian Guna theory that identifies human actions in terms of Tamas, Rajas and Sattava (TRS). Application of the TRS model from Gita, in strategic management implies three types of strategic thinking of policy making and strategic approaches *viz.*, tamasik, rajasik and sattavik. Spirituality in strategic thinking and strategic management implies bringing a sattavik touch to strategy formulation and implementation and make them SRIs (Socially Responsible Institutions). However this will depend on the expression of the Self of Leader in strategy formulation. A leader driven by sattava will bring this dimension into play in his organization. This is the Key note of 'Guna Theory in Strategic Management'.

Essence of **SSS** model is as follows:

S	S	S
Spirituality →	Society →	Strategy
Transcendent strategy →	Extended strategy →	Competitive strategy

15.6 Implications for Performance Scorecard

It was earlier indicated that Balanced Scorecard represented a breakthrough in performance measurement as it expanded the earlier concept of performance measurement from its narrow focus on financial performance. However, our discussion indicates that balanced scorecard has its own limitations as its view is limited to organization as an economic entity/business entity. Issues such as ethical performance, environmental performance, social responsibility and spiritual concerns are not included in this domain. There is a need base performance measurement system in the concept of corporate as social institution. While business entity concept led us to Balanced Scorecard, Social institution concept leads us to Holistic Performance Scorecard. Using the framework of Business House presented earlier and incorporating the 4 Es framework as well as STEPS framework, we arrive at a new foundational framework of Holistic Performance Scorecard, presented in Fig. 15.5. Using this framework we can develop specific metric for its various elements on the basis of SWAN analysis for each performance area. In fact, SWAN analysis can be combined with OMTAI (Objectives, Measures, Targets, Achievements, and Initiatives) for each performance area including CSR and Good governance. It may be indicated that a comparison of Targets and Achievements identifies the performance gap and initiatives indicate how this gap will be bridged. Thus, TAI (Targets, Achievements, Initiatives) when combined with Objectives and Measures (OM), gives a comprehensive view of performance.

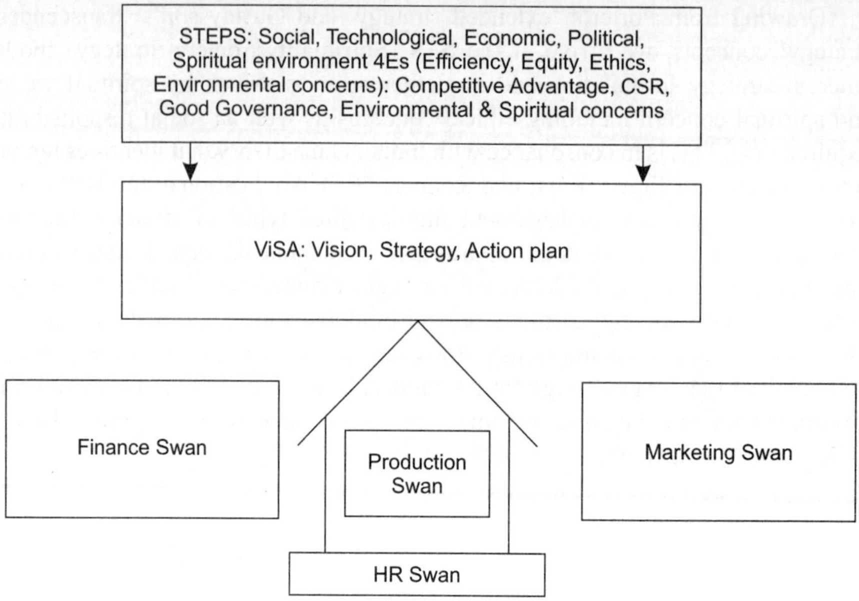

Figure 15.5. From Business Entity to Social Institution: Foundational Framework for Holistic Performance Scorecard

This framework presented above suggests that 'strategic vistas' of an organization should give due considerations to efficiency/competitive advantage, social equity/social responsibility, ethics/good governance and spiritual environment. Earlier performance scorecard was largely based on efficiency paradigm/competitive advantage paradigm of treating corporate as merely a business entity. This philosophy is also reflected in Balanced Scorecard developed by Kaplan and Norton. Our discussion indicated that this paradigm is undergoing a change and corporations are emerging as social institutions as a result of pressure from environment and many other social and spiritual movements. Therefore, need for Holistic Performance Scorecard to reflect the contribution of the corporate world towards environmental concerns, social concerns, good governance and betterment of spiritual environment. This implies that time has come to move beyond the Balance Scorecard (BSc) to Holistic Performance Scorecard (HPSc) to achieve a better symbiosis between corporate world, society and individuals.

Are there organizations that follow the ideas presented above? Balanced Scorecard has been in use in the corporate world and corporate world also recognizes the importance of CSR and good governance. Many corporations include a brief write up on their CSR activities and initiatives for Good governance in their balance sheet. This implies they are moving in the direction of Holistic Performance Scorecard (HPSc). This indicates that it is possible to have performance card that is in consonance with holistic perspective of organizations. In future, more corporations may adopt this approach as a result of pressures from social movements, environmental movements and spiritual movements.

❑

Part V

New Visioning and Envisioning

CHAPTER 16

Moon Ocean Strategy*

A few years back, water was discovered on the moon. Indian Space Research organization (ISRO) had a significant role in this discovery. This discovery of the water on the moon provides us the foundation for the idea of moon ocean strategy as a new concept in the field of Strategic Management. Further, going to the moon is also a metaphor for a giant leap. 'One small step for man, one giant leap for mankind', is a famous line from Neil Armstrong. In my poem, Step- by-Step (2001), which has become a popular 'corporate rhyme' I have captured this sentiment through the line, 'We go the moon and take a new step, Step by Step …'. These ideas provide us a new way in strategic thinking.

16.1 Moon as a Metaphor

Earlier poets used to draw heavily on the moon as a metaphor. Further, the metaphor of Full Moon has been widely used in many spiritual traditions as it symbolizes fullness and enlightenment. It may be indicated that Buddha had his enlightenment on a full moon day. Moon also has symbolic significance in various religions and regions. Once I took a 'full moon walk' in Grand Canyon, it invoked a link between moon, management and leadership. During recent years moon as a

*Moon Ocean Strategy: Beyond the Blue Ocean Strategy, Subhash Sharma, National Conference on Sustaining Competitive Advantage, Department of Commerce, Christ University, Bangalore, Nov. 29, 2011, Moon Ocean Strategy: A New Approach to Strategic Thinking, Subhash Sharma, 15th Annual Convention of the Strategic Management Forum (SMF), Indian Institute of Management (IIM), Indore, May 3–5, 2012, New Earth Shastra: Towards Holistic Development & Management (HDM), Subhash Sharma, IBA Publications, 2012, pp. 171–175. These ideas were also presented at the International Dialog amongst Research and Practice, School of Applied Psychology' Zurich University, Zurich, Sept. 1–3, 2014.

metaphor has also drawn attention of the academic community and has been used in academic writings. Prof. R.S. Deshpande (2004), Director, Institute of Social & Economic Change, Bangalore in his monograph, Moon in The Mirror: Farmers and MSP in Karnataka, has used moon metaphor in the field of Economics to describe price support. In my discussions with him, he highlighted the point that 'moon attracts many but is accessible to few'. In fact, moon also invokes the idea of Imagination and Imaginative Thinking (IT). Gary Hamel (2009) in his article, Moon Shots for Management, uses the metaphor of Moon Shot (A phrase that refers to America's landing on the moon program) to reinvent the discipline of Management. Sharma (2011) uses the metaphor of ocean on the moon, to develop the idea of moon ocean strategy to take us beyond the blue ocean strategy and has developed this idea further in his book, New Earth Shastra (2012). Mahapatra & Dave (2013) use the symbol of full moon to suggest their concept of full moon strategy.

Above discussion suggests, there are many illustrations of using moon as a metaphor in the academic literature. In fact, practitioners also tend to use this metaphor to set and achieve difficult targets. An interesting thing about the use of moon as a metaphor is that different researchers have used it differently to highlight different lessons that can be drawn from the powerful metaphor of moon. Thus, we see a shift in use of moon as a metaphor from philosophers, poets, saints and sages to researchers and also practitioners.

16.2 Three Approaches to Strategy: Red Ocean, Blue Ocean, Moon Ocean

Academic literature in the field of Strategic Management identifies two approaches to create USP (Unique Strategic Positioning) *viz*., 1. Red ocean strategy and 2. Blue ocean strategy. Red ocean strategy implies a fight for survival and growth in the market through 'head on collision' like the 'cola wars'. Blue ocean strategy implies search for new opportunities through 'discovery' of new markets and thereby new product – market spaces.

Drawing upon the idea of oceans on the Moon, Moon Ocean Strategy extends the idea of Blue Ocean and thereby takes us beyond the Blue Ocean concept. 'Going to places where no one has gone before', is an inspirational quote from Star-trek. This quote is at the root of Moon Ocean Strategy, which implies exploring those ideas and products, that very few have dared to explore.

In the corporate context, Steve Jobs is an excellent illustration of Moon ocean strategy. He imagined through his 'supra intuitional capabilities', a future that very few could visualize and convert into reality. In a way he had gone far beyond the blue oceans of the earth to the oceans on the moon. He simply 'jumped over the existing competition' ('quantum jumping') to create new competitive spaces far beyond the reach of Red ocean and Blue ocean thinking. Moon ocean strategy implies a revolutionary visioning and envisioning of the future of industry and thereby creating a complete transformation of the industry.

Three approaches require three different mindsets. Red ocean strategy needs 'Darwinian' mindset of 'survival of the fittest to eliminate the rest'. In contrast, Blue ocean strategy needs an 'explorer's mindset' like Columbus to explore 'new worlds'. In Moon ocean strategy we go a step further and it requires the 'star-trek' mindset to explore the spaces that nobody has explored before. This is represented by Steve Jobs mindset – a mind driven by imaginative thinking and Imagination. Thus, moon ocean strategy represents a 'radical' and 'revolutionary' approach to change in contrast to Red ocean and Blue ocean strategies. It may be indicated moon also has a spiritual significance and it represents the supra-intuitional powers of the mind and thereby power of 'charismatic creativity'. New age strategic thinking implies a shift towards Imaginative Thinking (IT) and Imagination in the field of Strategy.

Figure 16.1 presents above discussed three approaches to strategy in a diagrammatic form.

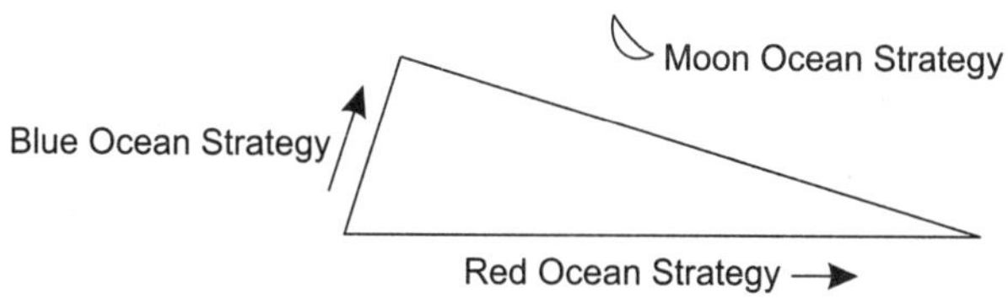

Figure 16.1. Three Approaches to Strategy - Red Ocean, Blue Ocean and Moon Ocean

Are there any examples of Moon ocean strategy from India? The following can be quoted as illustrations of this approach to strategy and they are known for their success and books and case studies have been written about them:

1. India's freedom struggle: The non-violent approach to achieve liberation is one of the best examples of moon ocean strategy exemplified by Mahatma Gandhi.
2. White revolution: Milk revolution in India that started with Amul way back in 1950s illustrates the idea of moon ocean strategy.
3. Indian spiritual movements such as Baba Ramdev, Art of Living, Brahamakumaries *etc*., represent the moon ocean strategy.
4. India's soft power represented through its music, dance, literature *etc*., *e.g*., re-mix revolution in music represents moon ocean type thinking.
5. Indian Cinema ('Bollywood') has quite often intuitively used moon ocean strategy in variety of ways.

Above stated examples go beyond blue ocean as they have a 'revolutionary' touch to create a change. Once more case studies are written on these illustrations and conceptual frameworks are developed based on such case studies, literature on strategic management will get enriched.

Krishnan (2010) emphasized the need to go beyond *Jugaad* to 'systematic innovation'. However, many times innovations originate from intuition and imagination and these processes may not be 'systematic' but 'chaotic and charismatic'. Strategic thinking is undergoing a shift from Red ocean to Blue ocean to Moon ocean thinking and also from *Jugaad* to 'systematic innovation' to 'moon ocean imagination'. Moon ocean imagination is rooted in VID (Visualization, Imagination, Dreaming). Steve Jobs represented actualization of the VID processes in the context of IT industry. VID actualizations also represents the essence of idea entrepreneurship'.

16.3 Three Eras of Strategic Management: Red Ocean Era, Blue Ocean Era, New Age Mantras Era

In general, the field of Strategic Management (SM) has witnessed following three eras in its evolution from 1960s onwards reflecting a shift from Michael Porter to Steve Jobs's influence:

Era I: Red ocean era – During this era academic literature focused on 'cola war' approach to SM. Accordingly the tools, techniques and frameworks of analysis were rooted in this 'ideology' of market wars with roots in zero sum market game. Darwin ruled the mindset of strategic thinkers. Academic literature generated during this period was largely rooted in rational – analytic / critical thinking approach to knowledge creation.

Era II: Blue ocean era – With publication of the book, Blue Ocean Strategy in 2003, academic literature started exploring new routes to strategic advantage. Thus, developing an explorer's mindset started having an impact on strategic thinkers and creative-intuitive approach to knowledge creation gained acceptance.

Era III: New Age mantras era – We have already entered a new era in SM *viz.*, new age mantras era, wherein many new mantras are entering the field of SM. Phrases such as out of box thinking, connecting the dot, disruptive technologies and reverse innovations *etc.*, have acquired common usage. Further, ideas such as Ideas Entrepreneurship, Sustainable Development, Inclusive Development, Corporate Governance, Social Responsibility, Responsible Business *etc.*, are also influencing the field of SM. Many such new mantras can now be heard in academic corridors as well as in corporate corridors. In fact, Strategy is increasingly becoming a search for connections and a search for new metaphors. Exhibit 16.1 provides some new metaphors in Strategic Thinking, Policy making, Management and Leadership presented in this book.

After Steve Jobs's impact, strategic thinkers are now experimenting with imaginative – visionary / imaginative thinking approach to discover new frontiers through VID (Visualization, Imagination, Dreaming) leading to new knowledge in Strategic Management. New age era can also be referred to as creativity era in Strategic Management. It implies creation of new models, new mantras, new yantras and a new vision of SM that takes us beyond the red ocean and blue ocean thinking to moon ocean thinking.

Above discussion also leads us to a typology of strategic thinkers in terms of following three types encompassed in the rainbow model of consciousness, intelligences and knowledge creation:

Rectangular thinkers: These thinkers are the red ocean type thinkers who always think within the box. Box can be represented by a rectangle. They think within rational – analytic framework of thinking and extensively use critical thinking approach.

Triangular thinkers: These thinkers are the blue ocean thinkers who always go beyond the box by taking a new creative route. They use creative – intuitive approach and extensively use creative thinking.

Radial thinkers: These are the moon ocean thinkers who think in terms of an 'expanding circle' representing the expansion of consciousness. These thinkers always think 'deep into the future' and use imaginative – visionary approach. They extensively use imaginative thinking approach. A moon ocean CEO is Creative, Enlightened and Organic (CEO) leader. He/she uses Theory O (Sharma, 2013) as a tool to expand his/her circle of consciousness from Rationality mode to Intuition & Insight to Imagination to arrive at a Vision that has the potential to transform the world.

Figure 16.2 represents the three types of strategic thinkers:

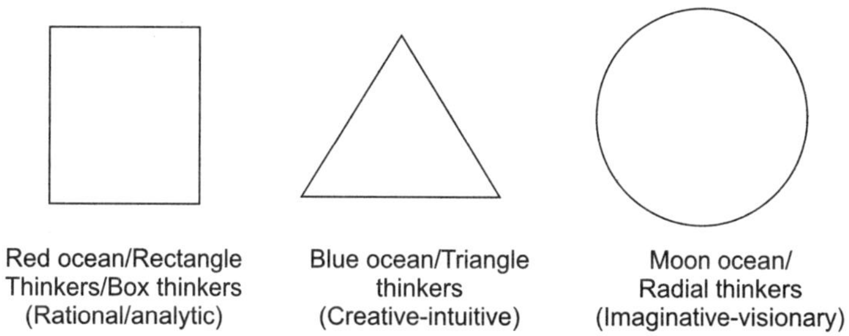

Figure 16.2. A Typology of Strategic Thinkers

16.4 Rambo, Rancho and Rishi Approaches

If we use some popular metaphors, Strategic Thinking and Management can be viewed in terms of Rambo, Rancho and Rishi approaches. Red ocean strategy is represented by Rambo approach, Blue ocean strategy is represented by Rancho (from the movie Three Idiots) approach and moon ocean strategy is represented by Rishi approach *viz.*, expansion of consciousness. Thus we arrive at the following three approaches to Strategic Management:

1. Rambo approach
2. Rancho approach
3. Rishi approach

In Corporate context, Rishi implies Re-See competence *i.e.*, ability to 'see' and re-see the events, threats and opportunities in new ways. In this sense, Steve Jobs was a Corporate Rishi. A Rambo uses his 'Head' (Rationality model) to fight his competitors. Rancho uses his 'Heart' (Creativity) to bypass the competition.

A Rishi uses his 'Spirit'/ 'Consciousness' to create a grand new vision and thus undertakes quantum jumping to jump over the existing competition. In fact, a new approach to strategic management implies a combination of the Head, Heart and Consciousness wherein rationality approach is combined with 3 Is *viz.*, Intuition, Insight and Imagination leading to new vision. Reason, Intuition, Insight and Imagination also represent a leader's expanding circles of consciousness. This is in consonance with Theory 0 of consciousness presented in this book, in terms of full circle rainbow. As a leader evolves from a Rambo leader to Rancho leader to Rishi leader, his/her consciousness expands and leader moves from lower circle of consciousness to higher circles of consciousness. An enlightened leader makes use of all the circles of consciousness as per the situational requirements.

Figure 16.3 presents above discussion as CH^3 (Consciousness, Head, Heart, Hand) model as an integrative model for strategic thinking and management. In this model, Hand symbolizes implementation aspect of strategic thinking and thereby reflects the grounded praxis approach to strategic management. Both Consciousness and Heart symbolize, Intuition, Insight and Imagination.

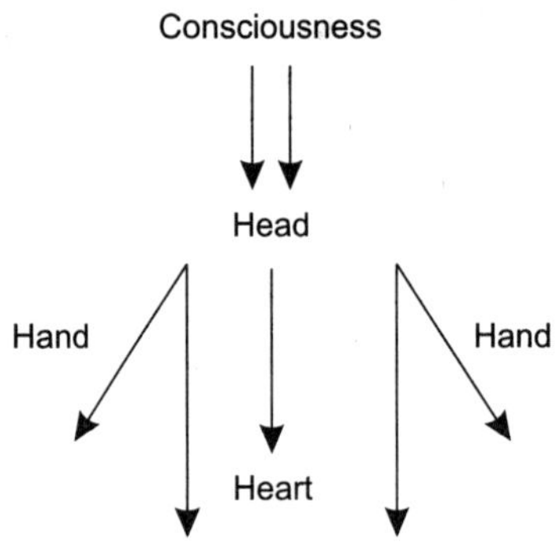

Figure 16.3. CH^3 Model for an Integrative Approach to Strategic Thinking & Management

Above discussion leads us to an integrative approach represented by R^3:

$$R^3 = \text{Rambo*Rancho*Rishi}$$

Thus, we arrive at a new framework for Strategic Management (SM) wherein there is a new synthesis of Red ocean, Blue ocean and Moon ocean strategies. This is a New Age Mantra for Strategic Management. For academicians and practitioners it implies, integration of rational-analytic, creative–intuitive and imaginative–visionary approaches to strategic management. In metaphorical terms it implies opening western windows, eastern doors and consciousness corridors in the field of strategic thinking and management, to arrive at holistic view of strategic management.

Exhibit 16.1 New Metaphors and New Models in Strategic Thinking, Policy making, Management & Leadership

	Metaphor	Model / Implications
1.	Four Ashokan lions	A model for Holistic Globalization
2.	Economic chapati making	A model for Holistic Development
3.	Empire Vs Umpire	Shift in role of State from Empire to Umpire
4.	Coconut model of society	Role of middle class in driving the society
5.	Capillary action	Grassroots model of development
6.	Swastika	Demand-supply swastika indicating high-low dynamics
7.	Dialectical Chakra	Understanding nature of dialectical intensities in society and organizations
8.	Rainbow	SHARMAN circles of consciousness, Seven tempers of mind
9.	Flying swan	SWAN (Strengths, Weaknesses, Achievement, Next step) analysis
10.	Moving clouds	SPOT (Space, Pace, Opportunities, Threats) analysis
11.	'Diya' (lamp)	Knowledge lamp indicating three research approaches – Quantitative, Qualitative, Creative
12.	Omega circle	Holistic integration in strategic thinking

❑

Concluding Word

Ideas presented in this book present a crystallization of conceptual models, frameworks, metaphors and 'theories' arising from field experiences and existing theoretical foundations in strategic thinking. Strategic Management Forum (SMF) of India provided an opportunity to the author to present most of these ideas during Annual Conventions. Other forums such as Association of Indian Management Scholars (AIMS) International, Chulalokorn University, Bangkok; Gaedda College, Bhutan; Assumption University, Bangkok; Curtin University-Pecth; Zurich University, Zurich and several Indian Universities and Management Institutes, also provided an opportunity to present these ideas. During presentations and discussions I received many useful comments and suggestions that led to further refinements. This was further supplemented by interactions with practicing managers during 'reach out programs' and other MDPs (Management Development Programs). Classroom discussions with MBA students and interactions with my doctoral students provided further opportunity to test these ideas. These processes led to creation of this 'knowledge bouquet' that presents some new metaphors, models and management mantras and management yantras.

Knowledge building in India with respect to Management in general and strategic thinking in particular, has largely been through cases and case studies. In this process, integrative indigenization (J.B.P. Sinha, 2000) has been the hallmark of Indian approach. Indian managers have also used 'grounded praxis approach' in modifying the ideas to suit the local conditions. This has also led to development of some Indian concepts. In this approach, focus has been on transfer of ideas from the West, either in their pure form or in their modification through application. During last two decades, this approach has been supplemented by a parallel innovative process of creating new concepts, new models and new mantras based on an integrative approach wherein 'Western Windows' (Western concepts and models) are supplemented with 'Eastern Doors' (Eastern concepts and models, originating from Eastern nations that include, India, China and Japan), to create a new house of knowledge. This is further supplemented by new consciousness corridors that are leading the world towards a new awakening of consciousness towards new issues such as social, environmental and spiritual concerns.

In general, reason, intuition and imagination represent three approaches to create new theories and new perspectives. These have earlier been referred to as rational-analytic, creative-intuitive, imaginative-visionary and in metaphorical terms as windows, doors and corridors of knowledge creation. In strategic thinking, all the three approaches play a complementary role. In offering this knowledge bouquet, all the three approaches have been used for developing new models, mantras, and yantras taking an integrative and synthesis approach of the knowledge creation in the West and knowledge creation in the East.

Metaphors are widely used in knowledge creation. Freud's iceberg model of unconscious, subconscious and conscious mind, Adam Smith's invisible hand, Maslow's hierarchy metaphor in his hierarchy of needs, C.K. Prahlad's Bottom of the Pyramid, Friedman's World is Flat, Porter's Diamond model, Butterfly effect in chaos theory etc. are well known examples of metaphors used for concept building and theory building. Taking a clue from this approach of knowledge building, this book presents some new metaphors drawn from Indian experiences. These include, Swastika theory of holistic globalization, dialectical chakra, Economic chapati making, Coconut model of society, Capillary action model of development, Empire Vs Umpire model with respect to the role of the State, Ashokan four lions metaphor to represent four forces of Market, State, People and Self, 'Diya' (knowledge lamp) metaphor of knowledge creation and research approaches, Rainbow model of seven types of mind and seven intelligence, flying swan metaphor leading to of SWAN analysis and moving clouds leading to the idea of SPOT analysis etc.

In Strategic thinking, many concepts and models have originated from consulting. Further, developing new conceptual models on the basis of existing theory and practice is another approach to knowledge building. Ideas presented in this book not only draw and extend received knowledge but also provide some new models based on the synthesis of the 'Western windows', 'Eastern doors' and 'Consciousness corridors'. Illustrations of the new models, mantras and yantras include, BEST analysis, Development STEPS, METRIC analysis, FATE analysis, CINE Matrix, SWAN & SPOT analysis etc. It may be indicated that these models have also been tested during Management Development Programs as well as in Faculty Development Programs and have been found useful and practical by the practitioners and academicians who participated in such programs.

In strategic thinking, Market, Society and Self, represent three key pillars of significance. In past, strategic thinking was largely focused which on Market and tools and techniques of analysis also originated from this focus. Now social concerns and social responsibility of business has become part of strategic thinking. Further, strategic thinking is also influenced by the mindset of the decision-makers. Hence an understanding of Self also becomes important. In this book, in addition to management models and mantras, some management yantras based on an integration of 'Western models and Eastern mantras' are proposed to enhance our theoretical and conceptual understanding of the inter-linkages between Market, Society, Self and Organizations. These include, TCP yantra (Focus on integrative view on Market, Society and Self), KTG yantra (Focus on Self / Leadership) and VSP yantra (Focus on Organization and Organization Development). When these three management yantras are combined together like three interconnected circles, we arrive at an integrated and unified view of strategic thinking and management in the context of the new corporate model which aims at transforming corproates from business entities to social institutions of significance to the nations and the world.

It is our hope that ideas presented in this book, will be found useful by management researchers, scholars, thinkers and practitioners. Readers are invited to participate in the 3D process of Discussion, Dialogue and Discourse, with the author for further enrichment of the ideas presented in this book.

❑

Researchers' Corner
Supporting Articles by the Author

For the benefit of students, researcher and practitioners, the following provides a select list of author's articles published in various journals, books, conference proceedings etc. that form the basis of this book. A number of them are accessible from google.

Sharma Subhash, 'Managerial Discretion and Organizational Slack: A Commentary', *Vikalpa*, April-June 1991, 16:2, 33–40.

Sharma Subhash, 'New Age Management'. AMA (Ahmedabad Management Association) News, August 1991, 19:8, 2–3.

Sharma Subhash, 'Management Mantras', AMA (Ahmedabad Management Association) News, June 1992, 20:6, 5–6.

Sharma Subhash & Vithal M.P., 'Management Control Models for Conditions of Organizational Discontinuity', *Decision*, Jan-March 1992, 19:1.

Sharma Subhash, 'Management Ideas in Arthashastra'. *Indian Journal of Public Administration*, April-June 1994, XL:2, 165–182.

Sharma Subhash, 'Forward Engineering of Public Institutions in Market Economy'. *Indian Journal of Public Administration*, October-December 1996, XLII:4, 633–641.

Sharma Subhash, 'CINE Matrix: A Model for Strategic Gearing'. *The Planters' Chronicle*, March 1997, 92:3, 133–138.

Sharma Subhash, 'Enlightened Leadership in Indian Ethos: The Way of the Theory K, *Management & Change*, 2 : 1 Jan-June 1998, 93–104.

Sharma Subhash, 'Social Discourse in a Globalized Era: Towards the Concept of Development Matrix'. *Indian Journal of Public Administration*, July-September 1998, XLIV:3, 328–338.

Sharma Subhash, 'From Factors of Production to Factors of Creation: 'Best' Model as a Strategic Management Framework, *Abhigyan*, FORE School of Management, October-December 1998, 16:4, 43–47.

Sharma Subhash, 'Sharpening & Strengthening Knowledge Competence of Corporates: Knowledge Management in Enterprise Context', *Decision*, IIM Calcutta, January-December 1999, 26:1–4, 147–162.

Sharma Subhash, 'Corporate Gita: Lessons for Management, Administration and Leadership', *Journal of Human Values*, Jan–June 1999, 3:1. 1–14.

Sharma Subhash, 'Total Resources Management (TRM): A Holistic Approach to Strategic Gearing'. *Sankalpa*, January-June 2000, 8:1, 81–94.

Sharma Subhash, 'Forward Engineering for Strategic Gearing: The Indian Tea Industry'. *Management Review*, IIM Bangalore, June 2000, 12:2, 57–65.

Sharma Subhash, 'Enterprise Performance Improvement Systems (EPIS): Value Chain Matrix and Forward Engineering Tools for Performance Improvement', *Sankalpa*, July-December 2000, 8:2, 34–54.

Sharma Subhash, 'Total Knowledge Management (TKM): Enhancing Competitiveness Through Knowledge Management Systems', *Journal of Scientific & Industrial Research*, *CSIR*, August-September 2000, 59, 673–682.

Sharma Subhash, 'Forward Engineering for Strategic Gearing: A Conceptual Framework', *Indian Journal of Public Administration*, October-December 2000, XLVI:4, 667–674.

Sharma Subhash, 'Routes to Reality: Scientific and Rishi Approaches', *Journal of Human Values*, January-June 2001, 7:1, 75–83.

Sharma Subhash, 'Technological Explosions and Knowledge Management: Towards A New Competitive Advantage of Nations', *Udyog Pragati*, *NITIE*, July-September 2001, 25:3, 1–4.

Sharma Subhash, 'Managerial Approach to Sectoral Analysis: Managing in a Global Mandi', *Sankalpa*, July-December 2001, 9:2, 12–23.

Sharma Subhash, 'Knowledge Generation Windows, Grounded Praxis and the TASK Learning Model: Knowledge Management and Learning Models in Knowledge Organizations', *Abhigyan*, FORE School of Management, April-June 2002, 20:2, 7–15.

Sharma Subhash, 'Corporate Rishi Leadership Model: An Indian Model for Corporate Development & Ethical Leadership', in Udai Pareek, Aahad M. Osman-Gani, S. Ramanarayan & T.V. Rao, eds., *Human Resource Development in Asia: Trends & Challenges* (New Delhi: Oxford & IBH, 2002), 291–296.

Sharma Subhash, 'Character Competence of the Corporation', *Journal of Human Values*, July-December 2002, 8:2, 107–118.

Sharma Subhash, 'Radical Change Management (RCM): From Managing Pyramids To Managing In Chaos', *Paradigm*, Institute of Management Technology (IMT), January-June 2002, 6:1, 1–9.

Sharma Subhash, 'Organization Development & Management (ODM): Five Forms of Capital as Holistic Development Framework', in S.K. Prasad, Siraj Ur Rahman and G. Pandu Naik eds., *Strategic Human Resources Management* (Bangalore: Institute of HRD, 2003), 3–11.

Sharma Subhash, 'Corporate VEDA: Indian Ethos & Corporate Development', *Journal of Human Values*, July-Dec. 2003, 9:2, 163–172.

Sharma Subhash, 'Corporate Shubhlabh: A Framework for Corporate Governance', *Indian Journal of Training & Development*, April – June, 2004, 34:2, 17–24.

Sharma Subhash, 'Creating Unique Strategic Positioning (USP) Through Creativity & Innovation: Strategic Management in Creation & Development of Institutions', *Strategic Management Forum Conference Proceedings*, Indore, May 2004.

Sharma Subhash, 'Three Roads to Development: A Framework for Society's Growth, Development & Progress (GDP)', *Southern Economist*, July 15, 2005, 44:6, 7–10.

Sharma Subhash, 'A Model for Corporate Development - A Holistic Approach', *Vilakshan, XIMB Journal of Management*, September 2005, 2:2, 71–78.

Sharma Subhash, 'Towards Holistic Globalization: Market, State, Society and Self', in K.B. Akhilesh, Anjula Gurtoo, Gopal Mahapatra, eds., *Enabling Execution Excellence: Global Agenda*, Himalaya Publishing House, Mumbai, 2006, 55–62.

Sharma Subhash, 'Three Roads to Development: Need for Grounded Praxis Approach to Strategic Management & Policy Making', in Proceedings of 8th Annual Convention of Strategic Management Forum on Strategic Issues in Development Organizations and Corporate Social Responsibility, Indian Institute of Forest Management (IIFM), Bhopal, April 2006.

Sharma Subhash, 'New Experiments in Institution Building: A Journey from Unknown to Well Known', in Shivprakash Agrawal, Omprakash Gupta, Prithvi Yadav (Eds), Managing Global Organizations: Challenges, Opportunities and Strategies, *AIMS International*, Houston, USA, 2006, 95–101.

Sharma Subhash, 'Ethical Foundations of New Corporate Model: Implications for Strategy and Leadership', in Atanu Ghosh & Gargi Banerjee (Ed.), *Strategic Management for Firms in Developing Countries*, Allied Publishers, New Delhi, 2007, 242–245.

Sharma Subhash, 'Corporate Rishi Model for Organizational Leadership', in Sunita Singh-Sengupta & Dail Fields (Eds), *Integrating Spirituality & Organizational leadership*, Macmillan, Delhi, 2007, 653–663.

Sharma Subhash, 'New Managerial Tools for Strategic Analysis: Towards Grounded Praxis Approach To Strategic Management', *Indira Management Review*, Feb. 2007, 21–30.

Sharma Subhash, 'Towards Holistic Performance Scorecard: A New Strategic Imperative', *Vilakshan, XIMB Journal of Management*, Vol. V, No. 2, Sept. 2008, 33–45.

Sharma Subhash, Towards a New Social Vision: Sacro-civic Society and the Calling of Holistic Globalization, *Vilakshan, XIMB Journal of Management*, Vol. 4, March 2007, 121–130.

Sharma Subhash, 'From Pyramids to Amoeba: Managing Organizations in Changing Times', *NHRD Network Journal*, July 2008, 18–23.

Sharma Subhash, 'Creative Meditative Research: Towards 'VITAL' Mode of Learning', in Global Recession, Survival and Growth, Selected Papers of AIMS International Conference on Management, Om Prakash Gupta, V Nagdevra, Subhash Sharma and Shivprakash Agrawal (Eds), *AIMS Houston*, 2010, 179–183.

Sharma Subhash, 'Coconut Model of Society and Rise of The Bottom for Holistic Development', *Southern Economist, Golden Jubilee Volume*, Vol. 50, No. 1, 2011, 7–11.

Sharma Subhash, 'Institution Building: Way of Theory J', 3 *D...IBA Journal of Management and Leadership*, Vol. 2, Issue 2, Jan.–June 2011, 95–102.

Sharma Subhash, 'Karma Kapital: Towords New Age ADAM Model for Prosperity, Justice and Peace (PJP)' 3D... *IBA Journal of Management & Leadership*, Vol 3, Issue 1, July-Dec. 2011, 138–147.

Sharma Subhash, 'Towards A New Earth Shastra–Rethinking Economics through Integration of Indian Thought and Economics', in Indian Economic Association Seminar Proceedings (Ed) Rekha Jagannath, Maharani Lakshmi Ammanni Social Sciences Research Centre, Bangalore, Jan. 2012, 73–81.

Sharma Subhash, 'My Experiences and Experiments in Teaching Corporate Governance and Related Ideas', 3D...*IBA Journal of Management and Leadership*, Vol. 3, Issue 2, Jan-June 2012, 94–104.

Sharma Subhash, 'From Indus (India is Us) Indus (India in Us): A New Age of India's Soft Power', *Values Based Management*, Vol 2, No. 1 June 2013, 1–11.

Sharma Subhash, 'Three Paradigms in Management: American, Japanese and Indian', *International Journal of Organization Theory & Behavior*, Spring 2013, 16 (1), 30–41.

Sharma Subhash, Candle Light Experiment for Inner Invocation: Lessons for Management, Leadership and Creativity, 3D...*IBA Journal of Management & Leadership*, Vol. 4 Issue 2, Jan-June, 2013, 33–41.

Sharma Subhash, 'Harmony through Joining of Heart and Spirit (JHS): Towards JHS Vision of Social Harmony without Hierarchy, Gandhi Marg Quarterly, 35 (1), April-June, 2013, 45–60.

Sharma Subhash, 'Per Capita Income, Per Capita Happiness, Per Capita Bliss: Integration of Economics, Psychology and Spirituality in Modern Societies, Southern Economist, Nov. 1, 2013, 8–10.

Sharma Subhash, 'Soil to Soul Philosophy of Holistic Education', in Reinventing Society – Search for a Paradigm, (Eds) Pramod Pathak, Radha Sharma, Saumya Singh, Macmillan, New Delhi, 2013, 196–206.

Sharma Subhash, 'India 2014: From Cross Roads to New Road, in India at the Cross Roads – The Way Ahead', *Lexis Nexis*, New Delhi, 2014, 1–9.

Sharma Subhash, 'Indian Social Analytics and Modern Western Society', *Southern Economist*, 52nd Anniversary Number, Vol. 53, No. 1, May 1, 2014, 7–13.

Sharma Subhash, 'Towards Theory O of Consciousness: Implications for Management, Leadership & Creativity', in Managing Organizations in Digital Era, Conference Proceedings of Eleventh AIMS International Conference on Management, (Ed. Shivprakash Agarwal and Omprakash Gupta), AIMS International Houston and Institute of Management Technology (IMT), Ghaziabad, 2014, 191–195.

❑

Books by the Author

1. Subhash Sharma (1993), Creation from Shunya, Anand Press, Anand
2. Subhash Sharma (1996), Management in New Age: Western Windows Eastern Doors, **New Age International Publishers, New Delhi**
3. Subhash Sharma (1999), Quantum Rope: Science, Mysticism & Management, **New Age International Publishers, New Delhi**
4. Subhash Sharma (2001), Arrows of Time: From Black holes to Nirvana Point, **New Age International Publishers, New Delhi**
5. Subhash Sharma (2007), New Mantras in Corporate Corridors: From Ancient Roots to Global Routes, **New Age International Publishers, New Delhi**
6. Subhash Sharma (2009), Market's Maya: Lotus Millionaire from New Madhushala, IBA Publications, Bangalore
7. Subhash Sharma (2010), Shunya Poems: My Experiments with Corporate Rhymes, IBA Publications, Bangalore
8. Subhash Sharma & Daniel Albuquerque (2012), Consciousness in Corporate Corridors: Management, Leadership, Spirituality, IBA Publications, Bangalore
9. Subhash Sharma (2012), New Earth Sastra: Towards Holistic Development & Management (HDM), IBA Publications, Bangalore
10. Subhash Sharma (2013), Wisdom & Consciousness from the East: Life, Living & Leadership, IBA Publications, Bangalore
11. Subhash Sharma, (2013), Leadership Par La Sagesse & La Conscience: Tresors & Secrets de l'Orient au Benefice de l' Humanite, IBA Publications, Bangalore (French version of Wisdom & Consciousness from the East: Life, Living & Leadership)
12. Subhash Sharma (2015), New Ideas in Strategic Thinking & Management: A Knowledge Tree of New Age Mantras, **New Age International Publishers, New Delhi**

Bibliography

Ackoff R. L. (1981), Creating the Corporate Future, John Wiley, New York.

Akhilesh K.B., Gurttoo Anjula, Mahapatra G. (Ed.) (2006), Enabling Executive Excellence: Global Aenda, Himalaya Publishing House, Mumbai.

Albuquerque Daniel (2 010), Business Ethics: Principles and Practices, Oxford University Press, New Delhi.

Anthony R. & Govindrajan V. (2007), Management Control System, McGraw Hill, Irwin.

Bansal Ipshita (2010), "Book Review: New Mantras in Corporate Corridors: From Ancinet Roots to Global Routes Subhash Sharma" 3 D … *IBA Journal of Management & Leadership*, Vol. 1, Issue 2, 130–131.

Bhuyan Nishigandha (2012), Character of the Leader and Organizational Integrity, 3 D…*IBA Journal of Management & Leadership*, IBA Publications, Bangalore.

Boatright John R. (1997), Ethics and the Conduct of Business, Prentice Hall, New Jersey.

Cappelli Peter, Harbir Singh, Jitendra Singh, Michael Useem (2010), The India Way: How India's Top Business Leaders Are Revolutionizing Management, Harvard Business School Press, Boston.

Chakraborty Meera (2011), Colors of Mind and Other Essays, New Bhartiya Corporation, Delhi.

Chakraborty S.K. (2001), Wisdom Leadership, Wheeler, New Delhi.

Chakraborty Souvik (2000), Antidote: Essays Against the Socialist Indian State, Macmillan, New Delhi.

Chandrankunnel Mathew (2008), Philosophy of Quantum Mechanics Quantum Holism to Cosmic Holism: Physics and Meta physics of Bohm, Global Vision Publishing House, New Delhi.

Chandra Ashok and M.K. Khanijo (2009), Knowledge Economy: The Indian Challenge, Sage Publications India, New Delhi.

Deshpande R.S. (2004), Moon in the Mirror, Institute of Social & Economic Change, Bangalore.

Friedman Thomas (2005), The World is Flat: A Brief History of Twenty first Century, Farrar, Straus and Giroux, New York.

Gamlath Isha, "Identity of Subhashism in Indian Business & Indian Management", 3D... IBA Journal of Management & Leadership, Vol. 3, Issue 1, Jan-June 2011, 103-106.

Ghosh Atanu & Gargi Banerjee (Ed.) (2007), Strategic Management for Firms in Developing Countries, Allied Publishers, New Delhi.

Ghoshal Sumatra, Gita Piramal & C. A. Bartlett (2000), Managing Radical Change: What Indian Companies must do to become World class, Penguin Books, New Delhi.

Giri Ananta (2004), Creative Social Research: Rethinking Theories and Methods, Lexington Books.

Giri Ananta (2013), Knowledge and Liberation: Towards Planetary Realizations, Anthem Press, London.

Govindrajan V., Trimble Chris (2010), Reverse Innovation: Create Far from Home, Build Everywhere, Harvard Business School Press, Boston.

Gupta Divya Kirti (2014), Journey of Management Research at Indus Business Academy (IBA), Greater Noida: 2006-2013, IBA Publications, Bangalore.

Gupta Rajen K (2002), Towards Optimal Organization: Indian Culture and Management, Excel Books, New Delhi.

Gustavsson B (2007), "Strategy – A Game of the Past", in Conference Proceedings of the Leadership Development Conference, IBA Bangalore, March 13-14.

Hamel Gary (2009), "Moon Shots for Management", Harvard Business Review, Feb. 2009.

Jain Neetu (2013), "Book Review, New Earth Sastra: Towards Holistic Development & Management (HDM), Subhash Sharma", Vision, Vol. 17, Issue 2, 193-194.

Kapadia Mala (2009), Heart Skills: Emotional Intelligence for Work and Life, Excel Books, New Delhi.

Kaplan Robert, Norton David (1996), Translating Strategy into Action: The Balanced Scorecard, Harvard Business Press, Boston.

Karki Rajnish (2008), Competing with the Best, Strategic Management of Indian Companies in a Globalizing Arena, Penguin Group (USA), New Delhi.

Kim W. Chan, Renee Maurborgne (2005), Blue Ocean Strategy: How to Create Uncontested Market Space and Make the Competition Irrelevant, Harvard Business School Press, Boston.

Krishna Kumar (1996), Cases in Strategic Management: Managerial Experiences, Global Business Press, New Delhi.

Krishnan Rishikesha (2010), From *Jugaad* to Systematic Innovation: The Challenge for India, The Utpreraka Foundation, Bangalore.

Kumar Satish (2012), Soil, Soul and Society, http://www.theecologist.org/blogs_and_comments/commentators/satish-kumar/1711652/soil_soul_and_society.html

Mahapatra A.K. and Chinmaya Dave (2013), "Full Moon Strategy: A Symbolic Derivation", *Pacific Business Review International*, Vol. 6, Issue 1, 78-81.

Maitreyi K.R. (1992), Ecological Movements: Strategies for Managing Conflicts Around Natural Resources, Indian Institute of Management, Ahmedabad.

Maira Arun (2002), Shaping the Future: Aspirational Leadership in India and Beyond, Johan Wiley & Sons (Asia), Singapore.

Maruthi Suresh (2010), "Strategic Response of Enterprises in Market Economy – An Examination Across Ownership Form: Case Study of a Cooperative Milk Producers' Federation Ltd. (RCMPF)", 3 D ...*IBA Journal of Management & Leadership*, Vol. 2, Issue 1, 97-107.

Menon Sangeetha, Being and Well Being in Upanishadic Literature 3D...*IBA Journal of Management & Leadership*, Vol. 2, Issue 1, July–Dec., 12-29.

Momaya K. (2011), "Cooperation for Competitiveness of Emerging Countries: Learning from a Case of Nanotechnology", *Competitiveness Review: An International Business Journal incorporating Journal of Global Competitiveness*, Vol. 21, Issue 2, 152 -170.

Nanjundiah M.S. (2013), Climate Change & Sustainability Issues: A perspective Adopting the Universal Message of Swami Vivekananda, Southern Economist, Bangolore.

Nankervis R Alan, Fang Lee Cooke, Samir R Chatterjee (2012), New Models of HRM from China & India, Routledge, London.

Narayana C.N., & Vidhu Shekhar Jha (2008), "Human Resource Management – A Flexible Strategy for the Future Organizations – A Conceptual Approach", *International Journal of Strategic Management*, Vol. 8, No. 2.

Nonaka I & Takeuchi H (1995), The Knowledge Creating Company: How Japanese Companies Create the Dynamics of Innovation, Oxford University press, Oxford.

Naqvi Farah (2010), Women Empowerment and the Collective Consciousness: Towards A New Model of Women Empowerment & Leadership, 3D... *IBA Journal of Management & Leadership,* Vol 2, Issue 1, July-Dec., 34-44.

Pathak Pramod, Radha Sharma, Saumya Singh (2013), Reinventing the Society: The Search for a Paradigm, Macmillan, Delhi.

Pillai Radhakrishnan (2010), Corporate Chanakya: Successful Management the Chanakya Way, Jaico Publishing House, Mumbai.

Porter Michael (1980), The Competitive Strategy, Free Press, New York.

Porter Michael (1990), Competitive Advantage of Nations, Macmillan Press, Hampshire.

Prahlad C.K., Venkat Ramaswamy (2004), The Future of Competition: Co-creating Unique Value with Customers, Harvard Business Press, Boston.

Prahlad C.K. (2005), The Fortune at the Bottom of the Pyramid: Eradicating Poverty through Profits, Wharton School Publishing, Wharton.

Rao G.P. (2014), Remaking Ourselves, Enterprise and Society: An Indian Approach to Human Values in Management, Gower Publishing Limited, Surrey.

Sadri Sorab, Dastoor D.S., Jayashree S. (2009), The Theory & Practice of Managerial Ethics, Jaico Publishing House, Mumbai.

Schon D A (1973), The Reflective Practitioner: How Professionals Think in Action, Basic Books, New York.

Senge Peter (1990), The Fifth Discipline: The Art and Practice of Learning Organizations, Currency, Doubleday.

Sinha Arun (2010) (Ed.), Changing Ideas in Strategy, Narosa Publishing House, New Delhi.

Sinha J.B.P. (2000), "Integrative Indigenous Management in India: Practices and Prospects", Indian Journal of Industrial Relations, 35:4, 439-460.

Sinha J.B.P. (2009), Multinational in India: Managing the Interface of Cultures, Sage, New Delhi.

Tripathi Shiv K (2009), Essentials of Effective Management and Srimad Bhagwad Gita: Towards Human Values Oriented Ethical Management, 3D ...*IBA Journal of Management & Leadership*, Vol. 1, Issue 1, 68-74.

Verma Pratima (2011), Two Gurus Shaping Indian Management: Lessons of LCM – SEED, Global Journal of Research in Management, Vol. 1, Issue 2, 10-34.

❑

Author's Papers Presented at Strategic Management Forum (SMF) Conventions

This book is primarily based on author's research papers presented at Strategic Management Forum (SMF) of India, Conventions held at premier management institutions in India. A list of papers presented in SMF Conventions is presented below:

Sharma, Subhash, *Forward Engineering for Strategic Gearing: A Conceptual Framework*, 2nd SMF Convention, Strategic Management: Looking to the Future, held at Indian Institute of Management (IIM), Bangalore, May 27-29, 1999.

Sharma, Subhash, *Character Competence of the Corporation*, 3rd SMF Convention, Perspectives on Strategic Challenges and Imperatives, held at Indian Institute of Management (IIM), Calcutta, Kolkata, May 4-6, 2000.

Sharma, Subhash, *Development Matrix and Development Discourse: Towards A Framework of Strategic Gearing of the NBUs*, 4th SMF Convention, A Decade of Liberalization & Globalization: Retrospect and Prospect, held at Indian Institute of Management (IIM), Ahmedabad, May 24-26, 2001.

Sharma, Subhash, *Towards A New Development Vision*, 5th SMF Convention, Competitiveness 2010: Prospects, Tasks and Challenges, held at Management Development Institute (MDI), Gurgoan, April 25-27, 2002.

Sharma, Subhash, *Towards A New Age Corporate Model: A Holistic Approach to Corporate Development*, 6th SMF Convention, Strategic Management in a Globalizing World: Perspectives from a Developing Economy, held at Xavier Labor Research Institute (XLRI), Jamshedpur, April 24-26, 2003.

Sharma, Subhash, *Creating Unique Strategic Positioning (USP) Through Creativity and Innovation*: Strategic Management in Creation and Development of Institutions, 7th SMF Convention held at Indian Institute of Management (IIM), Indore, May 13-15, 2004.

Sharma, Subhash, *Three Roads to Development: Need for Grounded Praxis Approach to Strategic Management & Policy Making*, 8th SMF Convention, Strategic Issues in Development Organizations and Corporate Social Responsibility, held at Indian Institute of Forest Management (IIFM), Bhopal, May 9-11, 2005.

Sharma, Subhash, *New Managerial Tools for Strategic Analysis*, 9th SMF Convention, Indian Institute of Management (IIM), Khozikode, May 18-19, 2006.

Sharma, Subhash, *Ethical Foundations of New Corporate Model: Implications for Strategy and Leadership*, 10th SMF Convention, Indian Institute of Technology (IIT), Mumbai, May 10-12, 2007.

Sharma, Subhash, *Holistic Performance Scorecard: A Strategic Imperative*, Strategic Management Forum, 11th SMF Convention, Indian Institute of Technology (IIT), Kanpur, May 8-10, 2008.

Sharma, Subhash, *Beyond Pyramid and Pyramid Thinking*, 13th SMF Convention, held at Indian Institute of Management (IIM), Lucknow, Noida campus, May 27-29, 2010.

Sharma, Subhash, *Holistic Thinking in Strategic Management*, SMF International Conference, Challenges to Inclusive Growth in Emerging Economies, held at Indian Institute of Management (IIM), Ahmedabad, Dec. 15-17, 2010.

Sharma, Subhash, *Moon Ocean Strategy: A New Approach to Strategic Thinking*, 15th Annual Convention of the Strategic Management Forum, Indian Institute of Management (IIM), Indore, May 3-5, 2012.

Sharma Subhash, *Economic Chapati making: A New Metaphor for Harmonic Capitalism*, 17th Annual Convention of the Strategic Management Forum, Indian Institute of Management (IIM), Calcutta, Kolkata, June 12-14, 2014.

❑

INDEX

R

S

T

U

V

W

❑